Labor's Troubadour

MUSIC IN AMERICAN LIFE

A list of books in the series appears at the end of this book.

Labor's Troubadour

Joe Glazer

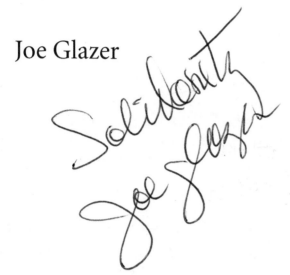

Solidarity
Joe Glazer

University of Illinois Press

Urbana and Chicago

Unless otherwise indicated, the photographs that appear
in this book are part of the author's personal collection.
Library of Congress Cataloging-in-Publication Data
Glazer, Joe.
Labor's troubadour / Joe Glazer.
p.   cm. — (Music in American life)
Includes discography (p.) and index.
ISBN 0-252-02612-8 (cloth : alk. paper)
1. Glazer, Joe. 2. Singers—United States—Biography. 3. Labor movement—
United States—Songs and music—History and criticism. I. Title. II. Series.
ML420.G56A3   2001
782.42'1593'092—dc21   00-009136

C 5 4 3 2 1

Publication of this book has been generously supported by grants from:
AFL-CIO (American Federation of Labor and Congress of Industrial
    Organizations)
American Federation of State, County and Municipal Employees (AFSCME)
American Federation of Teachers (AFT)
American Postal Workers Union (APWU)
California Labor Federation, AFL-CIO
Chicago Federation of Labor
Communications Workers of America (CWA)
Evelyn Bishop in memory of Franklin G. (Jerry) Bishop
Jonathan Grossman
Gail Klebanoff
Hotel Employees and Restaurant Employees International Union (HERE)
International Association of Machinists and Aerospace Workers (IAM)
International Union of Bricklayers and Allied Craftworkers (BAC)
International Union of Painters and Allied Trades
Los Angeles County Federation of Labor
New York State AFL-CIO
PACE International Union
Rieve-Pollock Foundation, Inc.
SEIU Local 585 (Service Employees International Union)
Service Employees International Union (SEIU)
Transport Workers Union of America (TWU)
ULLICO Inc.
Union of Needletrades, Industrial, and Textile Employees (UNITE!)
United Automobile, Aerospace, and Agricultural Implement Workers of
    America International Union (UAW)
United Food and Commercial Workers International Union (UFCW)
United Food and Commercial Workers, Local 588–Northern California
United Steelworkers of America (USWA)
Walter and May Reuther Memorial Fund

For Mildred,
my life-long partner

Contents

Illustrations follow pages 76 and 156

Preface

This book is full of my adventures in the field of politics and in the world of labor unions. It was through my music and guitar that I had those adventures.

My "day job" was first as a labor educator (seventeen years) and then as a labor specialist with the United States Information Agency (twenty years). But I became best known throughout the labor movement and political circles for my guitar and my use of music. I was soon tagged "Labor's Troubadour." And I was called in for organizing campaigns, picket lines and strikes, conventions, and demonstrations. During the same period I sang at political conventions, rallies, and political meetings. It all began in 1944 when I started singing for members of the Textile Workers Union, and I am still singing at union rallies and political meetings.

This odd occupation—"singer of labor songs"—brought me to forty-nine states and to sixty countries. My experiences have ranged from exhilarating to hilarious, from poignant to heart-warming, from gratifying to thrilling, and from frightening to frustrating.

I have sung labor songs to President Jimmy Carter at the White House; I have sung the songs of the martyred labor poet Joe Hill in the house where he was born in Gavle, Sweden; and I have exchanged notes about coal-mining songs with Merle Travis, the composer of "Sixteen Tons" and "Dark as a Dungeon." I sang at the closing convention of the Congress of Industrial Organizations (CIO) in 1955 in New York City and three days later at the first convention of the newly merged AFL-CIO. I sang at the 1956 convention of the Democratic Party. I sang for John F. Kennedy at his first major rally for the presidency.

I introduced Ralph Chaplin to a convention of lumber workers in Portland, Oregon, where we sang his song "Solidarity Forever," a composition that has been adopted as the labor movement's national anthem. I led two hundred guests at the LBJ Ranch in Texas in "We Shall Overcome," their arms linked, their bodies swaying to the rhythm of the great civil rights anthem.

I sang on the same platform with Eleanor Roosevelt, and when I stopped after two songs to give her more time to talk, she said, "Sing some more. I'd rather hear you sing than me talk."

I have had the good fortune to work closely with dozens of fine singer-composers of labor songs who are continuing a noble tradition. They are making a major contribution to American labor music, and I have devoted chapters 13 and 14 of this book to the careers and songs of fourteen of them.

But enough of that. Take this musical trip with me and learn about what I call the "true glory" of the labor movement. At its best, the labor movement gives working men and women a voice on the job, it provides workers with the clout to fight against injustice, and it gives them the opportunity to win a measure of dignity and security at the workplace.

It was my good fortune to make music for more than fifty years in and around the labor movement as well as in the political arena. This is the story of those years. Please sing along with me.

Acknowledgments

This book would never have seen the light of day if not for the tough love of my wife Mildred. She was relentless in getting me to put down the *New York Times* or close a book I had to finish or calling me out of the garden or shutting off the C-Span channel on television and sitting me down in front of a lined yellow pad. We discussed and argued about much of the content, and her numerous suggestions improved the manuscript immeasurably. She was also an eagle-eyed editor who kept me on track when I strayed from my mission and tried to write a monumental history of the American labor movement.

Archie Green, the guru of American industrial folklore, deserves special thanks. Archie introduced me to Ralph Chaplin, Merle Travis, and George Korson, the great collector of coal-mining songs and mining lore. He gave me scores of ideas to help make this book a more useful contribution to the story of America's working men and women. Archie has been an inspiration to me since the day I met him more than fifty years ago.

David Corbin, a labor and political historian, was particularly helpful when this project began in the early 1980s. David interviewed me at length a dozen different times, and the tapes from those interviews were invaluable when I began writing.

Judith McCulloh, assistant director and director of development at the University of Illinois Press, is worthy of special praise. She never gave up on me, even when I had long periods of little or no production. Her faith in the project never wavered. Her advice was invaluable.

Many friends read all or parts of the manuscript. They made useful suggestions and helped correct errors. Some helped to find old photographs, reminded me of events almost forgotten, or have helped in other ways. A roll call of these good friends follows. I thank them all: Joseph Ames, Laurel Blaydes, Elise Bryant, Hyman Bookbinder, John Brown, Abraham Brumberg, Jim Cebula, Olga Corey, Bobby Cumberland, Rocky Delaplaine, Hazel Dickens, Wilson

Dizard, Yael Eiran, Anne Feeney, Harry Fleischman, Douglas Fraser, Jon Fromer, Woodrow Ginsberg, Daniel Glazer, Emily Glazer, Nathan Glazer, Patti Glazer, Sam Glazer, Ellen Gonzalez, Elaine Graves, Martha Gray, John Haynes, Tom Juravich, Peter Jones, Si Kahn, Max Kampelman, Charlie King, Gail Klebanoff, Pat Knight, Liz Layton, Julie McCall, Don McKee, Paul McKenna, Abner Mikva, Tom Moran, Sarah Morgan, John O'Connor, Morten Parker, Larry Penn, Ronald Radosh, Jay Rosenthal, Helga Sandburg, Saul Schniderman, Roger Schrader, Pete Seeger, Harry Stamper, Eddie Starr, Sol Stetin, Holly Syrrakos, Marilyn Townsend, Gus Tyler, Joe Uehlein, Morris Weisz, and Kenny Winfree.

❖ ❖ ❖

"Stand by Your Union" by Harry Stamper. © Copyright 1987 by Harry Stamper. Used by Permission.

"We Just Come to Work Here" by Harry Stamper. © Copyright 1985 by Harry Stamper. Used by Permission.

"Scabs" by Anne Feeney. Used by Permission.

"War on the Workers" by Anne Feeney. Used by Permission.

"Fannie Sellins" by Anne Feeney. Used by Permission.

"Probationary Blues" by Eddie Starr. Used by Permission.

"I Am Union and I'm Proud" by Eddie Starr. Used by Permission.

"We Are the Working Class" by Eddie Starr. Used by Permission.

"Cotton Mill Dreams" by Kenny Winfree. © Copyright 1981 by Kenny Winfree. Used by Permission.

"Down at the Union Hall" by Kenny Winfree. © Copyright 1984 by Kenny Winfree. Used by Permission.

"I'm a Union Card" by Kenny Winfree. © Copyright 1984 by Kenny Winfree. Used by Permission.

"Long Live the I.A.M." by Kenny Winfree. © Copyright 1987 by Kenny Winfree. Used by Permission.

"Snake Oil" by Kenny Winfree. © Copyright 1984 by Kenny Winfree. Used by Permission.

The incidents and conversations in chapters 13 and 14, "New Voices, Part 1" and "New Voices, Part 2," appear as the author remembers them.

Labor's Troubadour

Introduction

"The Mills Weren't Made of Marble." That was the headline in the lead editorial of the *New York Times* on Labor Day in 1992. I had written a song called the "Mill Was Made of Marble," so the line immediately caught my eye.

Referring to America's first factory town, Lowell, Massachusetts, now the site of an unusual museum run by the National Park Service, the editorial continued, "These mills were not, like those in the old folk song, made out of marble nor the machines made out of gold." That was my signal to write a letter to the *Times*.

New York Times
Letters to the Editor

I wrote "The Mill Was Made of Marble," a song about the dream of a textile worker, in 1947, when I was on the staff of the C.I.O. Textile Workers Union, so it is not as old as you imply.

In the normal course of events a song is not considered a folk song until the composer has been long gone from this earth and the song, as the professional scholars say, enters tradition. This is the ultimate gift a people can give a creative artist. So I thank you for characterizing my song as an "old folk song." It is a nice Labor Day present.

Where had the *New York Times* editorial writer heard my song? I asked. A reply came from Jack Rosenthal:

You may have a dim recollection of your visit to cheer up the troops during the Portland Newspaper Strike in 1959–1960 of whom I was one. I vividly remember the concert you gave on our behalf. Among other things, on the spot you wrote a song about our strike along these lines:

Down in Multnomah County
In Portland, Or-ee-gon
Strikers march the picket line

Until the strike is won.
Which side are you on? Which side are you on!

And you sang the wonderful mill song, which has stirred around in my head ever since. I know you performed it beautifully but hadn't realized before that you wrote it too. Hats off!

At the time of the newspaper strike in Portland I had been singing in the labor movement for sixteen years and had become known as "Labor's Troubadour." Someone—I don't know who—slapped the label on me, and it has stuck. The complicated story of "The Mill Was Made of Marble" is developed fully in chapter 2.

Since I started to work in the labor movement in 1944 I have sung on scores of picket lines; at the White House and a hundred union conventions and rallies, union banquets and parties, and meetings in Madison Square Garden; before three hundred thousand workers at a Solidarity rally on Capitol Hill; and to janitors at an organizing meeting, students at Harvard University, professors at the University of Wisconsin, and labor arbitrators and company personnel directors.

How did I get into this odd occupation? I certainly did not major in "labor singing" at college. I never took a voice lesson, but I did have a pleasant singing voice as a youngster. I remember being picked out of an afternoon Hebrew class by the cantor when I was about nine and told that I would have the privilege of singing in the choir for the High Holidays. It was supposed to be an honor, but I didn't appreciate it because I had to rehearse every afternoon for weeks, which ate up all my ball-playing time. I did receive a gift of $10 for my efforts, but my mother appropriated the $10 bill to help pay the rent. Our four-room apartment in an East Harlem tenement at 215 East 103d Street in Manhattan cost $25 a month, and the seven kids in our family ranged in age from four to seventeen. A $10 bill was an important addition to the family's income.

The year was 1927, supposedly the height of the prosperity of the 1920s, but my family didn't see much of it. My father was a garment worker in an industry that had a chronic case of boom or bust. The "bust" was a slack season that could last two or three months, and there was no unemployment insurance in those days.

My parents were typical of the two million East European Jews who had poured into New York and other cities in the United States from the 1880s to the beginning of World War I in 1914.

My father, Louis, came over from Poland in 1911. In two years he was able to scrape together enough money to send for my mother, Tillie, and their two children, Sam and Rose. They settled in a tiny apartment on the Lower East Side of Manhattan, an area with the population density of Bombay and teeming with immigrant workers struggling to make a living in the "Promised Land."

Father was a member of the International Ladies' Garment Workers' Union (ILGWU), not an officer or leader but a good, solid, rank-and-file member. He read the Socialist-oriented *Jewish Daily Forward,* and when he became a citizen he voted for the Socialist candidates for president, Norman Thomas and Eugene Victor Debs. We didn't talk much about politics or trade unions. It didn't seem necessary. It was an act of faith that unions were a good thing for working men and women. You never, ever, crossed a picket line. Period. Socialism would ultimately provide a better life for all workers. In 1933, however, FDR and the New Deal replaced socialism as the New Political Religion.

I don't remember Father doing anything with music, but my mother had a lovely voice, and I learned some moving Yiddish folk songs from her. She didn't have too much time for music, however. She was busy from early morning until late at night, cooking, washing, ironing, darning, shopping, and getting us ready for school. I had six brothers and sisters: Sam, Rose, Freda, Henry, Gail, and Nathan. The older ones helped with some of the chores.

Money was scarce. Mother, who handled the family funds, had to count every nickel and dime. I don't remember going hungry, but I do recall crying my heart out trying to coax a dime from her so I could see a cowboy picture at the local movie house. My friends were going, and I just had to go with them. I was ten and couldn't understand that the dime had to help buy dinner for the family.

My eldest brother, Sam, had to quit high school when he was fourteen. He became a Western Union messenger. My brother Henry, two years older than I, never could find a job after graduating from vocational high school in 1932. He joined the Civilian Conservation Corps (CCC) in 1934, one of the most successful and useful New Deal programs. He was sent to western North Carolina, where he planted trees, dug fire trails, and helped to develop the Great Smokies National Park. He was paid $30 a month, $25 of which was mailed directly home. We checked the mailbox eagerly for that $25 check every month.

I was the fifth child in the family and the first to be able to go to college. How was I able to do it? The school I attended, Brooklyn College, a branch of the New York City college system, was absolutely free. I think I had to pay 50 cents a semester for a library card, but that was it. I also had to buy textbooks, but I was able to find used copies at a reasonable price. My earnings of $15 a month from a federal student work program also helped out. Mother doled out 15 cents a day to me—10 cents for the round-trip subway fare and 5 cents for milk to go with the sandwich I brought from home for lunch.

The older children sacrificed chances at a college education and went to work young, enabling the three youngest to attend college. My sister Gail, the sixth child, was a good student but dropped out because her clothes were so shabby (this was before jeans and a T-shirt became standard attire). My brother Nathan, the youngest and seventh child, also made it to college and ultimately became a distinguished sociologist, teaching at the University of California at Berkeley and Harvard University.

At college I majored in mathematics and physics, but I was more interested in music so I registered for a course in harmony in the music department. I paid no attention to the class's prerequisites, the ability to read music and play the piano, and I did well for the first three sessions. I learned the major and minor scales, how to form chords, and all about chord progressions. Then, during the fourth class, I ran into trouble. Our professor gave us the following assignment: Compose a three-minute classical piece and play it on the piano for the class. I had to confess that I couldn't play the piano. He indignantly crossed my name off the class list and said, "Please don't come back." As it turned out, those few lessons in music theory proved helpful when I learned to accompany myself on the guitar. But I am jumping ahead of my story.

I became fascinated with cowboy songs when I was in high school in the Bronx. It's hard to explain why. The nearest cowboy was about two thousand miles away, and the only horses I had seen were pulling wagons full of produce or blocks of ice. I also became interested in folk songs, called by many "hillbilly music" back then, and I would spend a lot of time twisting the radio dial, searching for programs with my favorite songs.

Of course, there were no cassettes or CDs and we didn't own a phonograph, so if I wanted to learn a song I had to scribble its lyrics as the song was being sung and then try to catch it another time or two to complete the job. My younger sister Gail became quite adept at jotting down songs from the radio, and with her help I soon had a notebook with fifty or more of my favorite songs, all of which I could sing from beginning to end without missing a beat.

It was 1933. I was fifteen years old and attending James Monroe High School in the Bronx when I discovered the school library. My eye caught upon *The American Song Bag* by Carl Sandburg. I couldn't believe it! Just about every one of the songs I had so laboriously collected were in Sandburg's book. There was "John Henry" and "Jesse James," "The Old Chisolm Trail," "The Streets of Laredo," "The Little Old Sod Shanty," "When the Work's All Done This

Fall," and dozens more. This was my first lesson in research. It dawned on me that I didn't have to reinvent the wheel if someone had already done it.

Next I had to learn to play the guitar. The Sears Roebuck catalog advertised one for $5.95, including a canvas case. It took me six months to save my pennies and nickels and occasional dimes, but I finally made it. The guitar arrived all in one piece, a decal of a cowboy on its front. I was flying high until I tried to play. The guitar was worth just about what I had paid for it. I took a few lessons from an unemployed musician who was picking up a few bucks by working as a music teacher for the government-sponsored Works Progress Administration (WPA). I can't recall now if the lessons were free or if I paid 25 cents for each.

Later on I got a better guitar, took a few more lessons, and finally learned how to accompany myself in a respectable manner. But I still didn't know a single labor song. I also knew very little about the labor movement in which I would spend fifty years of my adult life.

1

Textile North

I began working at the New York City headquarters of the CIO Textile Workers Union of America (TWUA) as an assistant education director in 1944 on May 1, traditionally a workers' holiday in many countries. It was a good date to start a job in the labor movement.

How did I, who had never worked in a mill or seen the inside of a textile mill, get to the Textile Workers Union? This is how it happened. During World War II, I was teaching physics and mathematics, my majors in college, to Air Force students at Truax Air Field in Madison, Wisconsin. I was a civilian instructor, having been rejected by the armed services because of a rheumatic heart.

I began taking courses part-time toward a master's degree in mathematics at the University of Wisconsin, where my wife Mildred was taking an undergraduate degree in labor economics. I soon found I was spending all my spare time reading her books. I became fascinated with the history of the labor movement and the struggles of workers to build unions. I switched my major from mathematics to labor economics and industrial relations.

When the war seemed to be winding to a close in the spring of 1944 the government closed Truax Air Field, and I was in the market for a job. I decided to try to find a place in the labor movement. Because I had experience as a teacher—and I knew I was a good one—and because I thought I knew something about the labor movement from reading a lot of books and taking some graduate courses, I thought I could fit into a union's education department.

Larry Rogin, the education director of the Textile Workers Union, one of the major unions in the CIO, decided to take a chance on me. I have always thought he hired me because of the graduate work I had done at the University of Wisconsin in labor economics and because he was impressed that I had plowed through all four thick volumes of John R. Commons's *The Labor Movement in the United States.* Years later, however, Rogin confessed that one reason he had hired me was because I had mentioned in passing that I had written songs and skits for shows at college and could sing folk songs and accompany myself on the guitar.

It seemed that an important part of the TWUA education program was a series of one-week summer training institutes for shop stewards and local officers. Rogin tried to put a lot of union content into the program, but he realized there was a limit to the amount of information that could be stuffed into a textile worker's head in one week. He knew that inspiring students and firing them up so they would want to do or die for the good old TWUA might be the most useful accomplishment he could hope for.

Rogin liked to open each evening session with a set of union songs and then later, when the formal evening program was over, get students singing while they socialized. There was only one problem. Rogin—as the saying goes— couldn't carry a tune in a bushel basket. He depended on me to lead the singing, but I didn't know any of the union songs except for "Solidarity Forever." That one was easy because it was to the tune of "John Brown's Body." When he tried to show me how other union songs went, it was all Johnny One Note. I didn't have a clue what he was singing.

Gradually I learned a dozen or more songs: "We Shall Not Be Moved," "Roll the Union On," "Union Maid," "Hold the Fort," "Which Side Are You On?" "Joe Hill," and others. Soon I was leading singing at training institutes every night. Music bounced off the walls; feet were stomping, hands were clapping, and union spirit was in the air. On the last night of an institute we would put on an elaborate show, and its music and drama charged up the students, who would sing "Solidarity Forever" until 2 A.M.

Few people know about the Larry Rogins of the labor movement. They have heard about strikes, picket lines, and union contracts. They may have read about union organizers or business agents or labor leaders (inevitably labeled "union bosses" by the media). But whoever heard of a union educator who conducted classes in parliamentary procedure, labor legislation, how to understand a union contract, and how to make a union more effective in the shop?

Larry Rogin was working toward a Ph.D. in political science at Columbia University in the early 1930s when his involvement with the American labor movement permanently interrupted his studies. Rogin was a democratic socialist who believed there had to be major changes in the American economic system if working people were ever to get a fair shake from society. Although he remained a democratic socialist for much of his life, he decided that the labor movement offered a more realistic vehicle for improving society than the hope of a "socialist revolution."

Rogin taught longshoremen in New York City; machinists, railroad workers, and hosiery workers in Pennsylvania; and textile workers and others in New Jersey and Maryland. He learned that students, workers who had little formal education, knew a lot more about shop problems and possible solutions and about relations with the foreman and fellow workers than he, the teacher, did.

"Start with the specific—start where the people are," he told me. "Students bring resources of their own to the class. They don't have textbook knowledge, but they have street and shop wisdom, they have life experience. You have to listen to them and you have to stop talking to find out how much they've learned."

When I started with the Textile Workers Union in 1944, Larry Rogin already had ten years of labor education experience under his belt, and I learned a lot from him. The first thing was that I didn't know much about the practical side of the labor movement.

On May 1, my first day on the job, when I sat down at my desk ready to do "labor education," Rogin called me into his office and told me he was sending me to New Jersey for a month. "We have some important organizing drives there and an especially big one among the woolen and worsted workers in Passaic. Sol Stetin is our New Jersey director. He'll take good care of you. You'll learn a lot from him."

In New Jersey, I handed out leaflets to textile workers more interested in scurrying to work on time than in reading the union's prescription for rescuing them from industrial serfdom. I knocked on doors of unorganized workers who told me to get lost. I attended the first "big" organizing meeting of a mill that had eight hundred workers to find that the number of organizers (four) outnumbered the workers (three) who had shown up. I met workers who were afraid of strikes and others who didn't want to pay union dues. Some were sure they'd be fired if the boss found out they had joined the union; others were worried about union racketeers. Many workers whose names were on my list of prospects were not home; others had quit the plant some time ago. One woman who seemed to be interested was told by her husband in no uncertain terms to forget about the union.

In one long week, knocking on several dozen doors, I signed up three members. Larry Rogin was right. I did learn a lot from Sol Stetin. I learned that this union business was going to be a lot tougher than writing reports on industrial relations in graduate school.

But things began improving when I started to concentrate on the campaign in the city of Passaic to organize the ten thousand woolen and worsted workers in the Botany, Forstman, and other mills concentrated there. Passaic was an industrial town of about sixty thousand and had large stretches of very modest or poor housing for mill workers, most of whom were immigrants or children of immigrants from Eastern and Southern Europe: Poles, Ukrainians, Serbs, Slovaks, Italians, and others.

Many remembered or had heard about the disastrous, occasionally violent, strike of 1926 that had dragged on for fourteen months and ended in complete defeat for the union. During that strike there had been noisy, continuous picketing, and hundreds, sometimes thousands, of workers paraded through town and in front of the mills, trying to prevent scabs from crossing the picket line. Police were kept busy arresting strikers, many of whom spent a night or two in jail.

Margaret Larkin, a writer who was sympathetic to the strikers' cause, observed the picket-line activity firsthand. One day she sat down on a park bench and scribbled some lines to the tune of "Polly Wolly Doodle." It became one of the most popular union songs. I have sung it at a hundred union rallies and meetings.

On the Line
Words: Margaret Larkin
Music: "Polly Wolly Doodle"

The union is the place for me,
The place for working men
Who want some time to sing and play
And money they can spend.

> On the line (on the line)
> On the line (on the line)
> Come and picket on the picket line.
> We'll win our fight, our fight for the right
> On the picket, picket line.

If you've never spent a night in jail
Come and picket on the picket line.
You'll be invited without fail
On the picket, picket line.

> Chorus

I am a union man because
I want a living wage.

We'll stick together, we'll fight together
We'll get that living wage.

Chorus

Note that despite the large number of women working in Passaic textile plants and on picket lines there, the song refers only to male strikers. And it was written by a woman!

Although eighteen years had passed since the 1926 strike, many workers were still gun-shy and wanted nothing to do with the union. But there were others who had seen workers in the silk mills and textile dye houses of Paterson and other cities organizing strong unions and improving their conditions. "Why should we be left behind?" Passaic workers thought.

During the three weeks I spent in Passaic I must have attended fifteen or twenty meetings with workers, who asked hundreds of questions. I learned more about the workings of the labor movement than I could have from twenty graduate school lectures.

It took another four or five months before the woolen and worsted workers in Passaic were organized. I was to return to the area a good number of times during the next few years to conduct union leadership training classes and other programs for the TWUA Passaic Joint Board, which soon had nearly ten thousand members in a strong organization.

My job in the union's education department was to write leaflets and pamphlets and conduct classes in such subjects as collective bargaining, public speaking, labor legislation, and parliamentary procedure. Because my labor music proved to be an effective solidarity-builder, I was assigned many times to tough strikes.

Maine

The first big strike in which I was involved concerned textile workers in Maine in November 1945. Thousands were on strike in towns I had never heard of—Lewiston, Biddeford, and Waterville—trying to obtain a minimum rate of 65 cents an hour and some improvement in working conditions.

The strike in Maine was a critical one for the union. Ten thousand textile workers were involved. None had been on strike before. The big textile companies were adamant: There would be no raise to 65 cents and no improvement in conditions. Take it or leave it. A cold Maine winter was around the corner. Workers were frightened. How long could they stay out on the picket

line? There was a good chance the union would be smashed as workers straggled back to the mills, hoping to preserve their jobs.

Larry Rogin had sent me to Maine to give local union leaders a hand in rallying workers and keep up their spirits. I was a pretty good rabble-rouser on the platform, and I could turn out snappy leaflets explaining the issues. Most important, I could lead workers in rousing labor songs in union halls and on picket lines. Rogin told me, "Go to Maine and see if you can build some union solidarity with that music of yours."

It was the first time I had been in Maine. Of course, I knew all about the state from reading and from the movies. Maine was full of Yankee fishermen who braved the cold Atlantic to catch the lobsters and good fish that rich folks ate in fancy New York restaurants. The fishermen wore heavy slickers and hats and looked heroic in magazine photos. They didn't say much; when they did talk, it was with an odd "down east" accent. There were also lumbermen and some farmers. That was the Maine I knew.

When I got to the city of Lewiston, which was to be my headquarters, I saw a piece of Maine I never knew existed. Everything was French. The names on the storefronts were Gagnon, Ouillette, and Carignon. There was a daily French newspaper and French radio stations. French was spoken in the streets, and parochial schools were conducted in French. As I walked down Main Street on my first day in town, a young man stopped me and rapped out a question in rapid-fire French. All I could understand was his first word, "monsieur." After that my high school French couldn't handle it.

There were five thousand textile workers in Lewiston, 90 percent of whom were French. French was the language of homes, mills, and union halls. I learned that not just Maine but all of New England was full of French Canadians who had come down from Quebec in the 1880s and 1890s to seek work in the cotton and woolen mills of Woonsocket, Rhode Island, Lawrence, Massachusetts, Manchester, New Hampshire, and dozens of other mill towns. The mills were run by Yankees, so there was a sharp division between the owners and managers and workers. Owners spoke English, and workers spoke French. Most owners were Protestant, whereas workers were Catholic. Owners were generally old settlers, and workers were new immigrants. It was "them and us." The boss lived in the mansion on the hill, and the workers lived in crowded tenements or tiny houses. Owners sent their sons to Harvard or M.I.T. Workers' children went to parochial school and then to the mill. They never saw the inside of a college unless they were working in its kitchens or mowing its lawns.

This strike—Brahmin mill owners against French textile mill hands—would

appear on the surface a one-sided affair. One factor, however, helped balance the equation somewhat—the union.

Local textile unions in Maine did not have much strength. Their unions were new, the leadership inexperienced, and their resources were meager. But they were affiliated with one of the major unions in the CIO, the Textile Workers Union of America, with 325,000 members in hundreds of local unions. The TWUA had skilled lawyers to match company lawyers. The union's economists and researchers could match charts and tables with the company's best. The union's top negotiators were veterans of a hundred struggles and contract negotiations and could go toe to toe with the shrewdest company management. Although the national union's resources could never match the deep pockets of big textile companies, it could feed strikers and their families for a period of time so they would not be starved back into the mills.

When I got to the union hall in Lewiston I saw that the strike was a mess. It was the most raggedy strike I have ever seen. Strikers milled around aimlessly. A long line of anxious workers waited to see the union's local director, George Jabar, for financial assistance. There were no committees, no regular meetings, and no written reports on negotiations going on in Boston, headquarters for most of the mills.

There wasn't a good strike kitchen or a soup kitchen, nor was there a systematic way to get assistance to strikers and their families. Hysteria was beginning to set in because people had been without a paycheck for several weeks. When you make 55 or 60 cents an hour, you don't have much money in the bank. We even lacked good picket signs, which should have been the first order of business.

As an education director from New York headquarters trying to develop activities and keep up strikers' spirits, the first thing I did was help establish regular meetings. At them I would talk and sing; I would also lead singing on the picket lines.

Fortunately for me, the French Canadians were great singers, completely uninhibited. They would let their emotions roll. They all knew a hundred French Canadian folk songs and would rap out tunes like "Allouette" and "Auprès de ma blonde" with plenty of stomping and clapping. Between the French songs, I would teach the crowd simple union songs. For example, we sang John Handcox's "Roll the Union On":

> We're gonna roll, we're gonna roll
> We're gonna roll the union on

We're gonna roll, we're gonna roll
We're gonna roll the union on.

If the boss is in the way,
We're gonna roll it over him, roll it over him
Roll it over him,
If the boss is in the way
We're gonna roll it over him,
We're gonna roll the union on.

Another favorite was Ralph Chaplin's "Solidarity Forever": "Solidarity forever, solidarity forever / Solidarity forever, for the union makes us strong." We seldom sang the powerful verses of "Solidarity Forever" because you learn quickly on a picket line or in a strike meeting to avoid sophisticated songs that have complicated music or wordy verses. You'll lose your audience on the second verse.

You need simple songs that people can pick up right away. And if you can work in one-line verses on the local situation, you can keep the song going as long as your voice holds out. For example:

We shall not be, we shall not be moved,
We shall not be, we shall not be moved.
Just like a tree that's planted by the water
We shall not be moved.

1. The union is behind us, we shall not be moved.
The union is behind us, we shall not be moved.
Just like a tree that's planted by the water
We shall not be moved.

Chorus

"The union is behind us" is basically a one-line verse that can be quickly changed. We sang it over and over in Maine. I remember one day as we marched around the giant Pepperell mill, makers of sheets and pillow cases, I led nearly a thousand strikers in verse after verse:

2. The union is behind us . . .

3. We're fighting for a contract . . .

4. We're fighting for our future . . .

5. We're fighting for our children . . .

6. We're fighting for our freedom . . .

7. We'll strike until we conquer . . .

8. We'll build a mighty union . . .

9. Come join us on the picket line . . .

We sang and we sang. We must have gone on for an hour or more on a picket line that seemed to stretch for miles around the plant. I would line out each new verse, and the strikers closest to me would pick it up. The new verse would roll like a wave through hundreds of others further down the line. Suddenly a striker began singing, "The hell with Mr. Jolly, we shall not be moved." I learned that Mr. Jolly was an unloved supervisor at the mill, and we all had a jolly time singing about him. I taught the strikers a useful variation for taking a swipe at a mean boss:

Mr. Jolly is a horse thief.
He shall be removed.
Mr. Jolly is a horse thief.
He shall be removed.
Just like the garbage standing in the alley
He shall be removed.

After singing for an hour or more in the snow and the bitter cold, we marched back to the union hall, exhilarated and ready to do battle with mill owners for another week or two—or for another month if we had to.

We began holding pep meetings twice a day. Emergency financial help was beginning to get out. During the following years the Textile Workers Union ran so many long strikes, especially in the South, that it became expert at distributing emergency aid. The union set up food distribution systems, worked out methods for meeting emergencies such as car and house payments, and developed all kinds of committees to run a strike.

I put out a mimeographed strike bulletin, usually one page and printed on both sides. It wasn't much, but it was important for workers to see their side of the story printed in black and white. As I look back on those early days, I realize I should have set up a newspaper or press committee of six or eight people and let them do most of the work under my supervision. I did a lot of things myself that I should have trained strikers to do. But I was young and gung-ho and had a lot to learn myself about running a big strike.

I would get back to the hotel each night about midnight, my adrenalin still flowing. Sleep was the last thing on my mind. There were lists of things to do: appoint a committee of good church-goers to visit the priest; line up speaking engagement at Bates College; get a committee to work on a dance benefit for the strikers; be sure to send copies of the newsletter to other striking locals, to the negotiating committee in Boston, and to the New York headquarters; prepare a news release for newspapers and radio stations; talk to the owner of the taxis that mill owners had hired to hustle scabs past picket lines; call Boston and New York to find out any new developments in the negotiations; call Mildred in New York and tell her everything is fine. It was two or three in the morning before I dozed off. Then I would be up at six or six-thirty to start all over again.

My talk at Bates College was an interesting experience. Bates was one of those small, private colleges that dot New England. It had an excellent reputation and attracted students from all over the country. It probably had about a thousand students. I talked about the textile workers and mills that were a stone's throw from the college's classrooms and dormitories. "Has anyone here ever been in one of those mills? Do you know what it is to breathe the cotton lint and dust eight hours a day, to have the clatter of a thousand looms ringing in your ears, to be pushed by the foreman to get out more and more production? To do all this for 60 or 70 cents an hour?"

The students were in a cozy cocoon, studying about the rise and fall of the Roman Empire, the Norman conquest, the Industrial Revolution, the Continental Congress, the Bill of Rights, the plight of the American Indian, the Civil War, and robber barons. All good stuff. These bright young men and women were learning all about the history of their country. But history was being made right under their noses, and they didn't know it. I passed out some literature that told the union story. I invited them to come to a union meeting and perhaps interview a spinner or weaver who had spent twenty-five years in the mills. Wouldn't that make a good report for a history or an English class?

I felt good after the talk. I should have brought a couple of strikers with me to tell their story, but it had gone well, and I felt I had made an impact. A number of faculty members were present, and that was important because they were permanent members of the Lewiston community and could be a positive influence in helping to get the union's story around.

I was floored when I got a message from New York headquarters. Someone in Lewiston had complained about an admitted communist making a speech at Bates College. That was puzzling. What were they talking about? Then it dawned on me. I had opened my talk with what I thought was a cute remark about why would the union send a communist like me to Maine to help with the strike? It was supposed to be a subtle crack at anti-union elements who were suggesting that the strike of the workers was a communist plot. Lesson learned: Don't try to be too subtle or smart-ass when trying to convince outsiders of the justice of your cause.

Almost every striker was Catholic, so the position of the church was important. We were excited when Father Drouin, the head priest at the cathedral-like church on the hill, announced that he would give a special mass on behalf of mill workers. At least a thousand workers marched slowly up the hill to the magnificent church, paid for in good part by the nickels and dimes of those same workers. It was cold, but the sun was shining brilliantly and that seemed a good omen. Everyone felt good.

Father Drouin was an impressive man, a power in the community and known to be friendly to the union. But he was careful. During the mass he blessed the workers not the union. He didn't say, "I hope you win this strike." He did say, "We don't want violence" and hoped there would be a settlement soon. I remember being disappointed that he didn't come out more strongly in favor of the union. This priest may be a friend of the union, I thought, but he sure is conservative. As I became more experienced in such matters I realized that he likely went as far as he could go without getting into trouble with the anti-union bishop in Portland, who could transfer him in a minute to a quiet country parish. The fact that he held a special mass for the workers and urged management and the union to get together was a helpful step for us. News of the mass was in all the newspapers, and everyone in town talked about it—one more bit of pressure on the companies to settle the strike.

One of the big events of the strike was the mass rally we had planned for the city auditorium. The union hall could hold only about three hundred workers, so we had to rent the auditorium because we expected at least two thousand to attend.

I remember all the excitement. We had some concern about whether we could fill a big hall. A lot of empty seats would not help morale, so we were a little nervous as the time for the meeting approached. But people began pouring in, with their children and their in-laws, with grandma and grandpa, and with friends and neighbors. Every seat was filled. We felt good.

I opened with a couple of union songs to help put everyone in the mood, and then we introduced the evening's speaker. We had brought up from New York our executive vice president, George Baldanzi, who had been a leader in the dyers' union in New Jersey. Baldanzi was one of the great orators of the labor movement. He was a powerhouse on the platform. Words and phrases flowed without hesitation—no uh-uhs, no searching for a word. He would jab the air at the right moments, and his language was colorful and earthy. His voice rose to dramatic heights and quieted to make a special point.

From the moment Baldanzi started talking, he captured the attention of every striker. He talked about the old days before the union, when workers earned pennies for back-breaking labor. "In those days," he said, "you could take a textile worker, hold him up by the legs and shake him for an hour, and you wouldn't get 50 cents falling out of his pockets." He went on in that vein to cheers, laughter, and applause. He told strikers that the union had brought some changes, but a lot more had to be done to bring workers the dignity and the conditions they deserved.

The meeting occurred the day before Armistice Day, and Baldanzi took advantage of that fact to make his final point: "Tomorrow is Armistice Day, a day of peace. But there is no peace in Lewiston, Maine. There is war! We are fighting for our lives, for our children. If you march together, if you fight together, you will win this war and in the years to come you will look back with pride at the role you played in bringing justice to the textile workers of Maine." People were on their feet, cheering and screaming.

After Baldanzi's great speech, which lasted for about forty-five minutes, the chairman announced that "Brother Chomelle will now translate." "What an anticlimax," I muttered to myself. But Brother Chomelle rose to the occasion. He must have been taking detailed notes because he made a good speech that was almost as long as Baldanzi's. He also received almost as much applause because a lot of the older workers had not been able to follow everything Baldanzi had said but were completely at home with the translation. I do not know how the handful of non-French workers felt. Some were Irish, and there were also a few Yankees, most of them skilled workers, and a small group of Lithuanians who had somehow found their ways to Lewiston. I guess they were used to being a minority. They sat patiently through the long translation.

My most outstanding memory of the strike is that a number of strikers seemed to come from nowhere—average spinners, weavers, and loom-fixers—to become strike leaders. Workers who had grade-school educations and had never made a speech spoke to hundreds with vigor, passion, and sometimes great eloquence. They had never taken a course with Dale Carnegie. In fact, they had never heard of him. But they rose to the occasion, fired by the justice of their cause and outrage at the arrogance of the mill owners.

There was a Mrs. Gay, a well-groomed woman in her fifties. She had spent perhaps twenty-five years in the mill but had managed to avoid the worn-out look so common among her peers. She was not a union leader, but just an average member who paid her dues and attended a meeting once in a while. I remember her on the platform at the union hall just before Thanksgiving. The strike had been dragging on, and progress in negotiations was very slow. When would this thing end? When would we get back to work? Bills were piling up.

Christmas was not far away. Would the strike last until then? People were worried, and many were afraid. How long could they hold out?

Mrs. Gay was speaking rapidly in French. Between my high school French and the three weeks I had spent in Maine I was able to catch quite a bit of what she said. She was trying to stiffen the backs of the strikers. She kept talking about "le work load," the importance of "le job control," and being under the thumb of "le boss" if they didn't win "le strike." Then she started talking about "l'amburger, l'amburger." It took me a few minutes to figure that out. She was talking about Thanksgiving: "If we can't afford turkey we'll eat hamburger. If we have to we'll eat hamburger for Christmas too but we won't go back to work until 'le contract' is signed."

I've run across workers like Mrs. Gay in dozens of strikes. I suppose it's like soldiers in a battle. Sometimes those who have not made much of an impression during maneuvers or routine training become heroes when the fighting starts. Something happens inside them, and they become leaders of men; they take charge, risking their lives for the cause. After all, in many ways a strike is like a war, although in most strikes people aren't killed or maimed. But people are fighting for their jobs, for their families, and for their future. Tensions are high as strikers try to keep scabs from entering a plant. I have known strikes where families have been split and one brother has told another, "If you cross that line I'll never speak to you again." I have seen couples divorced, parents estranged from children, and long-time neighbors and friends turned into life-long enemies, all because they took opposite sides during a strike.

One reason the mill owners were so hardheaded was that they were trying to establish the principle that northern New England (Maine, New Hampshire, and Vermont) was different from southern New England (Massachusetts, Connecticut, and Rhode Island). The cost of living was lower in the north; people didn't need as much and therefore should be paid less than workers in southern New England states. For example, Pepperell had agreed to the 65 cents an hour minimum in its Massachusetts mill but refused to grant the same benefit in its Maine mill.

We were able to fight this cost-of-living argument effectively with studies and figures from the union's research department. The TWUA research director was a brilliant, colorful economist named Solomon Barkin. He knew more about the American textile industry—wages, working conditions, production, profits, machinery, history, markets, and ownership—than anyone. His desk—a giant in-box—was piled with government reports, academic journals, company publications, newly published books, articles from dozens of magazines, and letters from staff representatives and local unions. But he could find any paper or report in a minute.

Barkin produced a big research study that showed that the cost of living for textile workers in Maine was the same as for workers in Massachusetts, that their productivity was the same, and that companies made the same amount of profits from mills in Maine as they did elsewhere. Why shouldn't they pay the same amount of money to the workers?

At our union meetings and in our newsletter I interpreted Barkin's report this way: "The union's research director has just made a major study. He measured the stomachs of the mill workers in Massachusetts and the mill workers in Maine. And you know what he found? Workers of the same size had the same size stomachs in each state. Prices in each state are about the same. Workers in Maine work just as hard as the workers in Massachusetts. They get just as hungry and they should be paid the same wage." Workers understood that kind of language, and it helped defeat the company's arguments.

After the workers spent six weeks on the picket line, the mill owners finally realized that "those French Canadians" were not as docile as they were supposed to be. Only a handful were crossing the picket line, and the numbers were not increasing as the weeks went by. They also realized that a strong national union was supporting local workers with substantial resources. I can imagine the mill owners and their lawyers and negotiators meeting in a well-appointed board room in Boston and saying, "We gave it a good try but it's not working. Who needs this headache? Let's give them the 65 cents and some of the other things they want and let's get production in those mills."

New England

I worked for the Textile Workers Union of America from 1944 to 1950 and spent a considerable amount of time in the textile towns of New England.

New England was the birthplace of the American textile industry, and Lowell, Massachusetts, was the first great American textile city. It was established in 1823, not far from Boston, and by 1833 had nineteen five-story mills with five thousand workers, 60 percent of them women.

Cotton mills, and woolen mills, too, spread throughout New England after Lowell showed there was money to be made weaving cloth. In Massachusetts, the cities of New Bedford, Fall River, and Lawrence became huge textile centers; in New Hampshire, imposing mills were built in Nashua, Dover, and Manchester; in Rhode Island, there were mills in Providence, Woonsocket, Pawtucket, and other cities; and in Maine, Lewiston, Saco, and Biddeford boasted about their mills. Connecticut and Vermont also had their share of textile production.

After scores of years without effective unions (there was a handful of weak craft unions), most mills had developed strong industrial unions by the late 1940s. They had orderly grievance procedures, guaranteed benefits, and union contracts. I conducted training classes in union halls, spoke and sang at union meetings and rallies, met with various union committees to plan activities, and showed labor movies to shop stewards and other leaders.

In each mill town I made it my business to tour one or more mill. I walked through dozens to get the feel of working conditions and become better acquainted with the complicated processes involved in turning a raw bale of cotton or wool into an attractive piece of cloth. I usually spent a couple of hours walking from the opening room, where bales of cotton or wool came off railroad cars, to the shipping room, where finished goods were packaged and moved on to customers. I was always relieved to get away from the dirt, lint, and head-rattling din of a thousand looms. Two hours in a mill were more than enough for me, and it was always a great relief at the end of a tour when the heavy door that separated operations from company office clanged shut behind me. Peace and quiet and fresh air to breathe! Was that how it felt when a prisoner was let out of jail?

Those two brief hours I spent walking through a mill perhaps once or twice a month reminded me of what it meant to be a textile mill worker, putting in eight hours a day, forty hours a week, year in, year out; tending the noisy machines; keeping a sharp eye open for defects or irregularities; taking care not to lose a finger or a hand; and satisfying a foreman who had to worry about production schedules. These were union mills. What could working life have been like in the "good old days" when the standard work day was eleven or twelve hours, six days a week?

When I walked the streets of Lowell, I thought of the young mill girls who were fired in the 1830s for reading "radical" newspapers or agitating for a ten-hour day. In Fall River the union had twelve thousand members in the late 1940s. In 1857, when mule spinners there drew up a petition for higher wages, they signed their names inside a circle so the one who had signed first could not be blacklisted. In North Adams, Massachusetts, I talked to work-weary Polish workers who had come to the United States as children. When they landed at Ellis Island, tags were pinned to their coats to indicate to which mill they were to be shipped. They went to work for pennies under the benevolent eye of William Plunkett, who owned the huge Berkshire Cotton Mills and was a good friend of President William McKinley. McKinley had been a guest of

Plunkett in North Adams, and I saw the statue that Plunkett had put up for him. It was paid for by the hard-earned pennies of mill workers. As I gazed at the statue of McKinley, I wondered how many of those workers had the courage or imprudence to say no when the foreman passed the hat to help pay for the statue.

As I walked through the towns in the late 1940s, staring at the huge red-brick mills, I was happy that the men and women who spent their working lives inside those walls had a union to speak for them and stand by them when they needed help getting justice on the job. In every town, history walked with me. The ghosts of union heroes looked over my shoulder, and the struggles of the past were always on my mind.

Lawrence

All through the nineteenth century and into the beginning of the twentieth, no one paid much attention to struggling textile workers. But in 1912, in the city of Lawrence, Massachusetts, a massive revolt of twenty-five thousand immigrant workers rocked the nation and put the problems of textile workers on the nation's front pages. Lawrence was the headquarters of the giant American Woolen Company. Over the years, the company had established twenty-four plants in seven states, and by 1948 the TWUA had organized twenty of them, including the big plants that dominated Lawrence.

During the 1940s, the union had fifteen thousand members in Lawrence with strong contracts and a structure of shop stewards and business agents who settled thousands of grievances each year.

Whenever I went to Lawrence to teach classes of shop stewards—classes on how to enforce the union contract, how to argue a case with a foreman or a supervisor, how the grievance procedure worked, and how to take a case to an outside arbitrator—I could never forget the arrogance and insensitivity of the mill owners who precipitated the historic walkout of 1912.

In my classes I devoted a lot of time to the 1912 strike, and it always amazed me how little the shop stewards knew about it. After all, their fathers or grandfathers or uncles or neighbors had marched for sixty-three days in the bitter cold and snow in what may have been the most momentous struggle in New England since the Revolution.

Perhaps I should not have been surprised by this bit of ignorance. The schools in Lawrence taught little or nothing about the struggle. More important, citizens of Lawrence did not want to talk about ancient history. They swept it under the rug.

At any rate, the shop stewards were eager to recapture this blanked-out piece of union history, and they listened eagerly to the story that starts with passage of a state law that made fifty-four hours a week the maximum for women and minors under eighteen, effective January 1, 1912. The regular work week in woolen mills was fifty-six hours, and therein lay a problem for mill owners. Men could still be worked for fifty-six hours, but mills could not work efficiently if some workers put in fifty-six hours and others worked only fifty-four.

The mill owners had a simple solution. Companies did not have to consult a union, so they cut everyone to fifty-four hours and cut pay accordingly. Average pay was $8.76 for the fifty-six-hour week; fifty-four hours' pay meant a cut of 31 cents a week.

When the workers received reduced paychecks on January 12, they stormed out of the mills. Soon, twenty-five thousand textile workers from a dozen mills were in the streets, and almost half were women and minors. The Industrial Workers of the World (IWW), commonly known as the Wobblies, moved in and took charge. The Wobblies were colorful and radical, and they knew how to run strikes. They believed in industrial unionism—one big union in each plant and one big union across the nation. They also knew how to bring together the dozens of different immigrant groups that worked in mills. From the beginning, they organized an effective committee of fifty-four, representing twenty-seven different languages, to run the strike.

One of the songs they sang, "In the Good Old Picket Line" to the tune of "In the Good Old Summer Time," calls on various ethnic groups to join the picket line:

> In the good old picket line, in the good old picket line
> The workers are from every place, from nearly every clime
> The Greeks and Poles are out so strong and the Germans all the time
> But we want to see more Irish in the good old picket line.

Thousands of members of the militia were called out, and students at Harvard University were given credits toward their midterm examinations if they agreed to serve in the militia. A young boy of sixteen was killed by a militiaman's bayonet. A young female striker was shot to death by a police officer, and mourners were prevented from attending her funeral by mounted troopers. Many strikers and their leaders were jailed. But the workers persevered despite massive opposition from state and local governments and the Massachusetts establishment.

After nine weeks, strikers beat back the wage cuts and won other important concessions, not only for themselves but also for 250,000 textile workers throughout New England. On March 14, twenty-five thousand men, women, and children gathered on the Lawrence Common and voted to approve the settlement. It was a time of cheers and joy, of victory against overwhelming odds.

Seventy-five years later, Lawrence reclaimed its heritage. In 1987 I was invited to that same Lawrence Common, where tens of thousands had gathered for a great festival commemorating the 1912 strike. Lawrence was learning about the struggles of the past and taking pride in those struggles.

During one of the many parades conducted by the strikers in 1912 young girls carried a banner with the slogan "we want bread and roses too." That inspired James Oppenheim to write a poem entitled "Bread and Roses" soon after the strike. Some time later, Caroline Kohlsaat set the poem to music. From the 1960s to the 1980s the feminist movement adopted the song, which had reference to "the rising of the women," as one of its own.

Bread and Roses
Words: James Oppenheim
Music: Caroline Kohlsaat

As we come marching, marching in the beauty of the day,
A million darkened kitchens, a thousand workshops gray,
Are touched with all the radiance that a sudden sun discloses
For the people hear us singing: "Bread and Roses! Bread and Roses!"

As we come marching, marching, we battle too for men,
For they are women's children, and we mother them again.
Our lives shall not be sweated from birth until life closes;
Hearts starve as well as bodies; give us bread, but give us roses!

As we come marching, marching, unnumbered women dead
Go crying through our singing their ancient cry for bread.
Small art and love and beauty their drudging spirits knew,
Yes, it is bread we fight for—but we fight for roses, too!

As we come marching, marching, we bring the greater days
The rising of the women means the rising of the race.
No more the drudge and idler—ten that toil where one reposes,
But a sharing of life's glories: Bread and roses! Bread and roses!

I sang the song during the festival, dedicating it to the courageous men and women who had fought the good fight seventy-five years earlier.

2

Textile South

After I had been with the Textile Workers Union for three or four months, my boss Larry Rogin asked if I had ever been in the South. I told him I had once been to Washington, D.C., which had a reputation of having a southern outlook in those days. He was not impressed.

Rogin was smart. He knew that before I could go into the South to educate textile workers I would need to educate myself. He assigned two books to me. One was *When Southern Labor Stirs* (1931) by Tom Tippett, a reporter's eyewitness account of several historic revolts by mill workers in the South in 1929 and 1930. Cotton mill workers in Danville, Virginia, and Gastonia and Marion, North Carolina, were striking against the twelve-hour day, the stretch-out and speedup, low wages, unhealthy working conditions, and mill owners' complete domination of workers' lives. The workers had a noble cause and a world of courage, but their unions were weak. They never had a chance. The mill owners had power. They controlled the community, the church, and the government that sent in the militia at the mill owners' request.

I read Tippett's book in one sitting. I cheered when the mill workers marched in solidarity and sang their hymns with new union verses. I cried and cursed as they buried their dead, nursed their wounded, suppressed their hopes for justice, and went back to looms and spinning frames, to the twelve-hour day, and the six-day week, praying on the seventh day to a God whose ministers on earth depended on the good will of mill owners to keep their churches open.

The second book Rogin gave me was *The Mind of the South* by W. J. Cash (1941), a brilliant sociological and psychological analysis of southern life, history, and culture. This was heavy, heady stuff. I did not read it in one sitting. Cash wrote about a region unified by the scars of a war lost in its own backyard. Its fields and its cities had been destroyed, a generation of young men decimated, and the system of plantation slavery crushed—at least theoretically. Anti-Yankeeism as a religion was second only to evangelical Protestantism, which dominated the entire region.

Cash's book, as did Tippett's, gave me sobering insight into what the union faced in organizing textile workers in the South. The South, however, was where the cotton textile workers were, at least a half million of them. Not more than 10 percent were organized. We knew that if the union was ever going to be an effective voice in the textile industry we had to organize the South.

When farmers came out of the hills to work in the mills at the turn of the century, the hours were long—from "can't see to can't see." They sang "Hard Times in the Mill," a song I sang dozens of times to textile workers at meetings, rallies, and training institutes:

Hard Times in the Mill
Traditional

Every morning at half-past four
You can hear the cooks hop on the floor.

   It's hard times in the mill, my love,
   Hard times in the mill.

Every morning just at five
You gotta get up, dead or alive.

   Chorus

Every morning at six o'clock
Two cold biscuits, hard as a rock.

   Chorus

Every morning at half-past nine
The bosses are cussin' and the spinners are cryin'

   Chorus

They docked me a nickel, they docked me a dime,
They sent me to the office to get my time.

   Chorus

Cotton mill boys don't make enough
To buy them tobacco and a pinch of snuff.

   Chorus

Every night when I get home,
A piece of corn bread and an old jawbone.

   Chorus

Ain't it enough to break your heart?
You hafta work all day and at night it's dark.

Chorus

The plight of southern textile workers struggling to live on low wages moved David McCarn, a mill worker from Gastonia, to write "Cotton Mill Colic" in 1926. When he recorded it in 1930 it quickly spread through the mill villages. It is another song I have sung many times in the South.

Cotton Mill Colic
Words: David McCarn

When you buy clothes on easy terms
The collectors treat you like measly worms.
One dollar down, then Lord knows
If you don't make a payment they'll take your clothes.
When you go to bed you can't sleep,
You owe so much at the end of the week.

No use to colic, they're all that way,
Pecking at your door till they get your pay.
I'm a-going to starve, and everybody will,
Cause you can't make a living in a cotton mill.

When you go to work you work like the devil,
At the end of the week you're not on the level.
Payday comes, you pay your rent,
When you get through you've not got a cent
To buy fatback meat, pinto beans,
Now and then you get turnip greens.

No use to colic, they're all that way,
Pecking at your door till they get your pay.
I'm a-going to starve, and everybody will,
Cause you can't make a living in a cotton mill.

They run a few days and then they stand,
Just to keep down the working man.
We can't make it, we never will,
As long as we stay at a lousy mill.
The poor are getting poorer, the rich are getting rich,
If I don't starve I'm a son of a gun.

No use to colic, no use to rave,
We'll never rest till we're in our grave.
I'm a-going to starve, and everybody will,
Cause you can't make a living in a cotton mill.

Although 95 percent of textile workers in the South were white during the 1940s when I worked there, you could not get away from the long shadow of race. I soon realized that the three most important considerations in organizing or conducting an education program (or any other kind of union activity) in the South were race, race, and race.

We had some members in the South who were Negroes (as we called African Americans in those days). They worked as floor sweepers, janitors, and laborers in opening and shipping rooms and in dye houses. But black hands could never touch a loom or a spinning frame, and black hands could never inspect finished cloth.

When we held a one-week training institute in the South we could expect perhaps forty or fifty shop leaders. Perhaps three or four of them would be African Americans, leaders among the few African American textile workers in the mills. The question was, Where do you find a site that will take both black and white union members? Hotels? Out of the question. Universities? All strictly segregated. Religious camp centers? There were a lot of them in the South. No blacks allowed.

The union's southern education director was Margaret (Pat) Knight, a native of Greensboro, North Carolina. Greensboro was the headquarters of the Cone Mills, a major textile chain with large plants in and around the city. Pat Knight had grown up in Greensboro, graduated from the University of North Carolina at Greensboro, and was thoroughly immersed in southern culture, customs, and language. Her father was a doctor whose patients included many from the mill community, and she understood the place mill workers held in southern class structure—close to the bottom but a cut above the lowest-ranking, African Americans. She knew all the rules about race that governed every aspect of daily life in the South. She was also one of those unusual southerners who knew the system was wrong, wrong, wrong and had decided to do something about it. Her way was to become part of the labor movement.

Pat Knight was gentle and courteous, but she was also firm in a ladylike manner. She was the perfect union representative to work on the sensitive task of finding a place in the South for a training institute where both our white and black members could attend. One conference center after another turned her down. It looked as though no place in the South was willing to accommodate a racially integrated group. Then she found the Methodist conference grounds at Lake Junaluska, North Carolina, about twenty-five miles west of Asheville. Thousands of white Methodists attended classes and meetings at the conference grounds each summer, but the facilities were available in September, and, yes, the Methodists would consider taking a union group if it didn't include too many blacks. Pat informed them that the union was expecting only a handful among the fifty or so textile workers. With some reluctance and considerable trepidation the Methodists accepted our training institute, and the deal was closed.

We slept and ate in one of the huge, rambling houses on the conference grounds. At the first dinner, we knew we had trouble. The white students came in on time and took their seats at tables set for six or eight, but not one black student could be found. I heard Larry Rogin mutter, "My god! Have they gone home already?"

But as soon as all the white students had sat down and begun eating, the four black students suddenly appeared. They came down the cafeteria line and sat at an empty table together. They knew the white textile workers had never sat at a dinner table with African Americans, and they didn't want to make trouble. Of course, they had never eaten with whites, and they were nervous.

Larry Rogin was a wise operator in crises like this. He got the staff together and gave us our marching orders: "When the bell rings for breakfast tomorrow I want every staff member to grab one of the Negro students, go through the line with him and sit down with him at a table with other students. Hang on to him and don't let him get away."

The atmosphere was a little tense when we sat down at breakfast the next day, but we talked union. We talked about working conditions, about union contracts, about the classes, and about the schedule. After a day or so the whites got to know the black union members as shop stewards who had the same kinds of grievances they did; they had become fellow union members who had names and jobs. The fact they were black was still an issue, but racial matters became just one aspect of the situation. The union story was the central focus of conversations and activities, and by the end of the week much of the normal racial tension had been set aside.

One fellow at the school came from Dalton, Georgia, and was named Dotson. I can still see his face. They called him Cotton because he had blondish-white hair, like a cotton patch. He was the kind of "good ol' boy" some would call a redneck or a cracker. He was also a heck of a nice guy and a good union man. He loved to play ball, and he was out on the softball field every day. Everyone was on the field, blacks as well as whites, all mixed up.

"How did you like the school, Cotton?" I asked at the end of the week. "Well, I tell you, Joe," he replied, "the classes were great, and I learned a lot about the union. That's gonna help me a lot. But when I get back to Dalton they just won't believe it when I tell them I slept in the same house with niggers, ate at the same table with niggers, and played ball with them. And I feel all right, I feel great! They just won't believe it back in Dalton."

One day I came downstairs to the living room of the big inn where we were housed. I saw four or five students around the piano, blacks and whites. They were singing a union song I had never heard—"Since I been introduced to the CIO / I ain't (no, I ain't) no stranger now."

They told me it was an old gospel hymn, "Since I Been Introduced to the House of the Lord, I Ain't No Stranger Now." They were making up all kinds of verses with nice arrangements. I threw in my 2 cents, and we wound up with a fine union song that I recorded on my first album, *Eight New Songs for Labor* (1950):

I Ain't No Stranger Now

I ain't (no, I ain't)
No stranger now (no, I ain't)
I ain't (no, I ain't)
No stranger now (no, I ain't)
Since I been introduced to the CIO
I ain't (no, I ain't) no stranger now.

I'm a union man (I feel so good)
In a union town (I feel so good)
I'm a union man (I feel so good)
In a union town (I feel so good)
I'm a union man in a union town,
I ain't (no, I ain't) no stranger now.

   Chorus

Run scab (run to the boss)
And hide your face (run to the boss)
Run scab (run to the boss)
And hide your face (run to the boss)
Won't you run to the boss and hide your face?
I ain't (no, I ain't) no stranger now.

   Chorus

Brother, sign (put your name down here)
A card today (put your name down here)
Sister, sign (put your name down here)
A card today (put your name down here)

Won't you come and sign a card today,
You'll be (you will be) no stranger now.

   Chorus

"I Ain't No Stranger Now" was played through several times with some good, swinging gospel arrangements, and before I knew it the group began to turn a second hymn into a union song. The hymn, "Let the Light of the Lighthouse Shine on Me," became "Let the Light of the Union Shine on Me":

Once I had no union, now I've got one
It's the CIO union, it's the only one
No starvation wages, no more misery
Since the light of the union has shined on me.

   Shine on me, oh brother, shine on me
   Let the light of the union shine on me.
   Shine on me, oh brother, shine on me
   Let the light of the union shine on me.

At the southern textile training institutes we always did a lot of singing. We would open each evening with a half-dozen union songs from the little union songbook I had put together. After the formal meeting, which might consist of a speaker or perhaps a movie followed by a discussion, there would be a lot of informal singing, more union songs plus lots of hymns that everybody seemed to know. Ninety-eight percent of the textile workers were Protestants—Methodists, Baptists, Church of God, Pentecostal, Evangelical, what have you—and they were all used to singing in church. No inhibitions here.

In my early days in the South I was hesitant when it came to the hymn singing. I had never heard even the most popular of these hymns. One, "Farther Along," became one of my favorites. We sang it every night.

Farther along, we'll know more about it
Farther along, we'll understand why.
Cheer up my brothers, live in the sunshine
We'll understand it all by and by.

Now where would I hear that song in the Bronx or in New York City? But if I walked down the main street of any town in North or South Carolina and asked a hundred people if they knew "Farther Along," ninety-nine would say, "Oh, yes."

I normally led all the union singing, but Pat Knight took the lead when it came to hymns. She knew them all. She would sit at the piano, fifteen or twenty textile workers crowded around her, and knock out one hymn after another: "Kneel at the Cross," "When the Roll Is Called Up Yonder," "Shall We Gather at the River?" "I Saw the Light," "What a Friend We Have in Jesus," "Almost Persuaded," and, of course, "Farther Along" and a dozen others. I soon learned all these hymns and could sing verse after verse along with the best of the singing Baptists or Methodists.

When textile workers at the Lake Junaluska Institute turned the two hymns into union songs, they may not have realized it but they were following an old union tradition. One of the most popular union songs, "We Shall Not Be Moved," is a direct descendant of the hymn "I Shall Not Be Moved." This is the original hymn:

> Jesus is my captain, I shall not be moved.
> Jesus is my captain, I shall not be moved;
> Just like a tree that's planted by the water,
> I shall not be moved.

In 1931, striking coal miners (black and white) in the Kanawha Valley of West Virginia, changed "I shall not be moved" to "we shall not be moved." "Jesus is my captain" became "Frank Keeney is my captain" after the popular leader of West Virginia coal miners. Another union song was born.

> Frank Keeney is my captain, we shall not be moved
> Frank Keeney is my captain, we shall not be moved
> Just like a tree that's planted by the water
> We shall not be moved.

Musically speaking, the line from the church to the union hall in the South is short and direct. In Tennessee, "Great Day, the Righteous Marching" became "Great Day, the Union's Marching." In Arkansas, "Roll the Chariot On" became "Roll the Union On." In Marion, North Carolina, the hymn, "We Are Climbing Jacob's Ladder" was turned into "We Are Building a Strong Union":

1. We are building a strong union
   We are building a strong union
   We are building a strong union
   Workers in the mill.

2. Every member makes us stronger . . .

3. We won't budge until we conquer . . .

4. We shall rise and gain our freedom . . .

5. We are building a strong union . . .

Many times I have led textile workers singing this version in a union hall, and I am sure it was just as moving and just as powerful in its way as when the original hymn was sung in church. I have been in textile strikes in the South where prayer meetings are held right on the picket line.

In one strike in Georgia, I was told, "Joe, this is Wednesday night. That's when we have our prayer meeting on the picket line. Can you bring your guitar and help us out with the hymn singing?" We sang "Kneel at the cross / Christ will meet you there / Smile while he waits for you." While we were singing, it suddenly occurred to me that it was Yom Kippur, the holiest Jewish holiday of the year. I felt a stab of conscience. "My father should see me now," I thought. "He would do a triple somersault in his grave." But I had not taken up the songs with any sense of religious identification. For me, the songs were primarily to build a sense of community and good spirit.

The most famous example of a hymn turned into a union song is "We Shall Overcome," which Charles Tindley wrote as "I'll Overcome Some Day" in 1900. Of course, most people know the song as the anthem of the civil rights movement of the late 1950s and early 1960s, which it was. But I sang it all through the South as a union song for years before it became a civil rights song.

The union version of "We Shall Overcome" came to me through a good friend, Agnes Martocci Douty, who visited me in New York City sometime in 1947 and told me she had picked up an interesting new labor song at Highlander Folk School in Tennessee. Highlander was a resident adult school in the Cumberland Mountains that actively recruited black and white labor, religious, and community leaders for its training programs. Under the leadership of Myles Horton, the school was a pioneer in efforts to improve racial relations in the South.

Douty was a fine singer and song leader, a labor educator who had taught at the University of Wisconsin and was currently teaching in a labor education program in Atlanta. Earlier I had learned two great labor songs from her: "The Death of Mother Jones" and "The West Virginia Hills," with union verses substituted for the words of the state song. She knew a good labor song when she heard it. The song she brought up from Highlander was called "We Will Overcome":

1. We will overcome, we will overcome
   We will overcome some day
   Oh, oh, down in my heart, I do believe
   We will overcome some day.

2. We will organize . . .

3. The Lord will see us through . . .

She had learned the song from Zilphia Horton, the music director at Highlander. Horton was an excellent musician who played the accordion while doing a beautiful job of leading students in labor and protest songs and folk songs of all kinds. She had learned the song from several black workers who were attending the school. The workers, members of the Food and Tobacco Workers Union, had sung it during a strike in Charleston, South Carolina, in 1945. The striking workers had taken an old church song, "I'll Overcome," changed the *I* to *we*, and ended up with a fine union song.

The tune was appealing, and the lyrics were simple and effective, but I thought the song was a little slow for northern textile workers. I successfully sang it at strikes, training schools, rallies, and meetings all over the South, however. After a while I was comfortable enough with the song to lead workers in the North in it. But it was in the South that my spine tingled and my spirit would be uplifted when several hundred textile workers filled a hall with soaring harmonies and those words of hope: "We will overcome, we will organize some day."

It was indeed ironic. I was teaching what later became the anthem of the civil rights movement to white textile workers all over the South. Remember, these workers were from small mill towns and probably strict segregationists, followers of the likes of George Wallace and Jesse Helms. For them, it was a union song, sung in a union hall. At the time it had nothing to do with civil rights.

The next step in the saga concerns how the union song "We Will Overcome" became the civil rights anthem "We Shall Overcome." Before I get into that story, I must describe the use of "We Will Overcome" in a film the Textile Workers Union made in 1950. It featured shots of a major strike—some 1,200 workers—at the Celanese Corporation in Rome, Georgia. One textile worker at a big outdoor strike rally shown in the film was leading people in "We Will Overcome." He likely had learned it from me because I had been down there earlier, working in that strike.

The film was made on the cheap, shot with no live sound and in 16-mm black and white film. We then added music and narration to complete it. For music, I gathered some twenty staff people at the TWUA headquarters in New York City and dubbed in my voice leading the group of "textile workers" singing "We Will Overcome."

There was one problem. The textile worker leading the singing was somewhat out of rhythm, and it was difficult to keep my song in sync with his lips. We had to play the film over about ten times as I tried to match his singing so viewers could not easily tell it was a dub. So there on film was a group of a thousand white textile workers in Georgia, singing the precursor of the civil rights anthem nearly ten years before "We Shall Overcome" became popular.

About the same time I was learning "We Will Overcome" from Agnes Douty, Pete Seeger was learning it from Zilphia Horton. And as I sang "We Will Overcome" to textile workers and other workers beginning in 1947, Pete was singing "We Shall Overcome" to audiences throughout the country. He made a critical change in the lyric. He substituted the word *shall* for *will*. "I liked a more open sound," Pete explained. "'We will' has alliteration to it but 'we shall' opens the mouth wider. The 'I' in will is not an easy vowel to sing well."

Pete tinkered a little with the music and added a couple of verses: "We'll walk hand in hand" and "The whole wide world around." Such adaptation was common with these "folk" songs. Somewhere along the line, "down in my heart" became "deep in my heart." In my singing I had dropped one of the original verses, "The Lord will see us through." My substitute verse was "We will build a new world," and that's the way I recorded it in 1950 in *Eight New Songs for Labor*. It was the first time a modern version of the song had been recorded.

The next major step in the development of "We Shall Overcome" as the civil rights anthem took place with the arrival of folksinger and sociologist Guy Carawan at the Highlander Folk School in 1959. Zilphia Horton had died several years earlier, and Carawan took her place as musical director.

Carawan was a first class folk-musician, accompanying himself on guitar and banjo. He was a good singer, a fine song leader, and an energetic song collector. As a sociologist coming from the outside he probably understood better than the participants the significance of the songs they were making up as part of the civil rights revolution.

He was the right man in the right place. Soon after he arrived in the South the first major student sit-in occurred at the Woolworth lunch counter in Greensboro, North Carolina, on February 1, 1960. Carawan was undoubtedly the catalyst in making "We Shall Overcome" and other civil rights songs known and sung throughout the South. He traveled everywhere, conducted song workshops, produced three LP recordings of civil rights songs, mimeographed songbooks for quick distribution to audiences, and ultimately issued with his wife, Candie, a magnificent collection of forty-six songs of the southern freedom movement.

There were many great songs in that collection. I have been asked many times why "We Shall Overcome" became the undisputed anthem of the civil rights revolution. No one knows. If some distinguished composer had been asked to write an anthem for the civil rights movement, you can be sure it would never have become the anthem. It would also not have worked had experts studied the songs in Carawan's book and tried to pick an anthem from them. Making a song from a book into the anthem for a movement is a matter of mysterious chemistry. "We Shall Overcome" had what it takes, and people made it their anthem without having a contest and without taking a vote.

It is quite a story. Starting out as a black church song, "We Shall Overcome" became a union song developed by black workers and sung for many years by white workers as their union song. It then became a civil rights song shaped and spread by three white musicians (Zilphia Horton, Pete Seeger, and Guy Carawan). Finally, it came home to the black community as the expression of its hopes and dreams.

Religion was always front and center in the South—right after race. Reading Tom Tippett's *When Southern Labor Stirs* had prepared me somewhat for the important role religion played in the lives of southern textile workers. In the Marion, North Carolina, strike of 1929 he describes union rallies that had the spirit of church revival meetings, with workers sending up prayers asking "God Almighty to help us drive the cotton mill devil out of this here village."

I had never heard such rhetoric up North, certainly not in a union hall. Northern textile workers, on the whole, were religious, but they were much more relaxed about it than their southern brothers and sisters. In the North, one rarely ran across the kind of intensity and fervor that southern fundamentalist Protestant churches exhibited, an intensity that easily crossed over into the union hall.

In the North, it was common for a priest or minister to give a perfunctory benediction at a union banquet or convention, but I never saw a prayer meeting with hymn singing on a northern picket line. I certainly never heard the kind of passionate, almost hypnotic, prayer a textile worker delivered at a strike meeting in Henderson, North Carolina, in November 1959.

At the time of the Henderson rally I no longer worked for the Textile Workers Union, having left nine and a half years earlier to work for another CIO union, the United Rubber Workers (URW). But it was the first anniversary of a bitter strike. Scabs had been recruited from far and near, and union members were dispirited. A mammoth strike rally was being planned, and supporters converged from all over the country. When they asked me to help out, I was eager to do what I could. L. S. Buckmaster, president of the United Rubber Workers, had always been generous in permitting me to take time away from my regular duties to assist other unions, and he okayed this show of solidarity.

A union organizer picked me up at the Raleigh-Durham airport, and during the hour or so drive to Henderson he gave me the plans for the afternoon's program. "We open up," he said, "with our two theme songs." I was sure that one of the theme songs had to be "Solidarity Forever," but what could the second one be?

"Our second theme song is 'Onward Christian Soldiers,'" he told me.

"Do you have union words to that?" I asked.

"No, we just sing it straight," he replied: "Onward Christian soldiers / Marching as to war / With the cross of Jesus / Going on before." "Then, Joe," he continued, "you go on for about twenty minutes, and you are followed by Miss Nannie Hughes, who will give us a prayer. After that we have the speakers and the donations, and you close the meeting with 'Solidarity Forever.'"

For this one-year anniversary of the strike, the union had organized quite a program. Hundreds of members were driving in from Massachusetts, New Jersey, Pennsylvania, Virginia, and other states with donations of food and funds for the striking workers. Only a handful of the original work force of a thousand workers had gone back to work, but the company had recruited a good number of scabs from the countryside. After a year on strike, the good union members needed something special to boost their morale. This meeting was planned to do just that.

The local song leader and the spirited strikers and their families performed the two theme songs vigorously. Then I was introduced. Some of the high school children of the striking workers had organized a four-piece rock band, and they were on stage to back me up. I was grateful for that support because we were in a huge city auditorium with about 1,500 people, and I needed all the help I could get.

I opened with "Give Me That Textile Workers Union," an easy-to-sing number Agnes Douty had adapted from "Give Me That Old Time Religion":

Give me that Textile Workers Union
Give me that Textile Workers Union
Give me that Textile Workers Union
It's good enough for me.

1. It will bring us higher wages . . .

2. It will bring us better conditions . . .

3. It stands by when we're in trouble . . .

Then I gave recognition to the faithful union members who had driven many hundreds of miles to show solidarity with the Henderson strikers. I made up additional verses and had each group stand as I mentioned their state:

4. It was good in Massachusetts . . .

5. It was good up in New Jersey . . .

6. It was good in Pennsylvania . . .

7. It was good in ole Virginny . . .

As I moved down the list of states, the audience picked up the volume and the pace of their clapping and stomping. After I sang the Virginia verse, I yelled, "We're coming on down!" There was a tremendous roar from the audience, and they joined me singing:

8. It's gonna be good in Carolina
   Gonna be good in Carolina
   Gonna be good in Carolina
   And it's good enough for me.

   Chorus

There was pandemonium—cheers, shouts, and yells of defiance. At that point I felt those strikers could stay out for another ten years if they had to. My backup band of high-schoolers had provided a good solid beat with their drums and bass, and that helped to fill the hall with a "joyful noise." They were all smiles as I had them take a bow, and the audience gave them a special round of applause.

I followed with a kind of churchlike, dignified "We Shall Not Be Moved," "The Mill Was Made of Marble," and several other union songs. I decided to close my set with "Solidarity Forever" even though they had sung it at the beginning of the meeting. I figured a double dose of "Solidarity" was good for anyone who had been on strike for a year.

When I sat down, the master of ceremonies announced, "We will now have a prayer from Miss Nannie Hughes." Nannie Hughes was a slight woman in her late forties or early fifties who had spent a lifetime in the cotton mill. I was not prepared for what turned out to be one of the most moving experiences I have had in any union hall.

The audience stood in respectful attention. Nannie Hughes closed her eyes and tilted her head toward the ceiling as if she was trying to make personal contact with her maker. She began in a clear, steady voice. She never hesitated and never stumbled. The words flowed from her, poured out of her, in a lilting singsong, one sentence building on the other. She started quietly but picked up speed and intensity as she rolled along. During the last minutes she was like a biblical prophet, a female Isaiah crying out for justice for her flock.

She went for four and a half minutes, and I was told later that she could carry on in that way for as long as necessary. She was moved by her faith, her knowledge of scripture, and her love for the union. She carried the entire "congregation" of 1,500 with her to new heights of belief in their struggle and belief in their ultimate victory over the forces of evil. I was relieved that I had preceded Nannie Hughes. She would have been a tough act to follow. Fortunately, the entire meeting was recorded, so we have the complete prayer:

> Jesus, Lord, our Father, we want to thank you for this Holy Sabbath day. We want to thank you for every privilege that's been our'n. We thank you Lord for every home that's here represented this evening. And Father, we can't begin to thank you for the good things that thou has provided for us.
>
> But Lord, you know every heart, and you know every desire, and you know how thankful we are today for the way that you've watched over us and cared for us. And Father, we thank you for the leaders of our union, and we pray that in some way, somehow you'll look down into the hearts of the ones that's so hard and so bitter and help them, dear God, to realize that you suffered and died for them the same as you did for us.
>
> And Father, we do pray this evening that in some way, somehow, that the way might be opened that we might go back on our jobs because you taught us in your word to earn our living by the sweat of our brow; and Father, you know today that we need our work, we need our jobs. And Father, looking back over the past year, knowing that the children have gone through the cold weather, dear Father, and how they've gone through the summer, dear Lord, and approaching the winter again, dear Father, but we know, dear God, this evening, that you're the God of a thousand cattle on a thousand hills, and we know that you watch over them and care for them and know that you love our children much more than that, and we know, Lord, that you'll not let our children suffer.
>
> This evening we want to thank you from the depths of our heart for every good word that's been spoken, dear Father; and the ones that have persecuted us, dear Father, we pray this evening that you'll bless them too. And especially, Father, we pray for management, we pray that you'll touch their hearts, dear Father, and help them to know what they've done.
>
> But as you hung on the cross, Father, and said, "Forgive them for they know not what they do," so can we this evening, dear Father, look back at the management and say, "Father, forgive them for they know not what they have done." Because they've pushed us out on the line. They've taken our jobs and give them to people that have come from far and near. And, oh God, we pray that you'll bless again every home that's represented. Bless our union, dear Father, especially we ask you to bless every visitor that has come from miles around. We pray that you'll bless everyone that has given one donation to the cause. And Father, we pray that you'll give each one a safe journey home and help them to have a glorious trip, dear Lord.
>
> Now, Father, we pray that you'll be with the speakers of the hour, that you'll give

them the very words that will inspire their hearts, and help us to be drawn together. Dear God, bless everything that we do and everything that we say. But most of all, dear God, help us to remember that you're a God of love and that your love extends from one end to the other. Dear Father, be with us throughout the day and help us to remember, whatever is accomplished, that you did it all in Jesus' name, we pray and ask it. Amen.

After Nannie Hughes's presentation, speeches were made and donations from many different unions were announced to prolonged applause. One speech put a lump in my throat. The representative of the International Ladies' Garment Workers' Union told the meeting, "We understand there are five or six daughters of striking workers who will be graduating from high school shortly. We know they do not have the funds to buy proper graduation dresses. The International Ladies' Garment Workers' Union hereby guarantees that it will pay for and deliver high-quality, union-made dresses for each of these graduates." I closed the meeting with still one more round of Ralph Chaplin's great labor anthem "Solidarity Forever."

> When the union's inspiration
> Through the workers' blood shall run
> There can be no power greater
> Anywhere beneath the sun.
> Yet what force on earth is weaker
> Than the feeble strength of one
> But the union makes us strong.

>> Solidarity forever,
>> Solidarity forever,
>> Solidarity forever,
>> For the union makes us strong.

> In our hands is placed a power
> Greater than their hoarded gold,
> Greater than the might of armies
> Magnified a thousandfold.
> We can bring to birth a new world
> From the ashes of the old
> For the union makes us strong.

>> Chorus

Despite these magnificent verses, despite the solidarity of the Henderson textile workers and families who stood 100 percent behind the strike even after a year of struggle, despite the support of a national union that must have poured a million dollars or more into the strike, despite the justice of the workers' cause (all they asked was a renewal of a contract they had held for fourteen years)—despite everything—the strike was defeated several months after the great rally that had lifted everyone's spirits. Those who could get their jobs back returned without a union contract and with scars on their hearts that would take many years to heal. Many had to leave their homes and search surrounding cotton mill towns for the elusive job.

The company was too powerful. When I asked a Henderson worker how long he had been in the mill, he replied: "I remember Mr. Cooper [the mill owner] coming into my class at school about forty years ago and asking everyone over twelve to follow him. I was twelve years old, so I joined the other kids and I followed him. He took us right into the mill, and I've been there ever since."

That kind of company power and control was still there forty years later. Some years after the strike was lost, a TWUA official summed up the company's opposition: "The company controlled the local government and had a great deal of influence in the statehouse. Company-provoked violence, National Guard troops breaking picket lines, and the mobilization of the town against the union followed—the company framed TWUA's southern vice-president and seven strike leaders for conspiring to dynamite company property. . . . These eight men were sentenced to terms of imprisonment from between two to ten years. The strike was broken, and the union disappeared from Henderson, North Carolina."

I had a liberal education in the South in the three Rs of union-busting: religion, race, and resistance by any and all means, whether legal or illegal, legitimate or illegitimate, vicious or paternalistic. Violent on occasion, resistance to unions was almost always brutally effective. In the textile mill villages of the South opposition to trade unionism was devastating because mill owners were the bosses in factories and the landlords in town. For all practical purposes they were also the mayors, chambers of commerce, teachers, preachers, school principals, chiefs of police, newspaper editors, and judges and juries. A song I learned from the singing of Carl Sandburg via his daughter, Helga, summed up the situation:

> We live in the company houses,
> We go to the company schools;
> We're working for the company
> According to company rules.
> We all drink company water,
> We all use company light,
> The company's preachers teach us
> What the company thinks is right.

You were born in a company house (or the company hospital), delivered by the company doctor, and taught in the company school. You worked in the company mill and shopped at the company store. If you got drunk, you were locked up in the company jail by the company sheriff. When you died, you were buried in the company cemetery by the company undertaker. In that atmosphere you had to be a very brave or very imprudent worker to take a position that might offend the mill owner.

Some owners prided themselves on how well they treated employees and how well-liked they were by textile mill hands. Paternalism was the boss's weapon, but it was still a weapon. A story is told about a paternalistic mill owner who was showing off his model mill village to a group of reporters. He pointed to the brick houses and the library, well-paved streets, and pleasantly landscaped yards. "There's something strange here," one reporter remarked. "You must have a couple of hundred houses here, and I notice that every single one of these houses has petunias in the front yard. Isn't that rather strange?" The mill owner taught the reporter the facts of mill village life: "What's strange about that? I *like* petunias."

R Is for Religion

Ministers of the gospel seemed to be especially susceptible to mill-owner pressure. In the great strike in Marion, North Carolina, in 1929, for example, most of the six textile workers killed by the militia were shot in the back while running away. But not one preacher from the scores of churches in the surrounding countryside accepted an invitation to say a few words at the burial ceremony for these good Christians. One mountain preacher stepped forward and cried out, "What would Jesus do if He were to come to Carolina?"

My union, the Textile Workers Union of America, was affiliated with the Congress of Industrial Organizations, known by all as the CIO. Some antiunion southern preachers told their flocks that the letters stood for "Christ is out" and "communism is on." Others were somewhat more sophisticated:

Cherryville, N.C.
February 7, 1953

Dear Friends:

Recently we have had it called to our attention that a CIO Labor Union election is to be held in your mill, Tuesday, February 10th. We realize this decision rests entirely with you.

However, we feel we would like to let you know our feelings in this matter. We are thoroughly convinced that it would be greatly to your disadvantage to have the

Union to represent you. Many of the benefits and special favors that you have had would no longer be yours under the Union.

We suggest that you consider this matter prayerfully before voting and may God guide you in your decision.

Yours in Christ's Service

The letter was signed by seven local ministers representing congregations of Baptists, Methodists, Presbyterians, Lutherans, and the Church of God. It was mailed to all persons on the company's payroll three days before the election. Union organizers felt that this piece of propaganda turned the tide in an election that had looked very promising.

One colleague, David Burgess, an organizer for the Textile Workers Union as well as an ordained minister of the Congregational Christian Church, conducted a major study, "The Role of the Churches on the CIO Southern Organizing Drive." He found dozens of incidents where local members of the clergy acted as instruments of employers in defeating union efforts. He found hardly any where the clergy had a kind word for the union.

R Is for Race

Southern mill owners were expert at exploiting white workers' fears of racial integration and did so to defeat the union. Although I came across numerous instances of mill owners who played the race card in organizing campaigns, two examples were particularly flagrant.

In the first case, a leaflet (generally mailed by employers to all workers before a labor board election) featured a photograph of Kathryn Lewis, daughter of the then-president of the CIO John L. Lewis, at a banquet honoring A. Philip Randolph, the distinguished black labor leader. She is seated at the head table, between Randolph and another black leader. The photograph's caption read:

Don't Let This Happen to You or Your Family

DEFEAT THE C.I.O.

If you think for one minute this can't happen to you, just go right ahead and vote for CIO. If they win this election, soon you will find colored laborers working side by side with you, taking over your jobs and asking for SOCIAL PRIVILEGES just as CIO has PROMISED THEM! Don't be a sucker! The CIO is promoting social equality through their F.E.P.C. and P.A.C. Don't let your WIFE or DAUGHTER or SISTER be found in the position of the woman above.

The second case involved a pamphlet published during World War II by the CIO's Committee to Abolish Racial Discrimination. The title of the pamphlet was "WORKING AND FIGHTING TOGETHER—Regardless of Race, Creed, Color or National Origin." Don McKee, a TWUA organizer, described how the pamphlet was used as a union-busting tool.

> We had an organizing campaign at the Aragon-Baldwin Mills in Rock Hill, South Carolina that was going great when a day or two before the election, workers living in the mill village received this pamphlet in the mail. The main union leader came up to the office and asked me, "Why in the hell did you send this thing out?"
>
> Of course, we hadn't sent it out. Textile mills bought up quantities of these pamphlets and sent them to their workers, (addressed the way TWUA offices used to send things out) just before an election. This pamphlet was used to kill organizing campaigns dead in their tracks all over the South. Because of this, the CIO Committee which had issued the pamphlet adopted a new policy: It refused to sell orders for the pamphlet unless it definitely knew who was getting them.

R Is for Resistance

In the South, with few exceptions, the trade union movement has not been accepted as a legitimate part of the American culture. Union-busting was the order of the day in the late 1940s when I was with the Textile Workers Union, and it is still the case as I write these words fifty years later.

A number of law firms in the South had well-deserved reputations as union-busting specialists. They could guarantee the company a "union-free environment." In my days with the textile workers we called this group "union-busting lawyers." In later years some had a more sophisticated name: "management consultants." We even had a special song for them, "Union Buster":

Union Buster (excerpt)
Words: Paul McKenna
Music: "Oh Susanna" by Stephen Foster

Let me introduce myself, Jack Gypper is my name
I'm a management consultant, union busting is my game.
I'm a master of the con job, I'm an expert at the hoax
And I make my living stealing bread from the mouths of working folks.

I'm a union buster, the bosses' trusty aide,
I help keep their employees overworked and underpaid.

A classic case of union-busting was that of J. P. Stevens, a huge conglomerate with fifty-three plants and some thirty-six thousand workers, most of them located in the Carolinas.

In 1963 the TWUA began a major campaign to unionize Stevens. Dozens of organizers were assigned to key plants, leaflets were distributed, meetings held, and workers were signed up. Then the company went to work. Supervisors threatened that "J. P. Stevens will close this mill if it goes union." Pro-union workers were harassed and sometimes discharged. The union filed charges with the National Labor Relations Board. After years of delays and appeals, the courts ordered Stevens to pay $1.3 million in wages to workers who had been discharged illegally. Stevens was forced to post notices in the plant, saying the company would discontinue its illegal activities. The company's defiant attitude toward the law was summed up in a memo to supervisors: "What must be impressed upon supervision is that the penalty for saying something may be the posting of a notice stating that the company will not say it again, while the penalty for saying nothing could very well be unionization."

Despite the unrelenting opposition of the company, the union finally won an election victory, although it took eleven long years. On August 23, 1974, in the mill town of Roanoke Rapids, North Carolina, workers in a group of J. P. Stevens mills voted 1,685 to 1,448 in favor of the union.

Many courageous workers deserved credit for the victory, but perhaps none more so than Crystal Lee Jordan, a thirty-four-year-old mill worker who had been born in a company house and whose mother, father, and several uncles all worked in the mills. Jordan is perhaps better known as "Norma Rae," the name of the motion picture made of her efforts to organize J. P. Stevens workers in Roanoke Rapids. It was a good movie, too, one of the few honest ones Hollywood has made about unions.

When I met Crystal Lee Jordan several years after the election, I noticed she was a fine-looking woman although not as gorgeous as Sally Field ("Norma Rae"). Jordan had a few more lines in her face than Sally Field, but then Field hadn't spent fifteen years sweating in cotton mills, breathing cotton dust eight hours a day.

Sally Field did a fine job of portraying the feisty, rebellious Crystal Lee Jordan, who threw in her lot with the union when everyone around her was afraid to do so. Jordan had worn a giant "I'm for TWUA" button to work. She had also attended one of the early union meetings at a black church (no white churches were available) where she and a friend were the only white workers present. "Cotton mill workers are known as trash by some," she said, "and I knew the union was the only way we could have our own voice, make ourselves better."

The most dramatic moment in the film occurs when Norma Rae is hassled by supervisors for her union activity. She climbs atop a table in her department and holds up a sign hand-lettered with the word *union.* She turns the sign around and around so every worker in her section can see it. That's just what Crystal Lee Jordan did, and it was a key factor in easing the fear of many workers.

The election was won in 1974, but when Sol Stetin called upon me in 1979 to sing at a huge rally of J. P. Stevens's workers in Spartanburg, South Carolina, the union still had not signed a contract. The company's "delay and stall machine" was well oiled and had been working overtime during the previous five years.

It was the same Sol Stetin to whom my first boss in the TWUA, Larry Rogin, had sent me thirty-five years earlier for on-the-ground organizing experience. Stetin had worked his way up to national president of the Textile Workers Union of America in 1972 and later merged with the Amalgamated Clothing Workers of America to form the Amalgamated Clothing and Textile Workers Union.

By 1979 Stetin had been chasing Stevens for sixteen years, but he still had a fire in his belly and a spark in his eye when he looked toward victory. The new, merged union mounted a massive campaign against J. P. Stevens that would force them to bargain with their workers. One of the new union's weapons was a nationwide boycott of Stevens's sheets and other consumer goods at major department stores.

The 1979 rally of J. P. Stevens workers in Spartanburg was an exhilarating affair. The big city auditorium was filled with more than a thousand workers from Stevens plants from across the Carolinas and from other southern states.

The textile industry had changed in one major respect since the 1940s. Blacks had entered the mills in large numbers. Twenty or 30 percent—or even more—of the workers in many mills were black. Nearly 50 percent of workers at the meeting were black. They sat side by side with white brothers and sisters, and nobody was nervous about it. At noon, box lunches were passed out to everyone. Blacks and whites ate heartily, talking and laughing among themselves. In my day, feeding blacks and whites at the same table was always a major problem. The segregation laws as well as the prevailing customs and attitudes of the time worked against races breaking bread together.

Speeches and cheers rang throughout the hall. Stetin pledged the continued support of the union until Stevens signed a contract. I closed the meeting with "We Shall Overcome," and black and white union brothers and sisters linked arms and swayed as the music bounced off the walls of the big hall:

We will organize, we will organize
We will organize, some day.

Oh, oh deep in my heart, I do believe
We shall overcome some day.

I never thought I'd live to see that kind of solidarity in the heart of the Confederacy.

It took one more year of struggle. J. P. Stevens finally signed a contract for the four thousand workers in Roanoke Rapids on October 20, 1980. Songs played an important part in the effort to organize Stevens by building a sense of cohesiveness and unity that helped lead to victory.

My First Recording

During the six years I worked for the Textile Workers Union I led textile workers, North and South, in old labor songs and wrote new songs and parodies for training institutes, rallies, picket lines, and meetings. A hair-raising ride in an airplane early in 1950 moved me to cut a record with eight of these songs. I was flying home to New York from a labor education program in Chicago when the plane bounced around like a ball in a lottery mixing bowl. I don't usually worry about plane flights but this one was scary. "This plane might really crash," I muttered. I wasn't worried about my wife and children. What did worry me was that if the plane went down the labor songs I'd been writing and collecting would go with me. Then and there I decided that if I survived I would rush into a studio and record a selection of the songs for posterity.

I picked eight songs that had never been recorded. I had written four of them: "The Mill Was Made of Marble," "That's All," "Too Old to Work," and "Humblin' Back." Two I had helped adapt from hymns: "Shine on Me" and "I Ain't No Stranger Now." The other two, "Great Day" and "We Will Overcome," had been developed at the Highlander Folk School.

I knew nothing about making a record, so I consulted the yellow pages. I found a studio that advertised "reasonable rates." That was for me. The studio suggested a music arranger, who copied down the music with ease as I sang it. Then he, in turn, recommended a male quartet for backup: the Elm City Four. My next job was to find a good guitar player because I knew I didn't play well enough for a recording.

The Musician's Union sent me a sophisticated jazz guitarist who played complex progressions that were incompatible for my simple folk-style tunes. Then I lucked out by finding Fred Hellerman, who was with a new group called the Weavers. Hellerman was just right for my record, and he agreed to charge me $100. It was only later that the Weavers went big-time with several hit records and became one of the nation's highest-priced acts.

We knocked out the eight songs in three hours, and they sounded pretty good. We put two songs on each side of a twelve-inch, 78-rpm record and had two such records. To pay for the project I canvassed friends and colleagues for an advance order of $5 for the album. The response was overwhelming. It was heartwarming to see their enthusiasm. I was able to pay the studio, the arranger, the Elm City Four, and Fred Hellerman. But I was running out of money for the pressing and the illustrated double jacket cover.

The CIO education and research department came to the rescue, like the U.S. Cavalry in the old Hollywood westerns. They agreed to take over production costs, promote the album, and mail the orders. After the CIO took over, we were able to cut the cost to $2.50 per album. Those who had sent me $5 in advance received two albums of *Eight New Songs for Labor*. One song on the record, "The Mill Was Made of Marble," has a story that should be told.

"The Mill Was Made of Marble"

I knew I had composed something special when a textile worker told me, "My grandfather used to sing that song to me when I was a kid." He was in his forties, so he believed he had heard "The Mill Was Made of Marble" nearly thirty years before I had written it. Professional folklorists talk about a song "entering tradition" or one that has been "taken over by the folk."

That seemed to be happening to my song, which was recorded, reprinted in union songbooks, and quoted in newspapers and books as if it had been written by that well-known composer A. Nonymous. After the *New York Times* referred to the song as an "old folk song" in its lead editorial on Labor Day 1992, I decided it was time to set the record straight and tell the complicated story of how "The Mill Was Made of Marble" was written.

My first memory of the song goes back to some time in 1947, when I was an education director for the Textile Workers Union of America. I remember eight lines I thought I had seen printed in the union's monthly newspaper, *Textile Labor:*

> I dreamed that I had died
> And gone to my reward,
> A job in heaven's textile plant,
> On a golden boulevard.
> The mill was made of marble,

The machines were made out of gold.
Nobody ever got tired
And nobody ever grew old.

I thought the lines had the makings of a good union song, and I remember
sitting down at a piano with Pat Knight and picking out a pleasant, simple folk
tune that seemed to fit the words. Years later, my young son Daniel remarked
that the tune sounded a lot like "The Death of Mother Jones," one of my favorite coal-mining songs. He was right. Perhaps I had subconsciously lifted that
melody and adapted it with some variations.

At this point the song had just eight lines and a melody. Then I, and perhaps others in the TWUA education department, began adding humorous
verses that we sang mostly at staff meetings—a kind of inside joke. The last
four lines seemed to work well as a chorus:

I dreamed that I had died
And gone to my reward.
A job in heaven's textile plant
On a golden boulevard.

    The mill was made of marble,
    The machines were made out of gold.
    Nobody every got tired
    And nobody ever grew old.

We had no business agents
To come on grievance day
Because when you looked at those grievances
They up and melted away.

    Chorus

What a job we had up in heaven
Conditions were mighty fine
And they fed you on scotch and on soda
When you marched on the picket line.

    Chorus

It was, oh, so lovely in heaven,
We never wore any shoes;
We never paid an assessment
And the company paid all the dues.

    Chorus

It was fun to sing the crazy verses and make up additional ones. The tune was catchy, and the idea was simple. I decided to try to work out some "straight" verses and turn it into a proper union song.

One day, riding on the New York City subway from Manhattan to the Bronx with Mildred, it happened. With her helpful criticism and kibitzing, I managed to scribble four additional verses by the time we reached our destination. I kept the first verse and chorus and wrote additional verses about the evil conditions—deafening noise, cotton dust, and lint—in a typical textile mill:

The Mill Was Made of Marble
By Joe Glazer

I dreamed that I had died
And gone to my reward
A job in heaven's textile plant
On a golden boulevard.

The mill was made of marble
The machines were made out of gold
And nobody ever got tired
And nobody ever grew old.

This mill was built in a garden
No dust or lint could be found
And the air was so fresh and so fragrant
With flowers and trees all around.

Chorus

It was quiet and peaceful in heaven
There was no clatter or boom;
You could hear the most beautiful music
As you worked at the spindle and loom.

Chorus

There was no unemployment in heaven
We worked steadily all through the year;
We always had food for the children.
We never were haunted by fear.

Chorus

When I woke from this dream about heaven
I knew that there never could be
A mill like that one down below here on earth
For workers like you and like me.

Chorus

I recorded this version of the song in 1950 and this is the way I sang it for the next few years. Somewhere along the way, however, probably in the early 1950s, I became uncomfortable with the pessimism in the last verse ("I knew that there never could be") and changed it to project some hope ("I wondered if someday there'd be"):

When I woke from this dream about heaven
I wondered if someday there'd be
A mill like that one down below here on earth
For workers like you and like me.

I've been singing it that way ever since. Now, where did the original idea for this song come from? I was sure I had seen the original eight lines in the union's newspaper in a story about an old textile worker reciting the poem during a strike in 1947 at the Safie mill in Rockingham, North Carolina. I told that story dozens of times when I introduced the song, so I must have believed it. Years later when I checked the newspaper to find the story it was nowhere to be found. It seems that no such story had ever appeared—a mystery!

The simple music seemed to have universal appeal, and everyone loved to fantasize about the wonderful world of work that was to be. The song had special meaning for textile workers, but it became an immediate favorite with autoworkers, steelworkers, rubber workers, school teachers, and others as soon as they heard it.

In October 1950, when I was scheduled to sing at the national convention of the CIO in Chicago, I planned to close my set with "The Mill Was Made of Marble." I was about to begin my program when CIO president Phil Murray, who introduced me, directed me in his rich Scottish brogue to "sing that song about the textile mill up in glory." Murray had been a coal miner and then was head of the steelworkers' union, but the textile song was his favorite. I explained that I planned to close the program with the song. He stared at me with those Paul Newman–blue eyes and said quietly, "Joe, I want you to sing it now." Although I believed my program would be better rounded if I sang the song at its close, I quickly made a switch and opened with it. Phil Murray was not the kind of man you argued with under such circumstances.

Although trade unionists in all kinds of industries loved "The Mill Was Made of Marble" even though it was a textile worker's song, I started to do parodies with a special set of words for the particular union I was singing to. Each industry had its peculiar headaches or problems, and the audience always enjoyed hearing how these problems were "solved" in heaven. For the Newspaper Guild I sang:

What a paper we had up in heaven
Our editor was Heywood Broun.
We started to work at eleven
The paper was printed by noon.

   The plant was made of marble
   The presses were made out of gold.
   And nobody ever got tired,
   And nobody ever got old.

No newspaper mergers in heaven,
We had jobs and papers galore.
Each city had five or six papers,
New York had twenty-four.

At a national convention of the Brotherhood of Maintenance of Way Employees, I sang another version:

There were no Greyhound buses in heaven,
No automobiles, not a plane.
If you wanted to travel in heaven,
You had to go by railroad train.

   The cars were made of silver
   The rails were made out of gold.
   And nobody ever got tired,
   And nobody ever grew old.

We maintained the railroad bridges—
They stretched from the moon to the stars.
And we painted the station buildings
On Venus, Neptune and Mars.

I also had versions for coal miners, school teachers, bricklayers, postal workers, and a dozen other groups. According to the song, in heaven their problems would float away on the nearest cloud.

"The Mill Was Made of Marble" was translated into Spanish, and I sang it in a dozen Latin American countries. In Germany, an American singer named Kenneth Spencer heard the song, had it translated into German, and recorded it. When I sang the song on the Island of Malta, a union leader there told me, "We have that song here in the Maltese language. One of our members heard it in Germany and brought it back. We translated it from German to Maltese." I always wondered how close the Maltese translation was to the original English.

An American historian, Jay B. Sorenson, claimed in *The Life and Death of Soviet Trade Unions, 1917 to 1928* (1969) that the song was sung in the Soviet Union. Sorenson wrote that even in an "ideal society" workers dream of having work that is "free from its drudgery, its 'clatter and boom,' and they are free from the fear of unemployment and hunger." If it was sung in the Soviet Union, I presume they sang it in a Russian translation. I could not verify any of this but find it intriguing.

In 1993 Pat Huber, a young folklorist working on a Ph.D. on southern textile songs, sent me a bombshell. He had found a poem in an April 1947 edition of the *Textile Bulletin*, a trade magazine for textile employers. The poem, written by James J. McMaham, was entitled "The Second Hand's Dream" (a second hand is a low-level foreman in a southern textile mill). The poem began:

I dreamed that I had died at last
And gone to my reward,
A job in heaven's textile plant
On a golden boulevard.

The mill was built of marble,
The machines were made out of gold,
No one there ever got tired,
And no one ever grew old.

This surely was the source of the first eight lines in "The Mill Was Made of Marble," but where had I gotten it? To refresh my memory, I contacted Pat Knight, who had been active in the Safie strike and had helped me work out the music. She replied, "During the Safie strike in Rockingham one of the old strikers gave me an eight line poem entitled 'The Mill Was Made of Marble.' I believe he had access some way to the *Textile Bulletin* and probably didn't want to admit he knew such an anti-union sheet so he copied off some of the words and gave it to me." Some months later, Pat came across the original version in the *Textile Bulletin*. She insists that she showed it to me, but I have no recollection of her doing so.

The version in the *Textile Bulletin* goes on for twelve four-line verses, not too different in tone than some of mine. For example:

They only worked four-hour shifts
And just three days a week;
They paid off every hour
And the wages were not cheap.

The sweeper drew the least of pay
And that was nothing slack.
He drew a million bucks a week
And no withholding tax.

Toward the end of the song its verses take an anti-union thrust, not surprising because it was published in a trade paper aimed at employers. The workers (angels) have very little to do, and they earn huge salaries—but they go out on strike anyway.

This is the full accounting of the origins of "The Mill Was Made of Marble," the most popular song I have written. Perhaps a musical Sherlock Holmes could tie up the loose ends of the puzzle.

3

The United Rubber Workers

In the summer of 1950 I went to work as education director of the United Rubber Workers (URW), a CIO union of two hundred thousand members that had headquarters in Akron, Ohio (the "rubber capital of the world"). I had six full and fruitful years as an assistant education director with the Textile Workers Union, but a chance to run my own program in a different kind of union appealed to me.

I learned quickly how different the textile industry was from the rubber industry. The Textile Workers Union had to deal with hundreds of small and medium-sized companies, although there were a few giants such as J. P. Stevens. The rubber industry, however, was dominated by five huge and profitable corporations: Goodyear, Goodrich, Firestone, U.S. Rubber, and General. These companies were nearly 100 percent organized by the URW, so they had strong union contracts, good benefits, high wages, and relatively good working conditions.

The difference between textile workers and rubber workers was brought home sharply in 1951 when I conducted classes for URW shop stewards at Goodyear Local 12 in Gadsden, Alabama. One evening when I was free I was asked to come across town to do a program of songs at a textile workers' union meeting. I was happy to give a hand to the brothers and sisters in my old union.

The contrast between the two groups of workers was striking. Almost all the rubber workers were men, younger than the textile workers and healthier looking. They walked and spoke with confidence. They drove good cars. Jobs at Goodyear were the best for fifty miles around, so the company could be selective. They hired high school graduates only. Those who seemed feeble or appeared run-down would never be hired. Textile workers were older, and a goodly number of bone-weary women undoubtedly had two jobs—one at home raising the children and one in the mill. Many of the men were bent over and had missing teeth. They were good union people but beaten down in a low-wage, poorly organized industry. If they made $1.50 an hour in the mill, Goodyear paid $2.50 or $3.00. I could see where a young, bright worker with some drive would try to get out of the textile mill and into the Goodyear plant. If he couldn't connect with Goodyear he would head north to a rubber plant in Akron, a steel mill in Cleveland, or an auto plant in Michigan.

I soon realized there was also an important difference between rubber workers and textile workers when it came to group singing. Many textile workers were in the South, and they were church-goers and hymn-singers. They came from the hills and the mountains to small textile towns. They were a folk community. Everyone worked in the mill, and everyone knew one another. They were uninhibited when it came to singing.

Quite a few rubber workers had come up from the South, and that made it somewhat easier to lead singing. At the same time, they were more sophisticated than textile workers and lived in good-sized industrial cities like Akron, Dayton, Detroit, and Buffalo. They were no longer in the small, comfortable mill towns. Among the various races, languages, and religions in the North were many Catholics from Southern and Eastern Europe. The group singing found in Protestant churches of the South wasn't a part of Catholic services.

Once when I was preparing a pamphlet on the union's history I asked L. S. Buckmaster, the union's president, "What turned a green country boy like you into a strong union man?" "It was the Firestone company that made a good union man out of me," he replied. "I worked for that company as a tire builder for eighteen years. I saw enough injustice to know that without a union we would never get fair treatment. When I was laid off during the 1920 depression I was making $1.25 an hour. When I came back seven months later I got 80 cents an hour for the same job. We didn't get a single raise in the eight or nine years before the big depression of 1929, and then things got worse."

There was a depression song, not as well known as "Brother, Can You Spare a Dime?" but with the same feeling of desperation and hopelessness, that told the story of workers hungry for a job. The song was obviously written before the consciousness of songwriters was raised to include the role of women.

When a Fellow Is Out of a Job
Words: Sam Walter Foss
Music based on the singing of Grant Rogers

All nature is sick from her heels to her hair
When a fellow is out of a job.
She's all out of kilter beyond all repair.
When a fellow is out of a job.

There's no juice in the earth, no salt in the sea,
No ginger in life in this land of the free;
And the universe ain't what it's cracked up to be,
When a fellow is out of a job.

Every man that's a man wants to help move the world
But he can't when he's out of a job.
He's left out behind, on the shelf he is curled,
When a fellow is out of a job.

His life has no laughter, his life has no mirth,
He wonders just why he was placed on this earth;
And he starts in to cussing the day of his birth,
When a fellow is out of a job.

The United Rubber Workers was born out of the misery of the Great Depression of 1929–33. When I taught labor history I didn't have to teach about the depression. I just let older workers tell their stories while younger workers listened quietly with wonder in their eyes at the cruelty and heartlessness practiced by foremen when there was no union to curb their excesses. A Firestone rubber worker recalled:

I can remember going to work every day trying to get a few hours' work. I'd pack my lunch, get on the trolley car, change to work clothes, and with dozens of others, wait for the foreman to tell us if we had any work that day. We'd sit on a bale of rubber and wait patiently for an hour or two, and then the foreman would tell us, "No work today, fellows, see you tomorrow." We'd change our clothes and take the trolley home. The same routine occurred day after day. One day I didn't come in. The next day the foreman said to me, "Where were you yesterday?" I told him that I was thinking as long as there was no work, I'd stay home and save the trolley fare. He said, "*I* get paid for thinking around here. Since you don't seem to be interested in working, you can take a two-week layoff."

The speedup was a killer, but you couldn't complain because there were a hundred workers outside the gate waiting for your job if you walked out. A worker at the U.S. Rubber plant in Detroit told me that when he came out of the plant he would sit down on the curb and wait for the trolley. He said, "Some days I was so tired from the speedup I would have to wait for two or three street cars before I had the strength to get up from the curb to catch the next car for home."

In 1933, section 7(a) of the National Recovery Act, and the Wagner Act in 1935, said workers had a right to join a union, but most employers didn't pay attention to the law. Rubber workers and later autoworkers developed a new tactic to fight employer opposition. Rex Murray, president of the URW General Tire local union in Akron where the first sit-downs developed, explained the new union strategy: "We were looking for some way to gain union recognition. We finally came up with the sit-down. I had read about strikers being beaten up by police. So I thought if we sat down at our machines it would be unhandy for the law to come and break our skulls. They might harm the machines. We had plenty of sit-downs at General from 1934–36. We didn't have a union contract or arbitration, and this was how we had to settle our grievances."

In Flint, Michigan, the United Auto Workers (UAW) won its first contract against General Motors in February 1937 after a historic forty-three-day sit-down strike. Maurice Sugar, a young labor lawyer in Detroit, captured the spirit of the times with a song:

Sit Down! Sit Down!
Words: Maurice Sugar

When they smile and say, "No raise in pay,"
Sit down! Sit down!
When you want the boss to come across,
Sit down! Sit down!

　Sit down, just take a seat,
　Sit down, and rest your feet
　Sit down, you've got 'em beat.
　Sit down! Sit down!

When the speedup comes, just twiddle your thumbs,
Sit down! Sit down!
When you want 'em to know, they'd better go slow,
Sit down! Sit down!

　Chorus

When the boss won't talk, don't take a walk,
Sit down! Sit down!
When the boss sees that, he'll want to have a chat,
Sit down! Sit down!

　Chorus

I had an eye-opening experience after being with the URW a couple of months that underlined two important points about the birth of the URW in 1935: the burning desire of rubber workers to build a union and the meager resources—except for their spirit—the workers brought to this task.

I was preparing to print a union educational pamphlet, so I asked for bids from several union printers in Akron. President Buckmaster called me into his office and told me he appreciated my desire to give the job to the lowest bidder, but "we don't follow that procedure when it comes to printing, we always use Alex Eigenmacht who runs Exchange Printing here in Akron." "How come?" I asked. "We had our first national convention in September 1935," he told me. "We didn't have a dollar in the bank. We did not have a single contract with a major rubber company. We had no staff. We had no money to print our constitution and the proceedings of our first constitutional convention. However, our printer, Alex Eigenmacht, never squawked about the bills. He told us, 'I know you have no money. If you do all right, that's fine. If you go broke, I go broke with you.'" I got the point of the story, and I appreciated it. All the URW printing business over the years, and it was substantial, went to Alex Eigenmacht.

I got to know Alex well. He had come from Yugoslavia as a young man and still spoke with a heavy accent. He told me about his first experiences with the rubber workers:

> You know, three or four of these young fellows come to my shop with a handwritten leaflet. It was 1934 or 1935. They don't know nothing about printing or layout. They want to pass out the leaflet to all the plants to tell the workers how to join the union. Everybody wants to join the union then. They ask for two thousand leaflets.
>
> I tell them, "That's crazy. You got maybe forty thousand workers in the rubber shops." But they tell me they only have enough money for two thousand leaflets. I tell them, "Look boys, I'll print you twenty thousand leaflets. If the union makes it you pay me. If you don't make it, the hell with it. We call it even."

As I write these words years later, when unions have to fight and struggle and scratch to sign up every single member, it is almost impossible to picture the scene in 1935 and 1936, when workers swarmed into the new industrial unions, fired by the rousing rhetoric and the leadership of John L. Lewis. Lewis was president of the Committee for Industrial Organization (CIO), which was established to unionize millions of unorganized industrial workers. Workers jammed union halls as they signed up in rubber, auto, steel, textile, electrical, and other industries. By tens and hundreds of thousands they rallied to the CIO banner. They sang, "The CIO's behind us, we shall not be moved." They sang, "Solidarity forever for the union makes us strong." Autoworkers sang "The Spirit of the CIO" set to the rousing music of the Marines' Hymn:

Oh we fought our union's battles
Won victories row on row.

And we never shirked a call to arms
We fear no danger or foe.

Yes, we'll fight when we must
For our cause is just
We will battle every foe.
And we'll never stop till we are on top
For we are the CIO.

> CIO! CIO!
> And we'll never stop till we are on top
> For we are the CIO!

But it would take more than stirring music to build permanent unions in the rubber, auto, and steel industries. The major companies were determined to keep unions out of their plants. P. W. Litchfield, head of Goodyear, the world's largest rubber company, said flatly in 1936, "The company will not sign any agreement with the United Rubber Workers, even if a vote of employees shows that a majority wish to be represented by the union."

Goodyear opposition to the union was unrelenting, culminating in a union hall in Gadsden, Alabama, in 1941 when company thugs with blackjacks brutally beat organizer John House, who was trying to organize the Goodyear plant. He required eighty-six stitches in his head, but he recovered. In 1956 House became one of my assistants in the URW education department, and even fifteen years later it was chilling to hear him tell the story of the beating that almost cost him his life.

John House survived the attack, but other workers were not so lucky during struggles to build industrial unionism in America's basic industries. On Memorial Day in 1937, the police killed ten workers at Republic Steel's South Chicago mill as striking union members marched peacefully in a parade. Seven were shot in the back and three in the side. Thirty more were wounded by gunshot, and more than fifty others were beaten or gassed so badly that they required medical attention. It was a tragic day in modern American labor history.

Earl Robinson, who composed the music for the "Ballad of Joe Hill," wrote a song to commemorate what became known as the Memorial Day Massacre. The Tom Girdler referred to in the song was the head of Republic Steel.

The Memorial Day Massacre
By Earl Robinson

On dark Republic's bloody ground,
The thirtieth day of May.
Oh, brothers lift your voices high

For them that died that day.
The men who make our country's steel,
The toilers in the mill,
They said in union is our strength
And justice is our will.

We will not be Tom Girdler's slaves
But free men will we be.
List to the voices from their graves,
"We died to set you free."
In ordered ranks they all marched on
To picket Girdler's mill.
They did not know that Girdler's cops
Had orders: Shoot to kill!

As they marched on so peaceably,
Old Glory waving high,
Girdler's gunmen took their aim
And the bullets began to fly.
That deep, deep red will never fade
From Republic's bloody ground.
The workers, they will not forget,
They'll sing this song around.

They'll not forget Tom Girdler's name
Or Girdler's bloody hands.
He'll be a sign of tyranny
Throughout the world's broad land.
Men and women of the working class
And you little children too,
Remember that Memorial Day
And the dead who died for you.

The song has a postscript. When I first came across "Ballad of the Memorial Day Massacre" in the early 1970s I did not know that it had been written by Earl Robinson. I had only a mimeographed song sheet with no music or author's name. When I decided to include the song on an LP album I was recording for the Steelworkers, I adapted an old folk tune that seemed to fit well with the words, and that's the way I sang it. Two days before going into the recording studio in Washington, D.C., I learned that Robinson was the author. I called him at his home in California to get the original tune. I then tried out my tune on Robinson, who said, "Your tune sounds better than mine, Joe. Use it." And that's how I recorded it.

Robinson was a generous and bighearted man with a fine talent. He died tragically in an automobile accident in 1991 in Seattle, Washington. He was eighty-one but still vigorous and active. He will be missed, but like Joe Hill he will live on through his music. Tom Girdler, the villain of the Memorial Day Massacre, signed a contract with the Steelworkers in 1942.

Throughout the 1940s unions won wage increases, good union contracts with grievance procedure and arbitration, vacations with pay and paid holidays, seniority protection against discrimination and unfair layoffs, protection against the speedup, and many other benefits. Workers in the huge industrial factories of America had won a measure of dignity and self-respect.

In 1949 and 1950 unions began talking about a new kind of benefit: company-paid pensions to supplement the meager Social Security benefits then paid by the government program. In 1949 Social Security paid about $32 a month. Walter Reuther, president of the United Automobile workers, said, "You can feed a canary on that, but you can't feed a hungry autoworker on $32 a month." I was at a large rally of autoworkers in Detroit in 1949 and heard Reuther make the case for company-paid pensions:

> The head of Ford gets a company-paid pension; so does the head of Chrysler and the president of General Motors. If an executive who makes $250 an hour needs a pension, how come an autoworker who makes $2.50 an hour can't get one? When I ask these auto executives about that, you know what they tell me? They say, "We can't give the workers company-paid pensions because that would be socialism." "Well, how about *your* pensions?" I asked. "Isn't that socialism?" "Oh, no," they tell me. "That's incentive." You see, the executives are so important they need an incentive to stay on the job. But autoworkers don't count at all. It's the old double standard, and we're going to put a stop to it.

Then Reuther told the story of how he grew up near the West Virginia coalfields. When the demand for coal had slowed, they laid off the miners. But he noticed they didn't lay off the mules who pulled coal out of the mines. The operators fed them, watered them, kept them out of the bad weather, and had them checked regularly by a veterinarian. Miners were on their own. Reuther wondered about that and finally figured it out. The coal operator took care of the mules because it cost $50 to buy one. But you could always get another coal miner for nothing. Then Reuther closed to the cheers of thousands of autoworkers: "I say when a worker gets too old to work and too young to die he deserves a decent pension so he can live out his life in dignity."

The phrase "too old to work and too young to die" stayed with me for months. General Motors and Ford agreed to company-paid pensions that were "fully funded, non-contributory, completely vested and jointly administered" as the UAW proposed, but Chrysler balked at some of the provisions, and there was a long strike in 1950. I wrote "Too Old to Work," put the song on tape, and sent it out to the picket line near the hundredth day of the strike. Four days later the company signed. The power of music? Maybe the solidarity of the workers and millions of dollars in the strike fund also had something to do with the victory.

It became one of my most popular songs and was reprinted in many songbooks and used by trade unionists and senior citizens groups all over the country. I even saw a German version of the song on a record in Berlin.

Too Old to Work
By Joe Glazer

You work in the factory all of your life,
Try to provide for your kids and your wife.
When you get too old to produce anymore,
They hand you your hat and they show you the door.

Too old to work, too old to work,
When you're too old to work
And you're too young to die.
Who will take care of you,
How'll you get by,
When you're too old to work
And you're too young to die.

You don't ask for favors when your life is through;
You've got a right to what's coming to you.
Your boss gets a pension when he is too old;
You helped him retire—you're out in the cold.

Chorus

They put horses to pasture, they feed 'em on hay
Even machines get retired some day.
The bosses get pensions when their days are through
Big pensions for them, brother, nothing for you.

Chorus

There's no easy answer, there's no easy cure;
Dreaming won't change it, that's one thing for sure.
But fighting together we'll get there some day,
And when we have won we will no longer say—

Chorus

Some years after I wrote this, it struck me that the first line in the second verse smacked of ageism. I substituted the word "work" for the word "life," and the revised line read "you don't ask for favors when your *work* is through." That was a big improvement.

During the 1950s the word *automation* frightened workers. At one of our union summer schools we had a lecture on automation by an economics professor. He told workers that there was nothing to worry about because in the long run machines would make more jobs by increasing productivity and raising the standard of living. One rubber worker muttered, "Nothing for him to worry about. Wait till they invent a machine to take *his* job."

During this period machines were developed that could give orders to other machines, "think" and correct their mistakes, translate foreign languages, and play chess. In one completely automated plant that produced concrete, any one of some 1,500 different mixing formulas could be loaded into ready-mix trucks with no manual labor.

Sure, it was progress, but it was frightening if you worked in a plant. I wrote "Automation" in one sitting. I knew it was a good song when I had to sing it five or six times the night I introduced it at a rubber workers' summer school.

Automation
By Joe Glazer

I went down, down, down to the factory
Early on a Monday morn.
When I got down to that factory
It was lonely, it was forlorn.
I couldn't find Joe, Jack, John or Jim
Nobody could I see.
Nothing but buttons and bells and lights
All over the factory.

I walked, walked, walked into the foreman's office
To find out what was what.
I looked him in the eye and said, "What goes?"
And this is the answer I got:
His eyes turned red, then green, then blue,
And it suddenly dawned on me,
There was a robot sitting in the seat
Where the foreman used to be.

I walked all around, all around, up and down
And across that factory.
I watched all the buttons and the bells and the lights

It was a mystery to me.
I hollered, "Frank, Hank, Mike, Ike, Roy, Ray, Don,
Dan, Bill, Phil, Ed, Fred, Pete!"
And a great big mechanical voice boomed out:
"All your buddies are obsolete."

I was scared, scared, scared, I was worried, I was sick
As I left that factory.
I decided that I had to see the president
Of the whole darn company.
When I got up to his office he was rushing out the door
With a scowl upon his face,
'Cause there was a great big mechanical executive
Sitting in the president's place.

I went home, home, home to my everloving wife
And told her 'bout the factory.
She hugged me and she kissed me and she cried a little bit,
As she sat on my knee.
Now I don't understand all the buttons and the lights
But there's one thing I will say—
I thank the Lord that love's still made
In the good old-fashioned way.

A Cleveland radio station wanted to use the song, and I said fine. When I listened to the program I was puzzled that they did not play the last verse. I complained to my contact at the station, and he was apologetic. The program director had thought the last verse too risqué and ordered it cut. I suppose "Automation" is the only labor song that ever received an R rating. Nearly fifteen years after I wrote it, a female trade unionist commented, "Joe, that's a great song, but don't they have any women working in rubber or auto plants?" Every single one of the seventeen names sung was a male's—and no one had ever complained. People sure were insensitive to the role of women. After that comment I always made sure to use plenty of female names every time I sang the song.

4

The United Automobile Workers

The subject of automation was a hot item in the United Automobile Workers Union (UAW), and I was asked to sing my automation song at their national convention in Cleveland in 1955. It was a great honor, but I had to catch a flight to California the afternoon of the day they wanted me to sing. UAW president Walter Reuther assured me that I'd have no problem getting away from the convention on time. They had only one big issue—a dues increase—to take up before I was scheduled to sing. "That won't take very long," Reuther said.

I had never heard of a union dues increase that could be passed in a hurry, but I thought Reuther knew what he was talking about. Two days later I was still sitting on the platform, waiting to be called. The dues debate went on forever. But Walter Reuther wasn't going to interrupt an emotional debate to hear a couple of songs by Joe Glazer. He was too good a politician for that.

I had to postpone my trip to California, but it was worth it because Reuther was a master at running the huge and volatile UAW convention. It was a pleasure to observe him at close range, playing those 2,500 delegates as if he was conducting a symphony orchestra. He knew the delegates. He knew the talkers and the squawkers. He knew the rabble-rousers, the nit-pickers, the frustrated lawyers, the agitators, and the effective debaters.

I can see him up at the podium, smiling, relaxed, and pointing his gavel: "The brother in the green T-shirt at mike three has the floor." He alternated the "for" and "against" speakers. "The sister in the red hat at mike seven is next." He would kill the opposition with kindness. Sometimes there'd be booing. "Wait a minute," he'd say. "Let's have some order here. Let the brother speak."

On a hot issue like a dues increase dozens of delegates would be lined up at the floor mikes. Even when the vote was a foregone conclusion, they had to get on record to show those back in the local that they were fighting for the local's position. After the convention and the speakers had pretty much exhausted an issue, Reuther would say, "Before the debate closes, the chairman would like the privilege of saying a few words on this resolution." Normally, each debater would be entitled to five minutes under the rules. But Reuther would take fifteen or twenty, and no one stopped him. He would bury the opposition in a snowstorm of statistics, logic, language, and rhetoric. He could be biting and sarcastic, but he never lost control. He was always cool. He was in his glory at the podium. He knew the autoworkers and the economics of the auto industry. He knew parliamentary procedure, and he was tough enough and smart enough to run a convention. It was a pleasure to watch him. He was better than Leonard Bernstein with his baton.

When the dues increase passed I finally had a chance to sing. In addition to "Automation," I sang a song about the guaranteed annual wage, a major UAW goal at the time. A rough version of the song had been sent to me by Ruby Williams, the talented wife of a Flint autoworker. I worked it over a bit, added a couple of verses, and came up with "The Song of the Guaranteed Wage" set to the tune of "Sweet Betsy from Pike." It fitted the occasion nicely and was enthusiastically received by the convention:

Song of the Guaranteed Wage
Words: Ruby Williams and Joe Glazer
Music: "Sweet Betsy from Pike"

I'll tell you the story of Jonathan Tweed,
Who had a good wife and four children to feed.
His wages bought food and a place they could bunk
But during a layoff poor Johnny was sunk,
Yes, during a layoff poor Johnny was sunk.

When Johnny was working, he'd get along fine,
But during a layoff he'd worry and pine.
He did not get paid but his bills did not cease,
No wonder poor Johnny could not sleep in peace.
No wonder poor Johnny could not sleep in peace.

Now Jonathan Tweed said there must be a way
To guarantee workers a regular pay
And that's when he thought of a guaranteed plan
And the boys in the union backed him to a man,
The boys in the union backed him to a man.

Said Jonathan Tweed, now there's one thing quite queer
The bosses get paid every week in the year.

But now when we ask for a guaranteed wage,
They rant and they roar and break out in a rage.
They rant and they roar and break out in a rage.

Now, wife, if we win it, our future is clear,
We'll draw up our budget with confidence, dear.
And, children, at last, you can live unafraid,
When you know that your daddy will always get paid.
You'll know that your daddy will always get paid.

Come all of you workers, pray listen, take heed,
For this is the message of Jonathan Tweed:
Though big corporations may bellow and rage,
We'll stand up and fight for a guaranteed wage.
Yes, we'll stand and we'll fight for a guaranteed wage.

In a historic, down-to-the-wire battle with the Ford Corporation, the UAW won a modified guaranteed annual wage without a strike in 1955. Soon after, unions in steel, rubber, glass, and other industries won similar contracts. Those plans, usually called supplemental unemployment benefits (SUB), added an amount to a worker's unemployment insurance check that provided a weekly take-home pay almost equal to regular take-home pay. The SUB generally lasted for two years.

People are always asking, "Where do you get the ideas for your songs?" Some come from a catchy phrase like "too old to work, too young to die." Others come from a need or a special campaign, such as the drive for a guaranteed annual wage. Sometimes you read a story in a newspaper or magazine and think, Now there's a song. After that there's not much to it—sweat, sweat, sweat; concentrate until your head hurts; write one draft, a second draft, then a third draft; and then throw it all away and start over.

"Fight That Line" started with an article in a weekly news magazine. The reporter had been asked to do a story about the assembly line. What better way to do that than from the inside, from the line itself? The reporter found a job on the assembly line at a General Motors plant. He was supposed to stay for a couple of weeks but had enough after a few days and quit. "I've got my story," he said and wrote a hellish tale about what it means to feel the line's steady, never-ending pressure. He had his story, and I had my song. I couldn't figure out a proper rhyme for "General Motors," so in the song I changed the name of the plant to Ford.

Fight That Line
By Joe Glazer

I left my home in Kentucky one day,
I heard up in De-troit you make good pay.
I got me a job with Mr. Henry Ford,
And when I saw that paycheck, I thanked the Lord (and the UAW too).

They put me to work on the assembly line;
My clock card number was 90–90–9;
Those Fords rolled by on that factory floor
And every fourteen seconds I slapped on a door.

　You gotta fight that line,
　You gotta fight that line,
　You gotta fight that line,
　All the time.

Those Fords rolled by all day and all night,
My job was the front door on the right.
The foreman told me the day I was hired,
"You miss one door, Mr. Jones—you're fired."
(I'll see my union representative about that.)

I slapped those doors on, always on the run,
Every fourteen seconds, never missed a one.
And I staggered home from work each night,
Still slappin' 'em on, front door right.

　Chorus

Couldn't turn around and I dasn't look back,
Those Fords kept a rollin' down the track.
If I stopped to scratch my ear or my nose,
I had ten guys climbing all over my toes.

You gotta move, man, move like a super-machine,
Gotta hustle, gotta rustle, it's a crazy scene.
Wanna scream, wanna holler, wanna call the cops
But it don't help none, 'cause the line never stops.

　Chorus

Now, one of these days when I'm tired and old
I'm gonna sail to heaven on a ship of gold;
And if they put me to work in that harp factory,
It won't be heaven—be hell to me.

'Cause I'll be working up in heaven eight hours a day
Assembling those harps for the angels to play.
I'll be working on the same damn string every time,
Even up in heaven I'll be fighting the line.

    Chorus

Now, if I was running heaven, tell you what I'd do,
I'd build a plant up there, brand-spanking new.
And that assembly line would be moving so slow,
You could do your job rocking to and fro.

You could take a little nap between each chore
On a bed right there on the factory floor.
And you would have your own button you could push any time.
Whenever you got tired of fighting that line—

    You could stop that line—
    You could stop that line—
    You could stop that line—
    Most anytime.

Did they hear my song in Japan? I understand that some assembly lines there can be stopped by workers whenever they feel something is wrong. So far, there are no beds on the factory floor.

The CIO

From 1944 to 1961 I worked for two unions: the Textile Workers Union of America and the United Rubber Workers, both of which were affiliated with the CIO (Congress of Industrial Organizations, formerly the Committee for Industrial Organization).

The CIO was founded in 1935 by a group of unions that split from the American Federation of Labor (AFL) because the AFL, which was dominated by craft unions, was either not interested or unable to organize the millions of workers in America's huge factories into industrial unions. The industrial union concept promoted by the CIO movement meant having one local union in each plant and one national union in each industry instead of having a series of different craft unions within the same plant, the way most AFL unions preferred to organize.

All efforts to heal the breach in the labor movement got nowhere until William Green, president of the AFL, and Philip Murray, president of the CIO, died suddenly in 1952 within a few weeks of each other. I never knew the bland and colorless William Green, but I met Phil Murray many times. I had an especially warm spot in my heart for him because he was a strong fan of my music. As the charismatic and colorful head of the CIO, Murray devoted his entire life to putting "carpets on the floor, pictures on the walls and music in the homes" of working men and women.

I recall Phil Murray lecturing a dozen or so top CIO leaders at a fancy dinner in Chicago where I had been asked to sing. The event was given by Arthur Goldberg, general counsel of the CIO, at a private club where the service was impeccable, the gourmet food savory, and the furnishings and atmosphere smelled of money. Murray spoke: "This is a beautiful dinner that Arthur has given us, and I thank him for his generosity." Then he wagged his finger, practically in the faces of his colleagues, and said, "We're all living pretty high on the hog in these luxurious surroundings, but let me remind each and every one of you not to forget where you came from and what your job as a labor leader means. We've been eating the shrimp and the lobster and the filet mignon, drinking the finest wines, and we're feeling well satisfied with ourselves. But don't you ever forget the rank and file, because if you do they'll be looking for new leaders, and you'll be out on the street."

I looked around and saw the group of tough labor leaders sitting with eyes cast down, their faces slightly flushed, as if they were children caught with their hands in the cookie jar. Right after that I sang a few rousing labor songs, and that eased the tension a bit.

Murray never lost the common touch. Small wonder that when he died in 1952, steelworkers everywhere mourned his loss. In Bessemer, Alabama, a group of black steelworkers who sang together as the Sterling Jubilee Singers wrote and recorded a moving gospel song, "The Spirit of Phil Murray," in his honor:

Let the spirit of Phil Murray live on and on,
  Let his spirit live right on.
  Let the spirit of Phil Murray live on and on,
  God has called Mr. Murray home.

Now in nineteen hundred and forty-two
The labor leaders didn't know what to do.
Mr. Murray advised them I'll be your friend,
I'll fight for the right of the workingmen.
When I die I wanna go straight
Where I can enter God's pearly gate.
Every workingman in this land
Don't forget the deeds of this wonderful man.

  Chorus (sung twice)

Well, in nineteen hundred and fifty-two
God called Mr. Murray, say your work is through.
Your labor on earth has been so hard,
Come up high and get your reward.
You been loved by everyone most,
You fought a good fight, now you've run your course.
The people everywhere began to worry
To see the message the Lord give Mr. Murray.

    Chorus

Later, when I was recording an LP album for the Steelworkers Union, I learned the song and had planned to include it in the album. Just before I went in to the studio, I listened once more to the original version by the Sterling Jubilee Singers. I compared it to the version I was singing and realized that I was imitating the real thing. Sure, it was a good imitation because I had been a big fan and follower of gospel music all my life. But it was still an imitation. As a result, "The Spirit of Phil Murray" was the only one of fifteen songs on the album that I didn't sing, and it was probably the best of the lot.

Walter Reuther succeeded Phil Murray as president of the CIO in 1953 while keeping his job as UAW president. George Meany succeeded William Green as president of the AFL in that same year, and on January 20, 1953, Dwight Eisenhower became president of the United States.

Now the labor movement confronted a hostile Republican administration for the first time in twenty years. Union leaders began thinking seriously about working together to face the common enemy instead of spending time and money fighting among themselves. The issue of craft versus industrial unionism, which split the labor movement in 1935, had become somewhat moot by the 1950s. The major mass-production industries had been firmly organized by the CIO, and many AFL unions, spurred by the successes of the CIO, also began organizing factories on an industrial basis. After the initial victories of the CIO, the reinvigorated AFL organized millions of workers and had nearly ten million members to the CIO's five million.

Thus many things began to fall into place, making a normally difficult merger of two large organizations possible. George Meany became its president, and Walter Reuther became president of the industrial union department, a new division of the merged organization that would coordinate and promote the interests of industrial unions.

The historic merger convention was scheduled for the Thirty-fourth Street Armory in New York City on December 8, 1955, after each organization had held its separate convention and closed its books for the final time. The new united labor movement was to be called the AFL-CIO.

There was exhilaration and excitement among labor people about the forthcoming merger. There was hope that a united movement would organize many more millions of unorganized workers. At the same time there was a feeling of nostalgia among CIO activists like myself, as well as concern that the bigger, older AFL would submerge the great social and political movement that the CIO had become.

We should go out with a roar I thought, singing and swinging, telling the story of our struggles and our achievements with music and drama and firing up our people for the battles to come. I proposed the idea of a pageant to Walter Reuther, who said, "Great idea! Go to it."

A committee headed by Victor Reuther, Walter's younger brother and a UAW veteran, decided on a relatively simple stage setting for the presentation of the CIO story. I would be center stage with my guitar to provide the appropriate union songs, and a group of actors to my left would portray the various roles of workers, labor leaders, employers, or public officials. At the right, a narrator at a podium would knit the entire program together, setting the framework for the actors and music.

We enlisted Hyman (Bookie) Bookbinder, a senior legislative aide at CIO headquarters, to write the script. Bookie was a good writer, and he knew the union songs and where they would fit into the CIO story. He came up with an excellent script with moving quotations on sit-down strikes, the Memorial Day Massacre, the fight for pensions, and other highlights of CIO history.

We were fortunate to have the distinguished actor Melvyn Douglas as narrator. We also hired a stage director and four or five professional actors and got the Workmen's Circle chorus of some twenty voices to back me up. We were off and running.

Rehearsals went smoothly, although we had to use Bookie as a substitute narrator. Melvyn Douglas would not be available until the dress rehearsal the night before the official presentation. Bookie was an excellent speaker and a good man on the platform. He knew the script thoroughly and made an effective substitute narrator. We all felt good about that, especially Bookie, who remarked half jokingly, "Well, if Douglas gets sick, I can fill in without any trouble."

At the dress rehearsal, however, Douglas showed us why he was a star of stage and screen. His voice was a marvelous instrument that could be mellow or harsh; it could be sarcastic or soothing, gentle or thundering. His delivery had fine shading, nuance, and perfect timing. I looked at Bookie. Bookie looked at me. "He's very good!" Bookie acknowledged. I smiled.

At 3 P.M. on December 5, 1955, I took my place at the center mike while the spotlight picked out Douglas at the podium on my right. Douglas's voice filled the hall: "We will now hear from Joe Glazer, who will call the roll of the CIO."

I had thought long and hard about my opening number. I wanted to work in the names of every one of the thirty national unions affiliated with the CIO, even the tiniest ones that were always ignored. I wrote a comprehensive, talking, blues-type song that ran a full five minutes. By the time the show opened I had completely mastered it, with its tricky timing and rhythmic twists. I socked the song in there without a glitch as the delegates cheered and applauded the lines mentioning their individual unions.

Let's Call the Roll of the CIO
By Joe Glazer

I'm gonna call the roll of unions in the CIO.
Got 'em right here on my old banjo.
I'm gonna call the big ones, call the small,
Gonna call the in-between ones, let's call 'em all.
Let's call the roll; let's call the roll,
Let's call the roll of the CIO.

We've got Uniteds, Amalgamateds, Internationals.
They've organized the workers in the shops and mills
In the stores and offices, the ships on the seas,
In the mines, on the buses, in the factories
Let's call the roll, let's call the roll,
Let's call the roll of the CIO.

Now down in Pittsburgh there's United Steel
And up in Detroit it's Automobile
And Aircraft and Agricultural Implement too
And on the seven seas, we've got the NMU
That's the CIO: Steelworkers, Autoworkers,
Sailors on the sea.

We've got the union with a smile, I mean Telephone,
Up in Vermont it's United Stone.
We've got Electrical and Radio, that's IUE
And the men who write the news—they're the ANG
That's the CIO—good looking telephone gals,
Quarry workers—sportswriters too.

Now in the inside pocket of your coat and suit
You'll find the Amalgamated Clothing Workers and a label to boot.

We've got Retail, Wholesale, Department Store
We've got Furniture and Wood and many, many more
In the CIO—tailors and lumbermen,
Laborers and store clerks,
All sizes, all colors, all CIO.

On the subways of New York we have the TWU
Scattered all around we have United Shoe.
We have the SOS boys known as ARA
And now we've got Oil, Chemical and Atomic
—I suggest you move out of the way
While I call the roll
Make room for those CIO atoms.

We've got Tool and Die Makers known as MESA
We've got a lot of CIO up Canada way
From Maine and Oregon to the Gulf of Mexico
Wherever you go there's CIO
Fishermen in Alaska, sugar workers down in Puerto Rico
Canal workers down in Panama.

We've got CIO barbers to cut your hair
And CIO tires will take you anywhere
You can light your home with CIO Utility
And the Transport Service Union handles your bags with agility—and ability
We've got Brewery and Textile and we can't forget
The Broadcast Engineers they call NABET.

The Leather Union tans the hides
While the Packinghouse Workers cut up the insides
Pork chops and pot roast
Rubber Workers and Radio Engineers,
Spinners and Weavers
Red Caps and Bottle Caps . . . all CIO.

We've got a lot more union in the CIO
Takes a lot of union to make the CIO go.
When the Shipbuilders Union makes a great big boat
The Marine Engineers make sure it'll float.
We've got Paper, Insurance, Lithographers, Glass
Government and Civic and now I'm gonna pass
Because I'm all through
Except for a few
Like the L.I.U.S.—State and City Councils,
The Ladies Auxiliaries—they're important too.

Every group has played a part in CIO
Every union's made a mark in CIO
Lots of people helped to build the CIO
And I'm proud to call the roll of the CIO
Let's call the roll—of brotherhood
Let's call the roll—of dignity
Let's call the roll—of solidarity
Let's call the roll—of the CIO.

The applause and cheers were tumultuous. Reuther said, "I'd like to thank my good friend Melvyn Douglas for a very brilliant performance. We've all been inspired—and Joe Glazer." "My big problem," Douglas replied, "was to keep from crying during Joe Glazer's songs." "Well," said Reuther, "if you kept from crying you did better than I did, because I couldn't keep from crying."

By popular demand I sang a duet with Walter Reuther. We did "Joe Hill" in front of the curtain while the stage was being reset. Reuther was singing "Joe Hill" too fast, and I couldn't slow him down. He was always in a hurry. At 4 P.M. Reuther closed the final convention of the CIO with a bang of the gavel. One more chorus of "Solidarity Forever" and the CIO was history. The next stop, Monday morning, was the AFL-CIO merger convention.

The week after the show, *Life* magazine ran a great photograph of the last moments of the CIO convention, with Walter Reuther and other CIO leaders lined up on the stage and the oval CIO logo above them. I was at the end of the row of distinguished labor leaders. Unfortunately, the photo was cropped, and I wound up on the cutting-room floor. Only one sleeve of my jacket made it into print. Fame is indeed fleeting.

Right after the show I met my friend Justin McCarthy, editor of the *United Mine Workers Journal,* who needled me because the show had downplayed United Mine Workers' president John L. Lewis, the founder and vital leader of the CIO. Without the inspiring leadership of John L. Lewis during the late 1930s, there would not have been a CIO. But we almost wrote him out of the script. The only mention given Lewis was: "The CIO had three presidents— John L. Lewis, Philip Murray, and Walter Reuther." The primary reason for such skimpy treatment was that Lewis was encouraging dissident autoworkers in Flint, Michigan—a piece of irresponsible political mischief on Lewis's part that Reuther did not appreciate. Nevertheless, we should have given him the credit he deserved despite the ongoing disagreement. Doing so would have upset Walter Reuther and others, but we all would have survived and the truth would not have been so badly distorted.

Joe Glazer's father, Louis, a tailor (standing, fifth from left) joins workers from his shop in Warsaw, Poland, for a formal photo, 1908. He migrated to the United States in 1911.

Joe Glazer, three (standing at left), poses with his parents, Tillie and Louis, and five brothers and sisters, Freda, Gail, Henry, Sam, and Rose, 1921. His youngest brother, Nathan, was born two years later.

George Korson records miners' music in a coal mine in Pennsylvania, 1946. (Courtesy George Korson Folklore Archive, Kings College, Wilkes-Barre, Pennsylvania)

Teaching a Textile Workers Union class in Cleveland, Ohio, 1947.

With CIO president Philip Murray at the 1950 CIO convention in Chicago. (Photo by Paul Vincent)

Joe Glazer's first album, two twelve-inch 78-rpm records. It includes first recording of labor version of "We Shall Overcome," 1950. (Photo by Karl Kosok)

With Harry Truman, Washington, D.C., 1952. (Photo by Nate Fine)

Composing a song at home, Akron, Ohio, 1952. (Photo by Charles Anderson)

With Illinois Sen. Paul Douglas, Washington, D.C., 1954. (Photo by Sam Reiss)

1954   1971

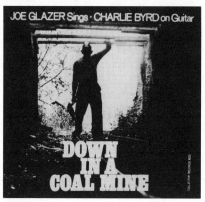

1974

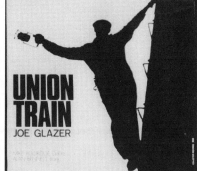

1975   1975

Several of the record covers for recordings made by Joe Glazer during his fifty years of working with labor. (Photos by Karl Kosok)

Members of the United Rubber Workers at one of the union's annual legislative institutes conducted by Joe Glazer, 1955. (Photo by Nate Fine)

Joe Glazer sings "Joe Hill" assisted by President Walter Reuther at final CIO convention in New York City, 1955.

During closing moments of the final CIO convention, December 1955, Joe Glazer leads Walter Reuther and delegates in "Solidarity Forever."

With AFL-CIO president George Meany at the first constitutional convention of the AFL-CIO, December 5, 1955. (Photo by Sam Reiss)

With John Edelman, a veteran labor lobbyist, and Esther Peterson, who became assistant secretary of labor for John F. Kennedy and consumer advisor to Lyndon B. Johnson and Jimmy Carter, in 1955. (Photo by Nate Fine)

With Minnesota Sen. Hubert Humphrey in his Washington office, 1955. (Photo by Nate Fine)

At a summer school of the United Rubber Workers in Rhode Island, 1956.

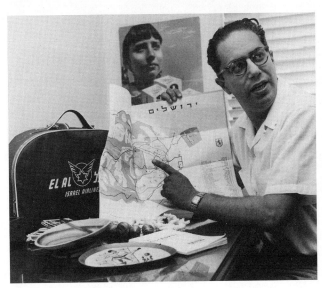

In Israel, 1956.

Sen. John F. Kennedy at a United Rubber Workers legislative institute in Washington, D.C., May 1957. Joe Glazer is seated third from Kennedy's right. (Photo by Nate Fine)

At the first anniversary of the Textile Workers' Union strike in Henderson, North Carolina, 1960.

Joe Glazer presents a copy of *Songs of Work and Freedom* to Ralph Chaplin, composer of "Solidarity Forever," Portland, Oregon, 1960.

As the labor information officer for the U.S. Information Agency in office at the American Embassy, Mexico City, 1963.

With Cesar Chavez, head of the Farm Workers Union, 1967.

Singing labor songs in English and Spanish at a union hall in Monterrey, Mexico, 1968.

At United Mine Workers Convention, Denver, 1968. (Photo courtesy of UMWA Archives)

5

The AFL-CIO

The merger convention opened on December 8, 1955, full of hope and the promise of great victories for a new, united labor movement. The occasion seemed to call for a celebratory song, and with the help of Hyman Bookbinder and Harry Fleischman I hammered out "All Together." The chorus went: "All together, all together, we are stronger every way, AFL-CIO / We will build together, work together, for a better day, AFL and CIO."

As it turned out, we were too optimistic about how long it would take to truly integrate the two federations. One major problem concerned the sharp differences between George Meany and Walter Reuther. Meany had been a business agent for the Plumbers Union, as was his father before him. The plumbers, like other skilled craftspeople, focused on job protection and restricting entry into the trade—many times to relatives or close friends who had similar ethnic backgrounds. Reuther, although a highly skilled tool and die maker, had come out of the industrial union tradition, where everyone in a plant, skilled and unskilled, black and white, men and women, was encouraged to join the same local union. Meany was blunt and direct, tough, smart, and able. Reuther was an agitator, an eloquent talker concerned with problems of other unions, civil rights, working conditions of farm workers, and human rights in general. Both shared an intense concern for improving conditions for workers and furthering democracy abroad, but their styles were radically different. During the 1957 recession, for example, Reuther wanted the AFL-CIO to mount a march on Washington to demand government action. Meany was opposed. He preferred a meeting at the White House or on Capitol Hill. They compromised. They would hold an all-day mass rally and conference at the Washington Armory, which could hold about three thousand people.

I was pleased when Al Zack, the AFL-CIO publicity director, asked me to sing a few songs about unemployment at the rally. I planned to sing "The Soup Song," which was sung to the tune of "My Bonnie Lies over the Ocean." It was written during the Great Depression by Maurice Sugar, but I had rewritten the verses to take note of the recessions that seemed to plague the country every few years:

The Soup Song
Words: Maurice Sugar (this version by Joe Glazer)
Music: "My Bonnie Lies over the Ocean"

Way back in the days of depression
I had very little to eat
But that didn't both me, mister
I was fed from head to my feet with . . .

  Soo-oop, soo-oop
  They gave me a bowl of soo-oo-up.
  Soo-oop, soo-oop
  They gave me a bowl of soup.

One day the depression was over
I almost was back on my feet.
But quickly there came a recession
So once more I start to eat—

  Chorus

We're striking this mill for a living
And one thing on which you can bet
Is that if we don't stick together
There's only one thing we will get—

  Soo-oop, soo-oop
  They'll give you a bowl of soup—(with a spoon).
  Soo-oop, soo-oop
  They'll give you a bowl of soup—(with no meat).

Zack told me I would go on right after lunch, which was a good spot. As the lunch break was coming to a close, I tuned my guitar and got ready on the platform as delegates began taking their seats. When George Meany got to the platform to start the afternoon session, he gave me a quizzical look that I translated as meaning, "What the hell are you doing here?" A conversation ensued:

Glazer: I was scheduled to sing a few songs about unemployment.
Meany: When was that supposed to be?
Glazer: Right now. Al Zack said I would go on right after lunch.
Meany: No. You were supposed to sing during lunch.

Glazer: I'm sure Al told me I would sing after lunch. Anyway, there was nobody here during lunch.

Meany [grudgingly]: O.K. One song.

Glazer: "How about "Solidarity Forever"?

Meany: No, we can't have the song of one union.

Glazer: Mmm. How about "Automation"?

He introduced me. I sang "Automation," and the afternoon session began.

While I put my guitar in the case, I tried to figure out what he meant by calling "Solidarity Forever" the "song of one union." "Solidarity Forever" was well on its way to becoming the anthem of the American labor movement. At first I thought he was thinking about "Solidarity Forever" as a song of the Industrial Workers of the World because it had been written in 1915 by the Wobbly poet Ralph Chaplin. On second thought, I realized that Meany wouldn't know the history of the song. Then it hit me. He probably thought that "Solidarity Forever" was a UAW song. The UAW's newspaper was *Solidarity,* and its headquarters building in Detroit was called Solidarity House. Walter Reuther always talked about "teamwork in the leadership, solidarity in the ranks." And, of course, they loved to sing "Solidarity Forever" at UAW meetings. That was as much "Solidarity" as Meany could stand at a rally that had been forced on him by Reuther. "Solidarity Forever" was out.

Another experience involving Meany and labor music occurred at the AFL-CIO convention in Miami in 1961. At the time, copper miners and refinery and smelter workers were out on a long, bitter strike against Phelps-Dodge, Anaconda, and other big producers. A majority of striking workers were members of the Steelworkers Union, and Joe Molony, vice president of the union, was chief negotiator.

Molony was a colorful and eloquent Irishman who understood the power of labor music as an inspirational weapon during a strike. During the 1930s he had helped organize the mammoth Lackawanna Steel Works of U.S. Steel outside Buffalo. Years later, he described that campaign to a reporter: "We sang songs and they came from our heart—that we shall not be moved. We faced Steel, the richest and most ruthless and most arrogant industry in the world. And we beat them to their knees. We did it singing on the picket line. When you stop singing the revolution is ended and so has the progress of the union."

Molony grabbed me outside the convention hall and started talking about the copper strike. "Joe, this strike has been going on for months, and we need something special to boost the morale of the strikers. We've got a strong resolution coming before the convention tomorrow pledging the support of the AFL-CIO for as long as it takes. We've got unions lined up prepared to make donations of $25,000 or $50,000 to the strike fund. Wouldn't it be great to have a song or two like 'Joe Hill?'"

I told him I thought it was a fine idea. "Joe Hill" would be perfect because it had a verse about copper bosses:

"The copper bosses killed you, Joe
They shot you, Joe," says I.
"Takes more than guns to kill a man,"
Says Joe, "I didn't die."
Says Joe, "I didn't die."

"I'll just check it out with the boss," said Molony, meaning George Meany. "Matter of courtesy. Should be no problem."

Molony, agitated, called me at my hotel that night. He sounded like he would burst, and his brogue seemed thicker than usual. "Joe, we've got trouble," he said. "I talked to George and you know what he told me? He said, 'Why waste time on songs? Pass the resolution and collect the money. Forget about the music.'" Molony was beside himself. "Can you imagine, Joe, you can't sing a union song at a union convention?" The next day the resolution was passed, stirring speeches were made, and hundreds of thousands of dollars were pledged. But music could have turned that convention into a revival meeting.

George Meany just didn't have the feel for this kind of thing, although he would react positively when he heard union songs that someone else had put on a program. Years later, when I sang at a convention dinner of the American Newspaper Guild where he was speaking, I could see Meany applaud and enjoy each song. When I sat down, he said, "Nice job, Joe." That was extravagant praise, coming from George Meany. For the occasion, the Guild put out an LP recording with Meany's speech on one side and my group of newspaper union songs on the other. They called it *Meany and Glazer Go on Record.* It remains a good memento.

George Meany was sixty-one at the time of the merger. One of my labor expert friends predicted he wouldn't last long because he was too heavy and smoked so many cigars. He was still going strong twenty years later but was beginning to slow down by the time he announced his retirement in 1979 at the age of eighty-five.

At his final AFL-CIO convention in 1979 he was in a wheelchair because of a bad hip, yet he made the best speech of the convention. The *New York Times,* reviewing his long labor career, called him the "lion of the labor movement." The article quoted a stanza from a song I had written about Meany's retirement and then pointed out that "even lions get old." Meany was wheeled out through a back door on the platform, through the hotel kitchens, and to a waiting car. Lane Kirkland, secretary-treasurer of the AFL-CIO and a member of the Masters, Mates and Pilots Union, became the new president. This was my farewell song for George Meany:

Big Union Daddy's Stepping Down
By Joe Glazer

Big Union Daddy's stepping down, do you hear?
Big Union Daddy is retiring this year,
It's the ending of an era, so let us shed a tear,
Big Union Daddy's stepping down.

No more we'll see that big cigar stuck in that iron jaw,
No more he'll pound the table for the labor reform law,
You just won't find a plumber like Big Daddy anymore;
Big Union Daddy's stepping down.

The president in the White House, sitting, working all alone,
No more will get that chilly feeling deep down in his bone,
When his secretary says, "I've got Big Daddy on the phone."
Big Union Daddy's stepping down.

He never was a diplomat—that everybody knows;
He said just what he had to say—he stepped on lots of toes;
But he was respected by his friends, as well as by his foes.
Big Union Daddy's stepping down.

One of these days Big Daddy's gonna cross the Great Divide;
He'll meet Gompers, John L. Lewis, and Walter Reuther on the other side.
What a union meeting that'll be—I wonder who'll preside?
Big Union Daddy's stepping down.

It's gonna be a job to fill Big Union Daddy's shoes.
A captain like Big Union Daddy's mighty hard to lose.
But I see the first mate on the bridge, and, brother, that's good news,
'Cause Big Union Daddy's stepping down.

Yes, Big Union Daddy's stepping down, do you hear?
Big Union Daddy is retiring this year.
It's the ending of an era—so let us shed a tear,
Big Union Daddy's stepping down.

6

Coal

Anyone interested in labor songs, as I am, is bound to learn and sing a lot of songs about coal miners. "Which Side Are You On?" was the first mining song I learned. It depicted, as graphically as any, the clash between miners determined to have a union and mine operators vehemently opposed to giving up any control over miners' lives. It was written in 1931 by Florence Reece, whose husband was a coal miner in Harlan County, Kentucky.

Which Side Are You On?
By Florence Reece

Come all of you good workers,
Good news to you I'll tell
Of how the good old union
Has come in here to dwell.

Which side are you on?
Which side are you on?
Which side are you on?
Which side are you on?

My daddy was a miner
And I'm a miner's son,
And I'll stick with the union
Till ev'ry battle's won.

Chorus

They say in Harlan County
There are no neutrals there;
You'll either be a union man
Or a thug for J. H. Blair.

Chorus

Oh, workers, can you stand it
Oh, tell me how you can.
Will you be a lousy scab
Or will you be a man?

Chorus

Don't scab for the bosses,
Don't listen to their lies.
Us poor folks haven't got a chance
Unless we organize.

Chorus

Although I had sung "Which Side" at hundreds of union meetings around the country for years, it wasn't until 1981 that I met Florence Reece in Washington, D.C., when we were both performing at the giant Solidarity Day Rally sponsored by the AFL-CIO. She was delighted when I told her how much I had used her song.

At the time, she was eighty-one and looked like everyone's grandma—white hair, eyeglasses, friendly smile, and plain cotton dress. When I asked if she had any fear of singing before three hundred thousand workers, she replied, "I wasn't afraid when I sang my song to the coal miners of Harlan County with all those gun thugs around, so why should I be afraid now?"

She explained how she came to write her songs: "I've always been at the poor man's side, and almost everything I write about leans toward that. We lived very poor and very hard. My father walked two mountains to get to work. He was killed in the mines. I felt that with a song, or a story, or a poem, the troubles was a little easier. I've heard that when the Negroes worked on the railroad they'd sing songs, and it would help them. I'd sing when I washed dishes; I'd sing when I'd rock my babies to sleep."

Not long after meeting Florence Reece, I wrote some new verses to the song and sang them at a protest rally held in front of the headquarters of the United Mine Workers Union. The miners then marched to the White House several blocks away to protest Ronald Reagan's attempt to cut the benefits miners received when they contracted pneumoconiosis (black lung disease). I think Florence Reece would have liked my adaptation of her song and the use to which I put it:

The miner's eating coal dust
Way down in the mine.

After years of eating coal dust
His lungs ain't worth a dime.

> Which side are you on?
> Which side are you on?
> Which side are you on?
> Which side are you on?

The coal miner's in trouble
When that black lung devil hits.
He can't live on jellybeans.
He needs his benefits.

> Chorus

Oh, Reagan, Ronald Reagan,
How could you be so mean
To steal the bread of a miner
And feed him jelly beans?

> Chorus

"Which Side Are You On?" is a great all-purpose rally and picket-line song. I have adapted it for low-wage textile workers, school teachers, and high-wage football players. When I sang an adaptation of the song to the convention of the National Football League Players Association (NFLPA) in 1972, I was not sure if these highly paid union members, many of them earning hundreds of thousands of dollars a year, could relate to it. But they risked their limbs and necks every Sunday on the playing field and were ready to fight for their fair share of the millions that owners collected from fat television contracts. The players bellowed out the chorus with the same spirit that coal miners or steel-workers would:

Come all you football players
Wherever you may be.
The time has come to take a stand
For solidarity.

> Which side are you on?
> Which side are you on?
> Which side are you on?
> Which side are you on?

Don't stooge for the owners;
Don't listen to their lies.
Football players can't fight back
Unless they organize.

Chorus

In this coming battle,
No neutrals can be found.
You'll stand up with your buddies
Or you'll crawl upon the ground.

Chorus

I'm standing by my union
For that's the only way.
I'm proud to be a member
Of the NFLPA.

Chorus

Another favorite coal-mining song I learned during my early days in the labor movement—"The Death of Mother Jones"—was radically different than "Which Side Are You On?" It was a song for quiet contemplation, not one for rallying the troops. I've sung it in labor history classes, at labor education conferences, at formal concerts, and in hotel rooms after a long convention day.

I learned the song in 1945 from Agnes Martocci Douty, who had picked it up in 1932 in West Virginia. After college graduation she and other young Socialists went to West Virginia to conduct educational and recreational programs for miners' children during a long strike. She was a fine singer and song leader, and the first time I heard the song I resolved to learn it.

The Death of Mother Jones
Author Unknown

The world today is mourning the death of Mother Jones;
Grief and sorrow hover around the miners' homes.
This grand old champion of labor has gone to a better land,
But the hard-working miners, they miss her guiding hand.

Through the hills and over the valleys, in every mining town,
Mother Jones was ready to help them; she never let them down.
In front with the striking miners she always could be found.
She fought for right and justice; she took a noble stand.

With a spirit strong and fearless, she hated that which was wrong;
She never gave up fighting until her breath was gone.
May the workers all get together to carry out her plan,
And bring back better conditions for every laboring man.

Not many labor leaders have songs written about them when they die, but Mary (Mother) Jones was the most remarkable woman produced by the American labor movement, and she deserved the song. "The Death of Mother Jones" began to circulate in West Virginia soon after she died in 1930, reportedly at the age of one hundred (although some researchers believe her true age was closer to ninety).

No one is sure of the song's origin, but it could have been written by any of the thousands of coal miners Mother Jones loved and fought for all her life. She shared their snacks and their meager food in dreary mine patches. She organized bands of women and marched with them for miles through the hills to help unionize scab miners. She inspired men with her eloquence, fearlessness, and devotion. And sometimes she helped bury miners' little children who had died for lack of food.

Mother Jones was buried, as she requested, in the union miners' cemetery in Mount Olive, Illinois, next to four coal miners who had been shot during a strike in 1898. Over the years, the original monument had deteriorated and cracked and the inscribed letters faded.

In 1992 a restored monument was officially dedicated, paid for with donations from local miners and others. At the dedication I sang "The Death of Mother Jones" to several hundred who had gathered there. It was probably the first time the song had been sung at her gravesite and the first time most of those who attended had heard it. I was thrilled to revive the moving, heartfelt expression of love for Mother Jones in the most appropriate place for it to be sung.

"Which Side Are You On?" and "The Death of Mother Jones" are only two of hundreds of memorable coal-mining songs composed and sung by miners. One man, George Korson, is to be thanked for collecting and preserving most of the songs. We met in 1961 and became steadfast friends.

Korson grew up in northeastern Pennsylvania, in the heart of the anthracite coalfields. Anthracite is a hard, shiny coal found in the United States only in northeastern Pennsylvania. Bituminous, the other principal coal, is a soft coal found in central and western Pennsylvania, West Virginia, Kentucky, Illinois, and many other states.

As a reporter for the *Wilkes-Barre Record*, Korson covered miners' weddings and christenings as well as their union's strikes and its victories. All too often he wrote about the mining accidents that brought tragedy to every family.

The early miners in Pennsylvania came from Scotland, Wales, England, and Ireland. Singing came as natural as breathing to them. They sang in barrooms, at family celebrations, and at gatherings at the company store. They sang about life in the coal camp. They also sang about mine disasters and the tragedy of lost lives and mourning widows.

Korson was stirred by such songs and decided to check the public library in Pottsville, Pennsylvania, for a collection of them. The year was 1924, and this is how he described his experience:

> I asked the librarian, Edith Patterson, for a book on anthracite miners' songs. I knew there were collections of lumbermen's ballads, cowboy songs, and sailors' chanties. So I was sure there were collections of miners' songs.
> "There aren't any," she said, "but I'll send out a search request to the Library of Congress just to make sure."
> I was surprised several weeks later when Ms. Patterson reported that there was no such collection. I said, "There certainly ought to be."
> "Why don't you try to collect those songs yourself?" she urged.

Korson picked up Patterson's challenge and never stopped until the day he died in 1967 at the age of sixty-eight. In 1927 he published his first effort, a modest book of forty-two songs that was entitled *Songs and Ballads of the Anthracite Miners.* In 1938 he produced a greatly expanded volume, *Minstrels of the Mine Patch: Songs and Stories of the Anthracite Industry,* which had more than a hundred songs and scores of stories about how the songs were made up and how miners lived and worked. He also included a dozen biographies of the minstrels who composed the songs. The dedication page read, "to Edith Patterson."

In the early 1960s, Korson and I took long walks, and over many a lunch hour in Washington we talked about the songs I wanted to learn and about the miners who made them up. I had read and reread Korson's *Minstrels of the Mine Patch* and his follow-up volume *Coal Dust on the Fiddle: Songs and Stories of the Bituminous Industry* (1943). In fact, I kept both books by my bedside. The books—eight hundred pages and 250 different coal-mining songs—are full of wonderful nuggets about miners at work and at play and about their families and lives in mining communities. Korson at times would lug a heavy recording machine right into the coal mines, connecting an electric cord of many yards a long distance to the nearest outlet.

The miners were honest and uninhibited when he turned on his big recording machine. Korson succeeded in getting the best from them because, as his daughter Betsy said, "Coal miners and their lives were as close to me as if I had been born and raised among them. Their songs, joys, sorrows, problems and sometimes the miners themselves filled our home ever since I can remember. Many of the miners whose songs Daddy recorded became lifelong friends."

Korson grew up in a poor family and had five siblings. His father, a Jewish immigrant from the Ukraine, was a house painter who could not make a decent living. Korson managed to get through high school and went to work immediately as a reporter in anthracite country. All of his early work, beginning with the fateful encouragement from librarian Edith Patterson through the publication of *Minstrels of the Mine Patch* in 1938, was supported by his work as a reporter, with help from his wife Rae. The couple married in 1926.

In 1938, to his credit, the president of the United Mine Workers Union, John L. Lewis, recognized the value of Korson's work on anthracite miners and provided him with a grant to research the songs and stories of bituminous miners. With Lewis's blessing and financial support, Korson worked three years full time on the task, traveling for hours over narrow, winding, mountainous roads or hiking to isolated mountain cabins. If there was no electricity for his portable recording machine, he would take the singer to a neighbor's house or into town. On one occasion, Korson recorded songs in a little crossroads store, where he disconnected a refrigerator so he could plug in the recorder.

Korson gathered hundreds and hundreds of songs, stories, legends, tales, sayings, and bits of coal-mining history that had never before been written down. Although he had no formal training as a folklorist, his tenacity in hunting songs and stories, along with his love and knowledge of the mining community, made him as effective as any academic specialist.

Much of his material appeared in his 450-page *Coal Dust on the Fiddle,* but Korson told me he could have filled another book the same size with the material he had to leave out. I understood what he meant when I visited him and Rae. Their small apartment on Sixteenth Street in Washington, D.C., overflowed with notes, files, folders, recordings, letters, photos, newspaper clippings, piles of UMW journals, manuscripts, and the other memorabilia he had collected during forty years of research. Rae Korson, who worked as a librarian for the Library of Congress, was of great assistance in keeping some order in what looked like chaos. She ultimately was made head of the Archive of Folk Song at the library and upon his death helped organize and codify his papers at Kings College in Wilkes-Barre, Pennsylvania, in the heart of anthracite coal country.

In 1945 the Library of Congress issued an album, *Songs and Ballads of the Anthracite Miners,* sung by miners Korson had discovered, many of whom were long past their singing prime. A second record, *Songs and Ballads of the Bituminous Miners,* followed a few years later. The recordings were made in the field—in barrooms, homes, and sometimes mines. The unaccompanied voices were rough and sometimes wavered, but they had the authentic quality of coming from the source.

One song, "When the Breaker Starts Up Full Time," was sung in Irish dialect and particularly interested me. In it, a miner's wife fantasizes about how wonderful life will be when the mine starts running again and money rolls in. The song also expresses one immigrant group's prejudice against another.

When I asked Korson to tell me what he knew about Con Carbon, the song's author, he smiled and dug a little booklet from a filing cabinet: *Con Carbon's Own Songster.* The publication must have been about sixty years old. Korson turned its fragile pages carefully until he came to "When the Breaker Starts Up Full Time" and said:

> Carbon sold the booklets for 10 cents a copy. But he never made any money from his music, though his songs were sung in every town in the anthracite region. He lived poor, and he died poor. He just loved to bring some joy to his fellow miners.

When the Breaker Starts Up Full Time
By Con Carbon

Me troubles are o'er, Mrs. Murphy,
For the Dutchman next door told me straight.
That the breaker starts full time on Monday
That's what he told me any rate.

Sure, the boss he told Mickey this morning
When he's 'bout to enter the mine,
That the coal was quite scarce down 'bout New York
And the breaker would start on full time.

And it's, oh, my, if the news be true,
Me store bill's the first thing I'll pay.
And a new parlor suite and a lounge I will buy
And an organ for Bridgie, hooray.
Me calico skirt I'll throw into the dirt
And in silk ones won't I cut a shine?
Cheer up, Mrs. Murphy, b'damn, we'll eat turkey
When the breaker starts up on full time.

I'll ne'er stick me hand in the washtub.
The Chineeman he'll get me trade.
I'll ne'er pick a coal from the dirt bank.
I'll buy everything ready made.
I'll dress up me children like fairies.
I'll build up a house neat and fine.
And we'll move away from the Hungaries.
When the breaker starts up on full time.

Chorus

In discussing the Library of Congress records with Korson, I expressed regret that, invaluable as they were to folklorists and other specialists, the scratchy pressings of unaccompanied voices would not attract general labor audiences and others who should be acquainted with the songs. As much as he had a special affection for coal-miner songs, Korson agreed that a high-quality studio recording would make them accessible to a wider audience. "But I don't want a big, fancy production," he warned. "I want you to keep the flavor and the spirit of the original recordings." I agreed.

We made a working tape of the songs, and I played them over and over until I mastered the various Scottish, Irish, or Slavic accents. I got the ace guitarist Charlie Byrd to back me up, which delighted Korson because Byrd could capture the various idioms. When playing a Scottish song, he was able to transport listeners to the Highlands, where the scent of heather was in the air. It was my Scottish accent for "Jolly Wee Miner Men" that displeased Korson. I kept mixing it up with an Irish accent, but after some intense coaching right there in the studio I got it right:

Jolly Wee Miner Men
Author Unknown

We're all jolly wee miner men
And miner men are we.
We have traveled through Canada
For many's the long dee.
We have traveled East and traveled West
This country round and round
For to find out the treasures
That lie below the ground.

For "Drill Man Blues," the music Charlie Byrd played was properly somber. The composer, George "Curly" Sizemore, had struggled for breath after developing silicosis from his years as a rock driller in the mines. Korson recalled recording Sizemore at his home in West Virginia: "There were frequent breaks in Sizemore's singing as he paused for breath. He told me new ballads form themselves in his mind as he drills, but he cannot sing them because he would get a mouthful of dust when he parted his lips." With that in mind, I tried to capture Sizemore's mood of fatalism and despair when I sang his song:

Drill Man Blues
By George Sizemore

I used to be a drill man
Down at old Parlee;

Drilling through slate and sandrock
Till it got the best of me.

Rock dust has almost killed me.
It's turned me out in the rain.
For dust has settled on my lungs
And causes me constant pain.

I can hear my hammer roaring
As I lay down for my sleep,
For drilling is the job I love
And this I will repeat

It's killed two fellow workers
Here at Old Parlee.
And now I've eaten so much dust, Lord,
That it's killing me.

I'm thinking of poor drill men
Away down in the mines,
Who from eating dust will end up
With a fate just like mine.

All together we recorded a dozen of Korson's best songs. We weren't able to press a record right away, but that turned out for the best. We were able to add several songs I sang a few years later at a UMW convention and came up with an expanded LP record, *Down in a Coal Mine.*

On that record I included "Sixteen Tons" and "Dark as a Dungeon," both written by Merle Travis, who was from a coal-mining family that worked in Beech Creek, Kentucky. "Sixteen Tons" is the most popular mining song ever written. According to folklorist Archie Green, it sold a million copies in twenty-one days after Tennessee Ernie Ford recorded it in 1955. By 1957 it had sold four million copies, a gangbuster record.

Eight years before it became Ford's super-hit, Jay C. Watkins, a UAW representative who was an old friend, had played Merle Travis's own recording of "Sixteen Tons" for me in his home in Buffalo. Watkins had worked in coal mines in Beech Creek for a couple of years in the 1920s and knew Travis's father, Rob, and his brothers, all of whom worked in the mines. The song was in an album called *Folk Songs of the Hills,* which contained eight songs on four ten-inch, 78-rpm records, most of which had a coal-mining theme.

I was captivated by Travis's swinging, virtuoso, finger-picking guitar style, his relaxed and friendly country music voice, and the folksy introductions to his songs. Most of all, he identified with miners and their working conditions. I must have listened to "Sixteen Tons" and "Dark as a Dungeon," another song on the record, ten times that evening. Long before Ford's recording of "Sixteen Tons," I learned the two songs and sang them for union groups all over the country.

I even copied Travis's introduction of "Sixteen Tons" from the record: "Yessir, there's a-many a Kentucky coal miner that pretty near owes his soul to the company store. He gets so far in debt to the coal company that he goes on for years without being paid one red cent in real honest-to-goodness money. But he can always go to the company store and draw flickers or scrip—that's little brass coins that you can't spend nowhere only at the company store. So they add that against his account, and every day he gets a little farther in debt."

Coal operators complained that any evils associated with company towns and stores were ancient history and the song was not fair to the current crop of coal operators. As it turned out, they need not have worried. Most people didn't know what a company store was. They liked the hard-driving, finger-snapping, rocking rhythm and musical arrangement as much as the song itself. When I asked a young clerk in a music store in Akron, Ohio, what she thought a "company store" was, she thought and thought and then said, "I guess it's like a Safeway food store."

"Sixteen Tons" was translated into Spanish, Japanese, and other languages. When I was performing overseas during the 1960s and 1970s for the U.S. Information Agency, I received requests for the song in a dozen countries. Surely in those places they didn't know about the custom of furnishing workers credit in company-owned stores and paying them in scrip rather than American currency. This is the original version as written by Travis:

Sixteen Tons
By Merle Travis

> You load sixteen tons and what do you get?
> Another day older and deeper in debt.
> Saint Peter, don't you call me 'cause I can't go.
> I owe my soul to the company store.

Now some people say a man's made out of mud,
But a poor man's made out of muscle and blood,
Muscle and blood, skin and bones,
A mind that's weak and a back that's strong.

> Chorus

Well, I was born one mornin' when the sun didn't shine.
I picked up my shovel and I walked to the mines.

I loaded sixteen tons of number nine coal,
And the straw-boss hollered, "Well, bless my soul."

    Chorus

Well, I was born one mornin', it was drizzlin' rain,
Fightin' and trouble is my middle name.
I was raised in the canebrake by an old mamma lion
Can't no high-toned woman make me toe the line.

    Chorus

Well, if you see me a-comin' you better step aside.
A lotta men didn't and a lotta men died.
I got a fist of iron, and a fist of steel,
If the right one don't get you, then the left one will.

    Chorus

Parodies popped up like mushrooms after a heavy rain. I heard one version from telephone operators who chafed under Ma Bell's tight control over their every move on the job:

Saint Peter don't you call me 'cause I won't be home,
I owe my soul to the company phone.

School teachers sang:

Saint Peter don't you call me 'cause I can't stay,
I gotta come back for the P.T.A.

I came up with a parody for members of Congress, "Congressman's Blues," that was reprinted in its entirety in the *Congressional Record*. It ended:

Saint Peter if you call me it will be in vain.
I gotta get ready for the next campaign.

Despite the song's wide circulation and scores of newspaper articles, commentary, and interviews with Travis and Tennessee Ernie Ford, no one ever asked about the significance of the phrase "load sixteen tons." I never thought of asking my friend Jay C. Watkins what it meant, but folklorist Archie Green did. The term *sixteen tons* refers to a specific on-the-job practice of initiating a new miner. In his book *Only a Miner: Studies in Recorded Coal-Mining Songs* (1972), Green explains that in the mid–1920s a man usually loaded eight to ten tons, and anyone who exceeded that informal quota was condemned as a "rate-buster." When a newcomer would come to work, however, old-timers would hold back on their production and encourage the new worker to "make sixteen" as a sign of manhood.

I loved "Sixteen Tons" and sang it wherever I could, but "Dark as a Dungeon," which was also on that early album of Travis's, appealed to me even more. No other coal-mining song portrays as well, and with such feeling, the constant presence of danger and potential death as well as the strange attraction that keeps a man working "down in the mines."

I liked that song so much that I put it on my first LP, *Songs of Work and Freedom*, in 1961. I was proud that it was my version of "Dark as a Dungeon" that CBS chose for a television documentary of the life of John L. Lewis ahead of versions by Harry Belafonte, Glen Campbell, Odetta, and even Pete Seeger—or for that matter the original recording made by Merle Travis or that of Tennessee Ernie Ford himself. I'm sure Charlie Byrd's sensitive accompaniment helped.

Dark as a Dungeon
By Merle Travis

Come and listen you fellows, so young and so fine,
And seek not your fortune in the dark dreary mine.
It will form as a habit and seep in your soul,
Till the stream of your blood is as black as the coal.

　It's dark as a dungeon and damp as the dew,
　Where danger is double and pleasures are few,
　Where the rain never fails and the sun never shines,
　It's dark as a dungeon way down in the mines.

It's a-many a man I have seen in my day,
Who lived just to labor his whole life away.
Like a fiend with his dope and a drunkard his wine.
A man will have lust for the lure of the mine.

　Chorus

I hope when I'm gone and the ages shall roll,
My body will blacken and turn into coal.
Then I'll look from the door of my heavenly home,
And pity the miner a-diggin' my bones.

　Chorus

One might assume that Merle Travis wrote the song after a mine accident such as the one his brother Taylor suffered. "He practically broke every rib in his body, and it changed his whole life," Travis recalled. But the fact is that Travis wrote the song in California many years after leaving the coalfields because he needed material to flesh out an album, *Folk Songs of the Hills.* Even though he was thousands of miles away from Beech Creek, Kentucky, images of life and work there had been burned into his memory, and he was able to recreate them when he composed the songs.

One summer day in 1973 when I was living in Washington, D.C., Archie Green asked if I'd like to meet Merle Travis, who was in town. Would I! When Travis came to the door of his hotel room, we saw a man who looked just like the publicity photo on the album cover of *Folk Songs of the Hills.* Of course, it was thirty years later, and he was heavier. His smooth, round face had acquired some lines, and his hair had a spot of gray here and there. But he still had a big, warm, friendly smile, his eyes still twinkled, and when he spoke his voice sounded like the spoken introductions on his record. At fifty-eight he had slowed a bit but was still picking and singing his way across the country. Wherever he sang, every audience wanted to hear "Sixteen Tons" and "Dark as a Dungeon."

I took the opportunity to ask about an aspect of "Dark as a Dungeon" that puzzled me. Travis had recorded three verses and a chorus, and that's the way it was sung everywhere. Once, however, I had heard him sing a fourth verse on a television show. Where did it come from? "When I wrote 'Dark as a Dungeon,'" Travis explained with a smile, "it had four verses, but when I got to the studio I could fit only three verses on the 78-rpm records we used in those days. So I had to cut out one verse right then and there. It's a good verse, and I sing it every now and then." I picked up a piece of Holiday Inn stationery and scribbled the verse down as he sang it:

Midnight or the morning or the middle of the day
Is the same to the miner who labors away.
Where the demons of death often come by surprise.
One fall of the slate and you're buried alive.

Travis autographed it for me, and that piece of Holiday Inn stationery remains one of my prized possessions.

Travis pointed out that despite their grim and dangerous job, coal miners laugh, joke, and tell stories as they get into the mine cage and go down into the earth. He wrote a number of humorous songs about their lives and loves and the trials of their trade. When I sing of unemployment and economic depression I frequently sing Travis's "Miner's Strawberries," which has wry, sardonic humor:

Miner's Strawberries (excerpts)
By Merle Travis

Them good old miner's strawberries
The best stuff that ever you seen,
I was twenty years old before I was told
That miner's strawberries ain't nothing but beans.

My maw was the queen in the kitchen,
And many a time she did say
That having good health was much better than wealth.
So we'd eat miner's strawberries three times a day.

Chorus

You can bake 'em or boil 'em or brown 'em
And cook 'em for hours in a pot.
And serve 'em up cold a week or two old
But if you're hungry enough, man, they sure hit the spot.

Chorus

There's many a lad just like I was
Who grew up in life and he found
That he was dern lucky them days in Kentucky
To always have miner's strawberries a-round.

Chorus

Travis explained that miners frequently enjoy their work and take pride in it, although some people don't have a clue about that aspect of a miner's character. In the 1970s I received a copy of a letter sent to the Waterloo Music Company of Canada. The company was promoting a record album called *Men of the Deeps* that featured a coal miners' choir from Cape Breton in Eastern Canada. They had received a letter from a New England distributor who refused to handle the record because it featured miners singing "happy songs." "Do you have any idea," the distributor asked, "how many people have died in the mines over the last hundred years? Well, I'll tell you it's a lot. . . . And you want us to distribute an album that has coal miners singing like happy little farmers or schoolboys or boy scouts or some such namby pamby claptrap. No thank you." The writer had likely never been in a mine or seen a coal miner, yet he believed he knew what veteran coal miners should sing better than they did.

❖ ❖ ❖

In the summer of 1964 I received a call from Justin McCarthy of the *Mine Workers Journal*. The conversation went something like this:

McCarthy: How would you like to be the substitute for John L. Lewis at our convention?

Glazer: Is this some kind of joke?

McCarthy: I'm dead serious. John L. was scheduled to be the main speaker at our convention banquet this September. We just received word that he can't make it. He's eighty-four years old and ailing, and his doctor won't let him travel. We figured it didn't make much sense to get just another speaker. We want something special since this banquet is a highlight of the convention. We thought a program of coal-mining songs dedicated to Lewis might be just right.

Glazer: I'd be happy to do it. But please don't bill me as a substitute for Lewis. Nobody but the good Lord himself could be a proper substitute for John L. Lewis.

John L. Lewis! Was there ever someone in the labor movement, or for that matter in the entire nation, who could match his eloquence, his poetry, and his power? In answer to public officials who, during a strike, questioned whether he was truly speaking for coal miners, he retorted:

I have laid down in a mine tunnel with my face in a half inch of water, and pulled my shirt up over my head, expecting to die the next minute in an explosion I heard coming toward me. And when God performed a miracle and stopped that explosion before I died, I think it gave me some understanding of what men think about and how they suffer when they are about to die in a coal mine explosion. So I understand some of the thoughts of the coal miners of America. And when I speak I speak the thoughts of the membership of the United Mine Workers of America because I understand them.

The 1964 convention of the United Mine Workers was held in September at the Americana Hotel in Bal Harbour, Florida. September was off-season, and hotel rates were lowered. The rugged coal miners and their wives from tiny coal patches and drab company towns delighted in the spectacular ocean view and the lush and plush settings of the huge lobby and fancy restaurants.

I had forty-five minutes to an hour and was able to give the delegates a full menu of songs and stories. Their spontaneous reactions swept me up and carried me along in a tidal wave of emotion. I opened with "A Miner's Life," which had "keep your hand upon the dollar and your eye upon the scale" as its refrain. The reference is to short-weighing miners' coal production, a common company practice before the union succeeded in appointing a union check weighman. When I said, "I want to dedicate this song to all the union check weighmen in the audience," a wave of cheers and approving laughter poured over me.

A Miner's Life
Author Unknown

A miner's life is like a sailor's
'Board a ship to cross a wave;
Every day his life's in danger,
Yet he ventures, being brave.
Watch the rocks; they're falling daily,
Careless miners always fail;
Keep your hand upon the dollar
And your eyes upon the scale.

> Union miners, stand together,
> Heed no operator's tale;
> Keep your hand upon the dollar
> And your eyes upon the scale.

You've been docked and docked again, boys,
You've been loading two for one
What have you to show for working
Since your mining days have begun?
Worn-out boots and worn-out miners
And your children growing pale.
Keep your hand upon the dollar
And your eyes upon the scale.

> Chorus

In conclusion, bear in memory,
Keep this password in your mind,
God provides for every worker,
When in union he combines.
Stand like men and linked together,
Victory for you'll prevail.
Keep your hand upon the dollar
And your eyes upon the scale.

> Chorus

Because I was "substituting" for John L. Lewis at the banquet, I thought I should do a song that mentioned his name. "Union Man" was recorded in 1946 by George Korson in the Newkirk Tunnel Mine in Tamaqua, Pennsylvania. I asked if anyone in the hall was from that region, and several delegates gave a whoop and holler, yelling, "Yessir, we're here!" The song was written by Albert Morgan, who sang it with a Slavic accent:

Union Man
By Albert Morgan

I tink I sing this little song,
Hope I say it nothing wrong.
Hope my song she bring you cheer,
Just like couple of shots of beer.

> Union man, union man
> He must have full dinner can.
> AFL, CIO,
> Call on strike; out she go!

We all got contract, she expire.
Mr. Lewis mad like fire.
Miners striking too much time,
Uncle Sam take over mine.

> Chorus

We signin' contract, we get raise,
After striking twenty days.
Butcher comes and ringin' bell
He raises prices—what the hell!

> Chorus

I'm drinking too much beer last night,
To go to work I don't feel right.
In my can some bread and meat,
I'm too damn sick I cannot eat.

> Chorus

I fire shot at ten o'clock
Tumble brushes full of rock,
Timber breaking o'er my head,
Jeepers cripes I tink I'm dead.

> Chorus

Of course, I also sang "Which Side Are You On?" "We Shall Not Be Moved," and "Solidarity Forever," all of which came out of the coalfields. For the delegates from Kentucky, I sang the then-popular "Sixteen Tons." I closed with "Coal Miner's Heaven," another version of my song "The Mill Was Made of Marble." I dedicated it to John L. Lewis, who, I said, had "done more than anyone to bring a coal miner's heaven down to earth and under the earth as well":

Coal Miner's Heaven
By Joe Glazer

I dreamed that I had died
And gone to my reward,
A job in a coal mine in heaven
On a golden boulevard.

    The coal mine was made of marble,
    The machines were made out of gold,
    And nobody ever got tired,
    And nobody ever grew old.

This coal mine was built in a garden
No coal dust or gas could be found
And the air was so fresh and so fragrant
With flowers and trees all around.

    Chorus

It was quiet and peaceful in heaven,
The atmosphere was so serene,
You could hear the most beautiful music
As you worked at the cutting machine.

    Chorus

There was never a rock fall in heaven,
The roof bolts went up to the stars.
St. Peter was boss of the haulage
And the angels ran all of the cars.

    Chorus

It was beautiful up there in heaven,
Our lamps were the sun and the moon.
The man trip began at eleven,
We always were finished by noon.

    Chorus

When I woke from this dream about heaven,
I wondered if some day there'd be,
A mine like that one down below here on earth
For miners like you and like me, where the . . .

    Chorus

I also sang at the 1968 convention of the United Mine Workers in Denver and was even pulled into rewriting a song of super-praise for Tony Boyle,

Lewis's successor to the presidency. Justin McCarthy had come up with a song, "The Ballad of Tony Boyle," sung to the tune of "Foggy, Foggy Dew," an old folk song. McCarthy was a good newspaperman, but he was no songwriter. I made the mistake of telling him that the song needed some work, and before you knew it I had agreed to fix it. The entire song, all seven verses, was printed in the *Mine Workers Journal,* and I was listed as coauthor. The song proved embarrassing some time later when Boyle went to jail for arranging the murders of his union opponent Jock Yablonsky and Yablonsky's wife and daughter. Hazel Dickens told the story of the Yablonsky murders in "Cold-Blooded Murder":

Cold-Blooded Murder (excerpts)
By Hazel Dickens

Clarkesville, Pennsylvania is not too far from here
Coal miners were hoping for a brighter new year.
But for Jock Yablonsky, his daughter and wife
The New Year brought an ending to their precious life.

Now it's cold-blooded murder, friend, that I'm talking about
Who's gonna stand up and who's gonna fight?
You better clean up that union; put it on solid ground.
Get rid of that dirty trash; keeps the working man down.

Coal-mining songs never stopped coming. In the 1960s and 1970s there were a lot of them about black lung. Jim Wyatt, a black lung victim, wrote and sang one song at rallies in West Virginia:

A young miner's lungs may be hearty and hale
When he enters the mines with his dinner pail,
But coal dust and grime
In a few years of time
Fills up his lungs and they begin to fail.
Black lungs, full of coal dust
Coal miners must breathe it or bust.
Black lungs, gasping for breath
With black lungs, we are choking to death.

Between the 1970s and 1990s, in addition to black lung songs, disaster songs, songs about fighting for a union, and those about dangers and working conditions, a new genre of songs came into being—those about women miners. Women in coalfields have always played a key role in the struggle to make a better life for their families. They have marched with their husbands on picket lines, braved the company police, and protested unsafe conditions in mines. They have also nursed husbands, sons, brothers, and fathers when the men's bodies were mangled in mining accidents. Now, with attitudes changing about women's rights, they entered the mines to work.

By the 1980s nearly four thousand women had become coal miners. Tradition held that it was bad luck to have women in the mines, but, Florence Reece recalled, "They told us if women went underground men would be killed. We didn't go underground and plenty of men were killed anyway." When women went to work in the mines they not only had to worry about the dangers of their workplace but they also had to fight against sexual harassment. Hazel Dickens, whose father and brothers worked in coal mines, writes and sings powerful songs about her Appalachian heritage. Her "Coal Mining Woman" captures the spirit of women who mine:

> I've got the woman coal miner blues.
> Just like you, I've got the right to choose
> A job with decent pay, a better chance to make my way.
> And if you can't stand by me, don't stand in my way.
>
> Well we had the babies, kept the home fires burning bright.
> Walked the picket lines in the thickest of the fight.
> Yes we helped you open doors, and we can help you open more.
> And if you can't stand by me, don't stand in my way.
>
> Well I'm entitled to work a job that is free
> From intimidations that are forced on me
> From men who are out of line, out of step with time
> And if you can't stand by me, don't stand in my way.
>
> Now union brothers, don't you think the time is right?
> That we all stick together and unite?
> Some better seeds to sow, and we'll help the union grow.
> If you stand by me, I'll surely stand by you.
>
> We must work together to change the things that's wrong
> For better conditions, we've waited much too long.
> Health and safety have to be a first priority,
> And the change can only come through you and me
> Yes, the change can only come through you and me.

I shall never forget Rocky Peck, a shy young man from the mining town of Varney, West Virginia. He played guitar and wrote and sang songs about the 1984–85 strike at the A. T. Massey Coal Company where he had worked.

I heard about Rocky through the United Mine Workers Union and wanted him to share his songs and heartfelt feelings with a wider audience. In 1985 I asked the union to send him to the Great Labor Arts Exchange at the George Meany Center near Washington. This annual three-day gathering attracted a hundred trade union singers and artists from across the country. It was sponsored by the Labor Heritage Foundation, an organization that I had chaired and helped found.

Rocky had never been away from the West Virginia coalfields and was anxious about the trip, so the union sent a UMW representative to accompany him. Although he had been on strike for more than a year, he certainly had not gone soft. When I met and embraced him, his arms were as hard as a tree trunk.

Rocky, who went by no other name, was a powerful singer who had a booming, country voice that reminded me of Johnny Cash. He captured the audience with simplicity, sincerity, and honesty when he sang about the strike at A. T. Massey. He'd written "UMWA" during long hours of walking the picket line:

UMWA
By Rocky Peck

Standing in the darkness
Out in the cold and rain
I guess we'll be a-standing
Till the snow flies again.

Everybody's wondering
Just how long we can hold on
Picketing for our union
It's a name we call our own.

The men drive for miles around
Standing in the snow
They've lost everything they own
And they've got no place to go.

Little babies asking, "Daddy
When are you coming home?
Me and Mommy are so afraid
To be alone."

    UMWA is fighting a battle
    And the hope is the contest won't last long.
    Massey has taken our jobs
    And given 'em to another.

And you can plainly see
Unmistakenly
That it is wrong.

Massey has taken over
At the Leslie mines
They're trying to take our union
Turn back the time.
Put us back in slavery
Like it was not so long ago.
We just can't sit around
And watch our union go.

Chorus

I got to know Rocky better when we shared a program at a labor music festival in West Virginia. I also got to know his wife, Debbie, who became my folk dancing partner at the festival because Rocky didn't dance. During the long months of the strike she had carried on, never complaining and always supporting him and caring for their home and daughter.

The strike was finally settled. The union held together and was able to beat back some of the company's harshest demands for concessions, but the results were mixed at best. Massey never reopened some of the company's mines, Rocky's among them. He was out of a job for a long time and finally forced to go to work in a small, non-union mine.

Rocky and I lost touch. Then, one day I had a message from the UMW: "Rocky Peck was killed in a mining accident on April 23, 1990." He was thirty years old.

Only a Miner
Author Unknown

The hard-working miners their dangers are great
Many while working have met their sad fate.
While doing their duties as all miners do
Shut out from daylight and their darling ones too.
He's only a miner been killed in the ground.
Only a miner and one more is found
Killed by an accident, no one can tell,
His mining's all over, poor miner, farewell.

7

Politics

My guitar turned out to be a useful weapon when it came to politics and political campaigns. I used it extensively during the one-week legislative institutes I developed as the education director of the Rubber Workers (1950–61).
The institutes were so successful that we had to run three of them each year.

We would bring twenty-five to forty shop leaders from all over the country
to Washington for five days to learn how the government works. The simple
quiz we gave them on the first day proved to us that delegates didn't know
much about how a bill becomes a law, how members of Congress do their jobs,
the roles of numerous government agencies, and how lobbyists operate. In fact,
they knew very little about labor's legislative program—and these were all
active union leaders who were supposed to make labor's legislative and political program effective back home. There was a lot of work to do.

We developed an intensive program that began with a speaker at an 8 A.M.
breakfast and didn't stop until 9 at night with a dinner speaker or panel. In
between, we attended congressional hearings, sometimes two in a day; listened
to members of Congress or their key staff members on hot legislative topics;
visited embassies to hear ambassadors discuss foreign affairs; talked with experts in the legislative and political action departments at AFL-CIO headquarters; were briefed by specialists in the Department of Labor; and toured the
Capitol Building and the Supreme Court. The goal was to provide information and inspiration so students would return to their communities and unions
as effective leaders.

We were able to get people to keep up with a packed schedule because we
picked speakers carefully. They not only knew their subject matter but could
also communicate effectively with factory workers. Our speakers included such
outstanding senators as Hubert Humphrey (Minnesota), Paul Douglas (Illi-

nois), Jacob Javitz and Herbert Lehman (New York), Wayne Morse (Oregon), Ralph Yarborough (Texas), and Philip Hart (Michigan). They were pro-labor and appreciated our efforts to educate key labor activists in the mysteries of government and politics.

I also had a secret weapon—my guitar. Most of the senators had heard me sing at fund-raising dinners or political rallies; I had even campaigned for several. I would pull out the guitar just before they spoke and, where possible, tailor a program to address the particular concerns of each speaker.

When Paul Douglas spoke to our meetings, I usually sang "The Giveaway Boys in Washington," which I wrote after hearing Douglas attack the Eisenhower administration's plans to "give away" the nation's natural resources to big oil, timber, and mining interests. The song was a Douglas favorite, and he always joined in the chorus with a big, hearty voice.

The Giveaway Boys in Washington
Words: Joe Glazer
Music: "Rambling Wreck from Georgia Tech"
(original version 1956, updated for subsequent campaigns)

The Giveaway Boys in Washington
Are busy as can be.
They're giving away the TVA
And the U.S. Treasury.
They're gonna take the tidelands oil
And, brother, they're not done.
The Giveaway Boys, the Giveaway Boys,
Way down in Washington.

> They're the Giveaway Boys, the Giveaway Boys,
> Way down in Washington.

The USA is getting smaller
Every single day
Because the boys in Washington
Are giving it away.
The National Parks are next to go
They'll take 'em one by one.
The Giveaway Boys, the Giveaway Boys,
Way down in Washington.

> Chorus

There's many a way to rob and steal
If ever you get the yen.
You can do it with a forty-four

Or with a fountain pen.
You can do a very thorough job
And never use a gun,
Like the Giveaway Boys, the Giveaway Boys,
Way down in Washington.

Chorus

The Giveaway Boys in Washington
Are giving away the dams.
They don't give a damn whose dams they am
As long as they're Uncle Sam's.
They'll take the public power lines
And then they will be done.
The Giveaway Boys, the Giveaway Boys,
Way down in Washington.

Chorus

We've had enough, it's time to change,
I'm sure you will agree,
What's good for General Motors
Is not good enough for me.
Get out and vote in '56
We'll have them on the run;
We'll chase those boys, those Giveaway Boys
Right out of Washington.

We'll chase those boys,
Those Giveaway Boys,
Right out of Washington.

The lines "you can do it with a forty-four or with a fountain pen" can be credited to Woody Guthrie, who first used the idea in his "Pretty Boy Floyd."

Several years after leaving the Senate, Douglas suffered a physically disabling stroke, but his mind was still sharp and agile. His wife, Emily Taft Douglas, would arrange for periodic seminars at their home in Washington and invite friends and former colleagues. I was invited to do several programs of Douglas's favorite political and labor songs. Those performances in the Douglases' living room gave me as much satisfaction as singing before twenty thousand people in Madison Square Garden. He was a beautiful person who had courageous ideals.

For each legislative institute we needed fifteen to twenty speakers, or between forty-five and sixty for the three institutes we ran each year. I was always on the prowl for speakers who had a good message and would not put hard-working rubber workers to sleep. I had good advice from top congressional assistants such as Max Kampelman, who worked for Hubert Humphrey; Frank McCulloch, who was Paul Douglas's chief of staff; and Ted Sorenson, who was then-Senator John Kennedy's administrative assistant. John Edelman, the longtime Washington representative of the CIO Textile Workers Union, was especially helpful in guiding me to freshmen legislators who had not yet made a reputation but were friendly to labor and could stir the students.

One day, when I was desperate for an evening speaker, I called John, who recommended a brand new member of Congress from South Dakota. "South Dakota?" I questioned. "John, we don't have a member within five hundred miles of the state. Why should he bother talking to us?"

"Try him," John said. "Even though he's from South Dakota he seems to know a lot about labor. He doesn't chair any committees, and he doesn't have too many visitors from South Dakota, so he ought to be available."

His name was George McGovern, and before coming to Congress he had been a political science professor. He had written his Ph.D. dissertation on the Ludlow Massacre. Ludlow, in the southern Colorado coalfields, had been the scene of one of labor's historic struggles in 1914. Miners' children, living in tent colonies, had been burned out and shot down by the company-controlled militia.

Because I was a labor history buff and familiar with the terrible events at Ludlow, we had a field day exchanging stories. I sang parts of Woody Guthrie's heart-breaking lament "The Ludlow Massacre" for McGovern:

It was early springtime that the strike was on
They drove us miners out of doors
Out of the houses that the company owned
We moved into tents up at old Ludlow.

Guthrie's verses describe how the militia fired machine guns at the tents and burned them. He ended with "'you killed these thirteen children inside.' / I said, 'God bless the Mine Workers Union' / And then I hung my head and cried."

McGovern spoke to our group almost every year after that. When he ran for the Senate in 1960 I wrote a radio jingle for him that was based on an old farmer's protest song:

The farmer is the man
The farmer is the man
Lives on credit till the fall.
With the interest rate so high

It's a wonder he don't die
And the banker is the man who gets it all.

I changed that to:

McGovern is the man
McGovern is the man
I'm voting for McGovern in the fall.
He will fight for you and me
Down in Washington, D.C.
That's why I'll vote for George McGovern in the fall.

He didn't make it that time, although he did in 1962 and again in 1968 and ran unsuccessfully against Richard Nixon for the presidency in 1972. But I always thought of him as the freshman congressman from South Dakota, happy to talk to union people about the Ludlow Massacre of 1914.

A visit to the House and Senate chambers was a must for our group at each institute, but they soon learned that the real day-to-day work of Congress took place in committees, consulting with staff in the office, or back home with constituents. We found that contrary to popular mythology, most members of Congress worked hard. They ran from one commitment to another, going day and night with little time for family and friends or for smelling the roses. I wrote a song that told the story:

Congressman's Blues
Words: Joe Glazer
Music: "Sixteen Tons" by Merle Travis

Some people think a Congressman has got it made,
He works short hours and he gets well paid;
But take it from me or ask the Congressmen's wives,
It's not an office job that goes from nine to five.

You work sixteen hours and what do you get—
Heartaches and headaches and stomach upset.
"Saint Peter, don't you call me until next week,
I've got two banquets and three luncheons where I must speak."

You get to the office 'bout a quarter to eight.
You answer two hundred letters from the people in your state.
Run off to a hearing for an hour or two,
You grab a bite while a constituent complains to you.

Now you and your constituent are doing swell,
When ding, dong, ding, goes the quorum bell.

You run to the chamber, yell aye or no
You vote a billion or two and away you go.

> You work sixteen hours and what do you get?
> Heartaches and headaches and stomach upset.
> "Saint Peter, don't you call me cause I can't stay.
> I've got three more subcommittee meetings today."

You're back in the office, it's a quarter to five,
You dictate till seven; you're just barely alive.
But you've got to shave and shower, pick up the missus too
To meet the ambassador from Timbuktu.

> You work sixteen hours running around,
> Meetings in the office, meetings out of town
> "Saint Peter, don't you call me for that heavenly ride.
> I've got a busload of high school students outside."

You stagger home; it's almost eleven,
You've got a breakfast caucus at half past seven.
But you can't go to bed until you check the news,
And you finally collapse with those Congressman's blues.

> You work sixteen hours and what do you get?
> Heartaches and headaches and stomach upset.
> "Saint Peter, if you call me, it'll be in vain.
> Because I've got to get ready for the next campaign."

When I sang "Congressman's Blues" at one of our luncheons at the Occidental Restaurant a couple of blocks from the White House, our speaker, Sen. Philip Hart, could hardly contain himself. When I finished, he pulled from his wallet a neatly typed card—his schedule for the day. The events listed seemed to have been stolen directly from my song. His day had begun with an 8 A.M. breakfast caucus with the Senate Democratic leadership, which was followed by no less than three hearings, all beginning at 10 A.M. Our rubber workers' luncheon was on the card from 12 to 1:30, followed by a meeting at his office with Michigan farmers and then a second meeting with Michigan educators.

At 4 P.M. he was scheduled for a photograph on the Capitol steps with twenty-five honor students from an Ann Arbor high school. At 5 there was an embassy reception to meet the new ambassador—not from the mythical Timbuktu in my song but from the very real nation of India. Hart's day closed with a fund-raising dinner for a Senate colleague. "I'm going to try to sneak away early from that one," he said, "so I can get home by 10 o'clock." Indeed, life follows art.

The Occidental Restaurant was in those days a weather-beaten, historic Washington landmark. Every inch of wall space was covered with signed, framed photographs of presidents, senators, governors, and Supreme Court justices who had eaten there over the decades. It must have been 1958 or 1959 when a delegate asked me, "How come they don't have John Kennedy's photo?" The maître d' explained:

> During JFK's first term as a Congressman, on a rainy night in 1947, he stumbled into the Occidental Restaurant, scribbled out a check for $100 to help pay for a waiting taxi, and asked to cash it. At that time he was a skinny, immature-looking guy and looked like a lost high school kid. He wasn't wearing a hat or coat and was absolutely drenched from the pouring rain.
>
> The cashier told him, "You can cash that check where you got your last drink."
>
> Well, Kennedy never set foot in the restaurant after that, and we never got his picture.

Probably more valuable than the speakers at our luncheons and dinner meetings were the congressional hearings we attended. A lively hearing was better than the best show in town. It made the law-making process come alive. I recall a hearing in the 1950s conducted by John McClellan, a dour, antilabor senator from Arkansas who loved to badger trade unionists. The day we were at the hearing McClellan was looking into alleged violence at a UAW picket line in Indiana. The exchange between the senator and an awestruck UAW worker from Indiana went something like this:

McClellan: Where do you work?
UAW witness: I work at the GM plant in Anderson, Indiana.
McClellan: Where is your home?
UAW: My home is in Anderson.
McClellan: Do you have a union in the GM plant?
UAW: Yes, sir. I'm the union representative in my department.
McClellan: You don't have a strike or anything like that in Anderson?
UAW: No, sir. We have a contract and good collective bargaining.
McClellan [his voice rising]: Then what were you doing forty miles away from Anderson, agitating on a picket line?
UAW: Sir, we weren't agitating. We were showing solidarity.
McClellan: Were you showing that solidarity by using force to keep workers who wanted to work away from their jobs?
UAW: No, sir. We were showing solidarity by marching around the plant and singing "Solidarity Forever" to convince the scabs not to cross the picket line.

At that point two men sitting directly behind me in the hearing room began whispering to each other. "What kind of song is 'Solidarity Forever?'" one asked. "Never heard of it," said the other. I resisted the temptation to sing a few verses for them.

The next witness was a tougher customer, not easily intimidated: Walter Reuther, president of the UAW. When he felt that Senator McClellan was crossing the line between legitimate interrogation and uncalled-for harassment he stopped him short: "Look here, senator. I've come here to state my position, and I'm going to have my say whether you like it or not. I'm not going to crawl into a hole and hide because you don't like the trade union movement. You know, this is my country, too." I was concerned that the thirty rubber workers in the hearing room would burst into applause and cheers, but they quietly savored the rest of the hearing as McClellan trod more carefully and showed respect for Reuther.

Some congressional hearings were harder to get into than a Broadway musical hit, particularly the hearings conducted by Sen. Joseph McCarthy of Wisconsin in the early 1950s. We'd skip our breakfast meeting and rush down to the Senate hearing room to sweat out a line until the hearing began at 10 A.M.

McCarthy was a mean-spirited bully, but he put on a colorful show. Early in his Senate career he discovered that the "communist menace" was a hot issue, and he exploited it ruthlessly, often ruining the lives and careers of innocent people. He muddied the waters by labeling as communists the liberals with whom he disagreed politically. At the time, I adapted and expanded a song called "Joe McCarthy's Band." It satirized McCarthy's witch hunts and was especially popular with the rubber workers, who had witnessed McCarthy's use of unscrupulous tactics while he enjoyed congressional immunity.

Joe McCarthy's Band
Words: Adapted by Joe Glazer from words by unknown author
Music: "MacNamara's Band"

My name is Joe McCarthy, I'm the leader of the band;
I don't play in the concert hall, but on the witness stand.
I have the finest orchestra in Washington, D.C.
And night and day I love to play McCarthy's symphony.
Jenner howls and Velde yowls and Mundt says pour it on;
The drums go bang, the symbols clang from Maine to Oregon.
And Hickenlooper tootles the flute as victims take the stand;
The finest music in the land is Joe McCarthy's band.

Toodle-dee-doo, just try to sue;
Toodle-dee-doo, just try to sue;

Toodle-dee-doo, I'll tell you more,
But I'll never, never, never say it off the Senate floor.

When I started chasing communists I claimed two hundred five;
Then I said 'twas eighty-one to keep the thing alive;
Then fifty-seven varieties of reds and pinks galore:
They're climbing on the ceiling and they're creeping on the floor.

Chorus

I'm the biggest headline hunter in the U.S.A.;
I'd rather chase a headline than a commie any day.
I've called them red and I've called them pink and everything in between
But the fact is that I'm color blind; I can't tell red from green.

Chorus

William E. Jenner was a senator from Indiana, Karl Mundt was a senator from South Dakota, Bourke Hickenlooper was a senator from Iowa, and Harold Velde was a U.S. representative from Indiana.

McCarthy began to self-destruct when he intimated that Gen. George Marshall and even Dwight Eisenhower and the army had been contaminated by communist influences. When the Soviet Union broke apart, papers were uncovered disclosing that some government workers were spying for the communists, but McCarthy and his wild and exaggerated charges was no help in exposing them. The fact was, he didn't know the difference between communism and rheumatism and didn't care.

I recorded the song on a single ten-inch, 78-rpm record, but McCarthy had been discredited by the time it was pressed and ready for distribution. There wasn't much interest in a satirical song about Joe McCarthy. I was stuck with a couple of thousand records. Topical songs can be quickly outdated by events, but in this case I didn't mind at all.

Campaigning for Adlai Stevenson

The first big national political campaign in which I did much singing was the 1956 presidential contest between Adlai Stevenson and Dwight D. Eisenhower. War hero Ike had easily defeated Stevenson in 1952, and 1956 was a rerun.

Some months before the Democratic Party convention in Chicago in the summer of 1956 I had put out a ten-inch LP record called *Ballads for Ballots* that contained four songs I had been singing at Democratic rallies and fundraisers. All four gave the Republicans various kinds of hell, and the Democrats loved them.

About two weeks before the convention was to begin I received a call from Mitch Miller's office in New York. Miller, a major pop music impresario and band leader, was in charge of the music at the convention. He wanted me to sing "I Like Ike," the lead song on the record.

I was scheduled to sing on Tuesday afternoon, so I flew out to Chicago Monday night. I assumed the Democrats would pay my expenses, but that was a naive assumption. It was considered an honor to be invited to sing at the convention.

They gave me a badge, and I went out to the convention hall early Tuesday morning. It was a madhouse, a regular boiler factory, with swarms of people talking and wandering the lobbies and aisles of the convention hall. No one paid the slightest bit of attention to what was happening on the platform. The only times the delegates were quiet was when the "Star Spangled Banner" was played and when the candidate for president was nominated. And then, of course, there were hordes of television, radio, and press reporters who covered every inch of ground in and around the convention hall, interviewing everything that moved. It was noise, noise, noise from the moment the gavel opened the convention until it closed ten hours later.

How was I going to sing to this crowd? I didn't go on Tuesday, and they couldn't fit me in on Wednesday. It was getting costly hanging around Chicago, and I was using vacation time from my job with the United Rubber Workers. I got hold of Mitch Miller and asked if there was any chance of my expenses being paid. He looked at me incredulously: "Nobody gets expenses here. Do you realize that Frank Sinatra flew all the way from Spain just to sing the 'Star Spangled Banner,' and he's not getting a penny for that?" Well, of course, if it was good enough for Old Blue Eyes I guess it had to be good enough for Joe Glazer.

While I had Miller's ear, I told him I was concerned about singing the song he had chosen. "I Like Ike" went on for a long time and had many subtle verses that needled members of the cabinet. All I had was my voice and a six-string guitar. I was outnumbered five thousand to one. I said, "Maybe I ought to sing something a little jazzier. I don't think I can hold this audience with that song."

Miller was impatient: "The hell with *this* audience. We don't care about them. Your audience is out in TV land. Do you realize you'll have twenty million people watching you? They'll be able to hear you. That's what counts." That was a whole new concept for me. I was used to singing to people who look at you, listen, and applaud. But twenty million people on television! I was warming up to the idea.

Finally, on Thursday morning before I could draw a breath, the convention chair was calling my name. Rep. Sam Rayburn kept the introduction simple: "We now have Joe Glazer, a singer from Akron, Ohio." I thought he could have built me up a little, but no one would have heard it anyway. I moved quickly to the podium and faced that sea of delegates, ready to do battle. They were walking around, talking, arguing, waving their arms at neighbors, taking notes, meeting in the aisles, and yelling at each other so they could be heard. They never looked at the podium.

As I sang, I kept thinking, "Glazer, what the hell are you doing up here?" But I forced myself to concentrate on Miller's admonition: "The hell with *this* audience. . . . you'll have twenty million people watching you." It was painful, but I did my job, strumming the guitar and singing verse after verse until I was able to escape to the quiet of the holding room. The cabinet members I sang about in "I Like Ike" are now forgotten footnotes of political history, but in 1956 they were front-page news and juicy targets for musical satire.

I Like Ike (excerpts)
By Joe Glazer
(sung talking-blues style)

Now, I like Ike, he's a friendly guy,
When things go wrong he doesn't moan and sigh.
His cheery smile and wide-open grin
Help you forget the mess you might be in.
A pal of mine lost his job and his car
While Ike was golfing, shooting for par,
He couldn't find a job for days and days,
But for good old Ike he's got plenty of praise—he says—
I like Ike—I like that smile—makes me forget my troubles.
Now the government's big and it keeps Ike busy,
He can't run it himself 'cause he'd get awful dizzy.
So he's got a lot of fellers kinda helping him out
While he's shooting a quail or catching a trout.

The number one helper in the whole shebang
Is a feller named Humphrey, the leader of the gang,
I don't mean Hubert, Minnesota's pride and joy—
I mean Trickle-Down George, the banker's boy.
George says *we* gotta balance the budget—And when he says *we*—
He means *you*—and *me*—but not *him*.
Now, Trickle-Down George is in charge of the taxes,
He's the big man in the Washington–Wall Street axis.

He wouldn't cut the taxes for you and me.
He says that's "irresponsibility."
But for the big fat cats he swings his axe,
And biff bang woosh—down comes their tax—
But don't worry, brother—you'll pick up a couple of drops
After awhile—when she starts to trickle down.

There's another little helper that Ike has got,
Who's the very best-looking of the whole darn lot.
That's Mrs. Hobby, as sweet as can be,
But how she ever got the job is a mystery to me.
The schools are jammed from the floor to the roof,
But Oveta Culp Hobby says, "That's no proof
That the schools must have some government aid—
We've got to have another great big study made—*grade by grade.*"
Well, by then the children will be wearing long pants
And it'll be too late for them to get another chance.
That's Ike's secretary of very little HEALTH—inadequate EDUCATION—and not
much WELFARE.
But I like Ike—I love that smile—makes you feel warm all over—

[Three more verses describe other cabinet members.]

There's one big helper we can't forget,
He's tricky Dick Nixon, Mr. Eisenhower's pet,
He's a fine-looking lad with a big sharp axe,
And he likes to plant it in other people's backs.
Now, Dick sneaks around spreading hate and fear,
Painting loyal Americans with a big red smear,
While Eisenhower smiles and says, "Dick's my boy,
He's the administration's pride and joy."
But I like Ike—love that smile—makes me feel so good.

Now I've told you all about the Eisenhower team,
The president holds them in the highest esteem.
They may pick your pockets and blacken your name,
And play you for a sucker in the give-away game,
But Eisenhower loves this motley crew
Which is doing such a job on me and you.
He says, "I'm with 'em—every single man,
They're backing my dynamic, conservative plan."
Yes, Ike's riding on the same old Republican track,
One step forward and two steps back—
But I like Ike—love that smile—crazy about that disposition,
Love that Ike.

Of course, I had alerted my family and friends when I knew I would definitely perform, and they were all watching. After Rayburn introduced me, Walter Cronkite, who was anchoring the CBS convention coverage, said, "There's nothing much happening on the platform—just somebody singing—so we'll have a message from Betty Furness." Betty Furness had become famous opening refrigerator doors on television and saying, "You can be sure if it's Westinghouse."

My wife was watching with friends in Akron, and when I suddenly turned into a refrigerator she started to change the channels to find me. I was finally located on another network. For the next twenty years I could not look at a Westinghouse refrigerator without thinking of how Betty Furness took away a good chunk of my twenty million viewers back in 1956.

During the 1956 presidential campaign I sang for Stevenson and his vice-presidential candidate Sen. Estes Kefauver in union halls, hotel ballrooms, and high school gymnasiums; at fund-raising luncheons and dinners; and at rallies in front of city halls. I worked this politicking in on weekends, used vacation days, or sandwiched the events in towns where I had legitimate union business.

The most spectacular meeting of the campaign for me was a rally in New York's Westchester County, where four thousand Stevenson supporters jammed into a huge auditorium. Westchester County, just north of New York City, was traditionally a Republican stronghold. Democrats were an endangered species there until Adlai Stevenson flushed them out with his elegant prose.

Most political rallies are run by politicians, and the program is inevitably loaded with candidates who talk too long even though they don't have much to say. The Westchester rally was different. It was run by professional show-business veterans who were able to tell the politicians how long they could talk. Every speech and act had a strict time limit, and the pacing kept the audience's spirits soaring.

Backstage I spotted Pare Lorentz, the legendary documentary film maker. Then, as I was tuning up I ran into a tall, slender man in tails, who was pacing up and down and rubbing his hands as if trying to get the blood moving. "Are you on the program?" I asked. "Oh, yes," he said, "I play the piano." I told him I was Joe Glazer and played the guitar. I was talking to Rudolph Serkin, one of the world's greatest piano virtuosos.

The program opened with bagpipers who marched down the center aisle in colorful kilts, wailing away as if they were marching into battle. The audience was on its feet, yelling, applauding, and cheering as the spotlight followed the pipers up to the front of the hall, around one of the sides, and out through the back doors. Then Serkin brought down the house with a brilliant performance of a Beethoven sonata. I was on next. I opened with a Stevenson rally song set to the tune of the old folk song "Pony Boy."

> Stevenson, Stevenson,
> If you vote for Stevenson,
> He will be, easily,
> U.S. president.

Then I launched into another rousing number to the tune of "The Yellow Rose of Texas." I sang it through twice and had everyone singing with me the second time:

> Oh, the Democratic Party,
> Is for you, and you, and you.
> It fights for all the people
> And not for just a few.
> On the farm and in the city
> For the big man and the small,
> The Democratic Party
> Is the very best one for all.
> So let's all vote together,
> And on election day
> We're voting Democratic
> All over the U.S.A.

I closed with "The Giveaway Boys in Washington," the big band swinging and rocking behind me. The musicians seemed to be enjoying themselves, and you could feel it in the music. The audience was screaming. They wanted more. But this was a tightly run ship. Orson Bean, the M.C., quieted the crowd with a promise: "If we have time we'll have Joe Glazer come back later with more of those wonderful songs. So let's give Joe a big hand." In show business, and the rally was being run as show business, "later" never comes. But the promise satisfies the audience, and you can move on to the next act.

Even Averill Harriman, the governor of New York, was made to toe the line. He was told he was allotted fifteen minutes to speak. A fierce argument with Harriman's chief assistant broke out. The governor had a prepared text, and it was half an hour long. Harriman got involved. His eyes were blazing. "Look here, young man, I'm the governor of the state of New York, and I'm going to speak for thirty minutes," he said angrily. I thought that Harriman might stalk out, but he caved in, made a fifteen-minute speech, and made way for Stevenson.

Stevenson was especially eloquent on that occasion. I was carried away by the spirit of the rally. Even though Ike was as popular in 1956 as he had been in 1952, maybe this time Stevenson could win. I had forgotten some simple wisdom my mother had once given me: "If you go to a hospital you see a lot of sick people." I had gone to a Democratic rally, and I had seen a lot of gung-ho Democrats.

The presidential contest began heating up as we approached Election Day. On the Friday before, I was scheduled to sing at a rally in Detroit sponsored by the United Automobile Workers (UAW) at one of the mammoth rococo movie palaces downtown. The theater was jammed to the third and fourth balconies with UAW members who had no love for Republicans and the Eisenhower-Nixon ticket. I peeked out from behind the stage curtain and saw a sea of UAW windbreakers and caps. They were a rugged-looking lot, ready for some old-fashioned, fire-eating, anti-Republican rhetoric.

My contact was UAW education director Brendan Sexton, an old friend who was in charge of the program. Just before I was to go on and do maybe three songs, Sexton grabbed me. "I've been expecting a planeload of Hollywood celebrities for the program," he said, "but they are stuck in a snowstorm in Milwaukee."

"What does that mean?" I asked.

"That means we've got time to kill," he replied. "You get out there and sing every damn song you know. Pep this crowd up."

It seemed to me the crowd needed calming down more than pepping up, but I told him I would get them properly primed for Stevenson and the other politicos scheduled to speak. A big band was in the pit, and I told Sexton I'd like to have them back me up. "Fine," he said. "Arrange it with the leader."

The leader informed me that his contract did not include backup for singers. That was an extra chore, he said, that would cost an additional $4 per man. The total for the fifteen-piece band would be $60. Sexton was incensed. "We're paying these guys good union rates, and they're trying to hold us up. Fuck 'em. Go out there with your guitar and start singing." I was just as angry. Because I was a long-time member of the Musician's Union I understood the logic of the rule, which was designed to avoid abuses that had been prevalent in the music business. The band could have gone ahead and backed me, however, because it wasn't a case of having to come in early to rehearse with the singer.

I went onstage with just my voice and my guitar and gave it all I had. The response was overwhelming. But it could have been earthshaking if the beat of the big band was bouncing along with me.

Because it was a union crowd, I was able to mix a lot of labor songs with political songs. "Solidarity Forever" shook the rafters as five thousand voices boomed out the chorus. With "We Shall Not Be Moved" they stamped and clapped in rhythm as I made up new lines: "We need Adlai in the White House . . . / We're gonna win on Tuesday . . . / Goodbye to Ike and Nixon . . ." Then, to change the pace, I sang a satirical solo, "The Ballad of Richard Nixon," which I normally reserved for low-key occasions. I was inspired to write the song when I heard Thomas Finletter, a distinguished public servant, respond to a question: "Don't you think that Nixon's experience as vice president now qualifies him for the presidency after Eisenhower leaves office?" His response was, "I don't believe the office of vice president should be used as a reform school."

Nixon had an unsavory reputation for unjustly smearing opponents as communist sympathizers during his campaigns for the House and again for the Senate. At the Republican national convention in 1952 he became Eisenhower's running-mate by delivering a number of California votes to Ike rather than support California's governor and state favorite Earl Warren. Nixon referred to his dog Checkers in a television appearance during the campaign.

The Ballad of Richard Nixon
Words: Joe Glazer
(parody of "Ruler of the Queen's Navy" by Gilbert and Sullivan)

As a very young man I was asked to run
For a congressman's seat in Washington.
I called my opponent a pink and a red,
It wasn't true at all but I came out ahead.
It wasn't true at all, but I won you see
And now they say I'm ready for the presidency.

[Repeat last two lines of each verse.]

Next for the Senate I made my try
And the very same tactics got me by.
I conclusively demonstrated that it pays
To work in the gutters and the alleyways.
I worked in the gutters so assiduously
That now they say I'm ready for the presidency.

At the fifty-two convention of the G.O.P.
No paper or reporter took notice of me.
Till I switched my vote and I double-crossed Warren,
Then I made every paper both domestic and foreign.
I've done my double-crossing so effectively
That now they say I'm ready for the presidency.

Unfortunately my enemies discovered
My secret fund which they gleefully uncovered.
But I went on television and I saved the day.
With a little help from Checkers I explained it all away.
I explained it all away so logically
That now they say I'm ready for the presidency.

All the columnists write how I've matured
From my youthful habits they say I'm cured.
I won't use my axe I quite agree
Unless I find it's absolutely necessary.
I've covered up my work successfully
And now they say I'm ready for the presidency.

If you want to do as well as me
Here's a bit of advice, gratuitously.
Use plenty of mud and plenty of dirt
But be sure to wash your hands and be sure to change your shirt.
If you make this change quite thoroughly
You too may be considered for the presidency.

The song that really brought down the house was "The Giveaway Boys in Washington" because of its reference to General Motors in the last verse. Charles Wilson, the head of General Motors, had made a well-publicized statement: "What's good for General Motors is good for America." That hit a nerve with the autoworkers, and they roared when they heard the verse:

We've had enough; it's time to change,
I'm sure you will agree
What's good for General Motors
Is not good enough for me.
Get out and vote in fifty-six.
We'll have 'em on the run.
We'll chase those boys, those Giveaway Boys
Right out of Washington.

After the Detroit UAW meeting I got back to my hotel about midnight, exhausted and exhilarated. There was a message from home—urgent! Someone must be sick I thought. When I telephoned my wife, she said, "A fellow named Earl Bush called. He's the public relations man for Mayor Daley in Chicago. He just heard your record *Ballads for Ballots,* and he wants you to come to the big Chicago election rally Saturday night—tomorrow. He said to call him at home no matter how late it is."

Bush was enthusiastic about the songs on my record. "Be sure and do 'The Giveaway Boys,'" he urged, "because Paul Douglas is on the program. And I love your Nixon song. And can you write a song about William Stratton, the Republican governor of Illinois who just got caught milking a milk fund for poor children?"

Bush was really charged up. He proposed giving me twelve minutes just before Douglas and Stevenson went on. "We've got national live TV coverage," he said, "beginning at 10 o'clock sharp when Eleanor Roosevelt introduces Adlai Stevenson. You'll go on about twenty minutes to 10, just before Douglas."

I was too excited to sleep and began working on the Governor Stratton song. Fortunately, Bush had mentioned that Stratton was called "Billy," and that gave me my hook. I recalled a song about the infamous outlaw Billy the Kid, one of the meanest characters in the Old West, and I patterned my song after that.

I'll sing you a true story of Billy the Kid.
I'll sing of the terrible deeds that he did.
In the city of Springfield, in the state of Illinois,
Stole the milk fund money from the poor girls and boys.

Bush met me at the airport with a big car and over a steak dinner explained that this was the traditional preelection rally always held on the Saturday before Election Day. It would start with a big parade before the rally, and people would march right into Chicago Stadium beginning at 6 or 6:30. At 8 o'clock the program would begin. I looked at Bush quizzically, "How big is this stadium?" "It can seat about twenty thousand," he said. "That's a lot of seats," I replied. "Can you guys fill it?" He looked at me with disdain. "We can fill it just with the organization."

As we drove to the Stadium I told Bush about my problem with the band in Detroit. He smiled. "We won't have that kind of problem here. Lou Breeze and his orchestra are very cooperative."

I reviewed the songs quickly with Lou Breeze and his big band and could see we were going to fill the stadium with bouncy, high-volume music. Bush went crazy over the three or four verses I had on Governor Stratton to the tune of "Billy the Kid." "Save it for last," he said. "The crowd will love it."

As I sat in one of the front rows of the Stadium I saw the awesome power of the Chicago "organization" in action. The afternoon began with a giant parade of Democratic workers and activists that wound through the streets. They marched straight to the Stadium and began pouring into the hall by the hundreds after 6:30 P.M. Marchers carried scores of signs and placards—"Stevenson for President," "Douglas for Senator," "Vote Democratic." Most prominent were colorful banners such as "Park District 34" and "Sanitation District 22." What was that all about?

I soon learned that these districts were the heart and sinews of the Chicago Democratic organization. They employed thousands of workers who were not covered by civil service regulations. These were purely patronage jobs controlled by the committeemen and precinct captains in each ward. Naturally, these workers and their families would come to a rally like this one. Most were happy to participate, to demonstrate loyalty and support to the organization that made their jobs possible. Moreover, if they didn't show up their committeemen would be very unhappy.

I went over the program with Earl Bush and the master of ceremonies. What was going to happen was listed minute by minute. At 7:30 a Ukrainian chorus would sing; at 7:36, Congressman so-and-so would speak; and at 7:40 Serbian dancers would dance. A politician will speak next. Then would come a Polish polka band, Albanian jugglers, Irish cloggers, and Swiss yodelers. It was one big parade of ethnic Chicago, dancing across the stage in colorful costumes. I don't recall a black singer or musician being on stage, however, although thirty years later blacks evened the score with the organization by electing Harold Washington as mayor. As the last half hour of the program shaped up:

9:35   Pop singer—song: "There'll Be Some Changes Made"
9:40   Joe Glazer
9:50   Mayor Richard Daley introduces Sen. Paul Douglas
10:00 Eleanor Roosevelt introduces Adlai Stevenson on national television
10:30 Program ends.

I had no complaints. I had the best spot on the program. As the program developed, however, I noticed one disturbing problem. We were losing a minute here and a minute there as one politician after another exceeded his allotted time limit. Normally, that would not have mattered, but we had an absolute 10 P.M. television deadline. Something would have to give.

At 9 Earl Bush came over to me, looking somewhat harried. "We've got to cut one of your songs," he said. "We're running behind schedule." At 9:25 Bush was back. He was sweating. "Those damn politicians are talking too much. We've got to cut another song. At least you'll be able to do that Billy the Kid thing." As I feared, he was soon back again. It was 9:42. "We're in trouble, Joe," he said, shaking his head. "We're in trouble." I went over the list with him once more. Two items were left before Mayor Daley went on at 9:50 to introduce Paul Douglas. One of the acts was me, cut now to one song. The other was what we called in those days a "girl singer" who was going to do "There'll Be Some

Changes Made." "What's the problem?" I said (using language I would not use today). "Let's get rid of the broad and there'll be time to do my song." Bush winced. "We can't do it. She's the M.C.'s girlfriend."

She sang her song, Mayor Daley introduced Paul Douglas, and at 10 P.M. Eleanor Roosevelt introduced Adlai Stevenson, live and on television. At 10:30 I closed my guitar case and headed for the hotel, shaking my head in disbelief.

Several days after the election, I received a check for my expenses and a nice letter from Mayor Daley, undoubtedly written by Earl Bush. He said he was sorry I was squeezed off the program: "Please drop in to see me the next time you're in Chicago." That ended that.

The album I recorded for the 1956 campaign, *Ballads for Ballots,* also ran into a streak of bad luck and several major distribution foul-ups during the election campaign. It all started with a major distributor in New Jersey who had an exclusive contract to sell the record across the country. The distributor soon found that retail stores and record chains were leery of handling a highly partisan Democratic record without a Republican equivalent to display as well. The distributor hired a commercial songwriter to knock out songs bragging about the G.O.P. The songs were awful, but the colorful cover matched the one on my record and assured customers that the store owner was properly nonpartisan. Nearly six weeks of distribution time were lost with this exercise.

Then came the knockout blow. Just when the distributor was ready to launch a national promotional campaign for the two records, he was forced into bankruptcy. He owed money to CBS, Capitol, and other big record producers. All his assets were frozen, including his warehouse, which contained hundreds of thousands of records, including mine. The government said that nothing could be moved from the warehouse except "perishable items." As much as we tried, we could not convince the government that political records were as perishable as fresh strawberries. After the election, they would be worthless. But the records were not released until several weeks after the election.

Several months later I encountered an advertisement in the Sunday *New York Times* for "the record that might have won the election for Adlai Stevenson!" It was my record being advertised. As much as I believe in the power of music, I would say that claim was an exaggeration.

The Party Line

Throughout the years, I used my songs and guitar to campaign for many worthy candidates. One of my early recordings, however, dealt with politics of an entirely different kind. It was a musical satire on the twists and turns of the U.S. Communist Party line.

I became involved in the topic because I had met a number of communist activists during the course of my trade union work, and many of them were dedicated, hard-working trade unionists. They helped organize workers, supported strikes, and fought against racial discrimination. As communists, however, they followed the party line even when it disagreed sharply with the policies of the trade union movement.

I had experienced the Soviet influence on songwriters early in 1941 when I joined the Theatre Arts Committee (TAC). During the period of the Nazi-Soviet pact (August 1939–June 1941), we were instructed to write peace songs declaring that "the Yanks are not coming." Then, on June 21, 1941, Hitler turned on his ally and invaded the Soviet Union. Peace songs were out. The new slogan was "open up the second front." The *Daily Worker,* in confusion, stopped publication for a day while the party line was being reworked. That kind of thought control was not for me.

Once the Soviet Union was involved in the war, the communists wouldn't support A. Philip Randolph, who proposed a march on Washington to force President Roosevelt to issue an executive order for a Fair Employment Practices Commission. Randolph wanted war plants to employ blacks and treat them with equality. The communists contended that such a march against racial discrimination could interfere with the effort to get war materiel to Russia and the Allies.

In 1947, when the United States proposed the Marshall Plan to help revive the economies of devastated European countries, the American trade union movement overwhelmingly approved. The Soviet Union opposed the plan, hoping to expand control over those countries. Communist-dominated unions in the United States followed the party line. In 1949, after a number of such ideological clashes demonstrating strict adherence to Moscow's dictates, the CIO voted to expel them.

The record I made in 1952 about the zigs and zags of the Communist Party line was called *Ballads for Sectarians.* I recorded it with Bill Friedland, a staff member of the Michigan CIO who later became a sociology professor at the University of California in Santa Cruz.

One of the songs, "Our Line's Been Changed Again," reflects the slavish adherence of American communists to the shifting ideology of the Soviet Union. It was written during the Popular Front period (1935–39), when the Soviet Union ordered followers around the world to shed their revolutionary mantle and court former adversaries, including socialists and bourgeois liberals. The "Browder" in the song refers to Earl Browder, general secretary of the American Communist Party, who was purged in 1945 after a radical change in the party line.

Our Line's Been Changed Again
Words: Alton Levy
Music: African American spiritual

United fronts are what we love
Our line's been changed again.
From below and from above,
Our line's been changed again.

We must appear to be sedate
Our line's been changed again.
The Revolution it can wait
Our line's been changed again.

   I knows it Browder
   I knows it Browder
   I knows it Browder
   Our line's been changed again.

We're now a party with finesse
Our line's been changed again.
With bourgeois groups we'll coalesce
Our line's been changed again.

Bourgeois tricks we'll have to use
Our line's been changed again.
Our women must not wear flat shoes
Our line's been changed again.

   Chorus

We're simply communists devout
Our line's been changed again.
We're not sure what it's all about
Our line's been changed again.

Kaleidoscopic what I mean
Our line's been changed again.
Now we're red and now we're green
Our line's been changed again.

   Chorus

One of my favorite songs on the album was "In Old Moscow," which high-lights the period of the Nazi-Soviet pact (1939–41).

In Old Moscow (excerpts)
Words: Walter Cliff
Music: "Clementine" by Percy Montrose

In old Moscow, in the Kremlin
In the fall of '39
Sat a Russian and a Prussian
Writing out the party line.

Oh, my darling, oh, my darling,
Oh, my darling party line
Oh, I never will desert you
For I love this life of mine.

Now the Nazis and the Fuehrer
Stand within the party line.
All the Russians love the Prussians,
Volga boatmen sail the Rhine.

Chorus

The party line kept twisting and turning, so in 1962 I issued an updated and expanded version of the record, "My Darling Party Line," with the collabora-tion of Abe Brumberg, a noted Sovietologist. The recording was attacked in a lengthy review in *Sovetskaia Kultura,* a major Soviet cultural magazine, as be-ing "nothing but anti-Soviet material in rhyme stuffed with boisterous Rus-sian vulgarisms."

I never could understand how some folksingers in the United States who made real contributions with songs about liberty, justice, and freedom could nonetheless give unwavering support to the Soviet Union, a nation of tyran-ny, dictatorship, slave labor camps, and phony trade unions. How could oth-erwise-dedicated trade unionists ignore the evidence that Soviet unions could not strike or bargain collectively?

The Soviet Union folded in 1989, and its state archives were opened in 1992. A mountain of evidence—letters, cables, memos, and reports—documented beyond question that the American Communist Party was financed by and took orders from the Soviet Union at every turn.

Perhaps it is because I am a singer that one brutal, suppressive incident es-pecially distressed me. The distinguished composer Dimitri Shostakovich in *Testimonial,* his autobiography, related that during the mid-1930s communist authorities in the Soviet Union convened the First All-Ukrainian Congress of folksingers, many of whom, by tradition, were blind men. Shostakovich wrote, "Here were these blind men walking around singing songs of dubious content. The songs weren't passed by the censors and what kind of censorship can you have with blind men?" Shostakovich reported that several hundred attended the Congress, and almost all were shot and killed right there.

8

Campaigning in Presidential Elections

Hubert Humphrey was one of my very special heroes. I first met him in Minnesota in 1947 when I was conducting training classes for the CIO Textile Workers Union and he was the young reform mayor of Minneapolis. He spoke at one of our meetings and set everyone afire, including me, with uninhibited political rhetoric that combined eloquence, humor, idealism, and optimism. I became an unreconstructed Hubert Humphrey fan right then and there.

When Humphrey lost the presidential election in 1968 by an eyelash to Richard Nixon I had a pain in my heart. And when he died of cancer in December 1977 I felt driven to write a song to give him a proper send-off to that big political meeting hall in the sky. For weeks after his death ideas fought with each other inside my head, but nothing came together until months later when I saw a film about Hubert Humphrey at the national convention of the State, County and Municipal Workers Union in Southern California. The film closed with Walter Mondale's moving eulogy at Humphrey's funeral: "He taught us how to laugh and how to cry; he taught us how to win and how to lose; he taught us how to live, and finally he taught us how to die." I said to myself, "My God, there's my song." I polished it off for the dinner being held that night. I don't normally write songs that bring tears to people's eyes, but this one did:

The Man from Minnesota
By Joe Glazer

There's a man from Minnesota
I never will forget.
I know that I will always be
Forever in his debt.

He was a preacher and a teacher
A man of great renown.
He always picked me up
When I was down.

> He taught us how to win
> He taught us how to lose.
> He taught us how to laugh and how to cry,
> He taught us how to love
> And he taught us how to live
> And finally—he taught us how to die.

It was cold and it was bitter
On that sad December day.
Tears were falling, hearts were aching
When I thought I heard him say:
"Stop your weeping, stop your mourning,
There are good deeds to be done.
The greatest songs have never yet been sung."

> Chorus

I do believe the Lord above
Has got a master plan.
And every now and then
He makes a special kind of man.
The man from Minnesota
Had that magic touch from birth:
A man who made a difference on this earth.

> Chorus

Humphrey was in the U.S. Senate in the 1950s when I was conducting legislative institutes for the United Rubber Workers. Although his schedule was always full to overflowing from early morning to late at night, he was generous with his time and energy and would speak to our group. He would invite us to his office, where he would squeeze us between appointments for a "fifteen- to twenty-minute chat" that invariably stretched to forty or fifty minutes. Humphrey, a former political science professor, would lecture on labor law legislation; the role of the federal government in education, agriculture, civil rights, and nuclear disarmament; the United Nations; and his Food for Peace plan. He would have us laughing and crying, ready to fight evil and feed the hungry. We walked out on clouds. Many's the time a delegate said, "That's my man for president." No one would disagree.

Late in 1959 I received a call from Max Kampelman, Humphrey's legislative assistant. Humphrey had definitely decided to enter the 1960 Democratic primaries for president. Would I be willing to help the campaign with my music and my contacts in the labor movement? Max was an old friend, a brilliant lawyer and political science professor from the University of Minnesota who had worked with Humphrey in Minnesota and now was one of his closest advisors.

I told Max that my guitar had been tuned and ready to make music for Humphrey since practically the first time I heard him back in 1947 in Minnesota. Joe Rauh, a Washington civil rights and labor lawyer, worked on the details. He asked me to come to Washington to help set up a Labor for Humphrey Committee and be part of it.

"You can stay at my house," he said, "and save the hotel bill. I'll put you in the room where Marilyn Monroe once slept." He wasn't pulling my leg. Rauh was the attorney for Arthur Miller, the distinguished playwright called up by the House Un-American Activities Committee on a contempt charge. Rauh reported that he and Miller, who was married to Marilyn Monroe at the time, had the following telephone conversation:

> Miller: I'd like to bring my wife with me when I come to Washington to testify.
> Rauh: No problem. I'll get you a reservation at the Hilton.
> Miller [after an embarrassed hesitation]: But we can't stay in hotels.
> Rauh: How come?
> Miller: Well, when I'm traveling with Marilyn, we get mobbed.
> Rauh: Oh! Why don't you stay at my home?
> Miller: That's great.

So there I was, sleeping in Marilyn Monroe's bed, but Marilyn wasn't there.

Rauh was a great civil rights and labor lawyer and a sophisticated activist but not well acquainted with the phenomenon of Hollywood celebrities. On another occasion, his secretary told him that Marlon Brando was on the line and wanted to participate in a Washington, D.C., civil rights rally. "Who's he?" Rauh asked.

We set up the Labor for Humphrey Committee in Joe Rauh's living room. The chair was Joe Karth, a former union staff representative who had become a respected member of Congress from Minnesota. I became secretary. We put together a list of labor leaders from across the country who were strong Humphrey supporters, printed some stationery, and we had a committee.

When I look back at it, the operation was pretty small potatoes. We had no money and no staff. Our headquarters was my dining-room table, from which I sent out an occasional mailing to a list of several thousand key labor people. I put out a newsletter bragging about Humphrey's labor record and asking for contributors. The prepaid envelopes came back with $5 and $10 checks and the occasional $25 or $50 contribution from true believers.

Our children became involved with the daily take. One day when returns were slim, my eight-year-old daughter Patti pulled a quarter from her pocket and asked, "Will this help?" I told her that Senator Humphrey appreciated every contribution, no matter how small. When I told him about the incident, the senator sent her a warm letter, thanking her for the contribution and inviting her to have a soft drink with him when she visited Washington. She still cherishes the letter.

When I think about current political fund-raising operations that have highly paid consultants, computerized lists of hundreds of thousands of names, and sophisticated, automated mailing equipment, I wince at the comparison. We did, however, manage to inform influential trade unionists everywhere of the Humphrey campaign, and we always raised enough to pay for the next mailing. Our efforts didn't cost the Humphrey campaign a dime, which was good because it didn't have a dime to spare.

The first big test for Humphrey was the Wisconsin Democratic primary, which came immediately after the first primary in New Hampshire. I had to attend to my full-time job as education director of the United Rubber Workers, but the union had important locals in Wisconsin. I could arrange legitimate union meetings on a Friday, run around the state with Humphrey during the weekend, and get back to my office in Akron by early Monday morning. It was an exhausting routine, but the Humphrey campaign couldn't afford to put me on the payroll. I became good at napping on airplanes, and it worked out. My trusty Martin guitar was always with me, and I must have sung at a couple of hundred meetings before the Wisconsin campaign ended.

Humphrey, of course, was still in the Senate. He was an active member of half a dozen committees and took his duties seriously. He'd fly into Wisconsin on a Friday night, campaign furiously all day Saturday and Sunday, and rush back to Washington on Monday morning to take care of Senate business.

Humphrey's rival in the Wisconsin primary was John F. Kennedy, who was also in the Senate. Kennedy, however, focused all his energy on the presidential campaign and had begun to prepare for the 1960 primary in 1957. He never stopped. I had tried for years to get Kennedy to speak to a Rubber Workers' legislative institute, but he always turned me down. In the spring of 1957, however, he accepted, made a short speech, shook everyone's hand, posed for photographs, and was off to the next meeting. It was then I realized he was running hard for the presidency.

Humphrey would make five, six, or seven meetings a day. For example, he would get into Milwaukee on a Friday evening, in time for a fancy cocktail fund-raiser at some friendly Democrat's big house. That would be followed by a strategy meeting late that evening with key supporters. At 8 A.M. on Saturday it would be a meeting with black ministers at a Milwaukee hotel. Then it was off to one town after another in the beat-up Humphrey campaign bus for meetings in union halls, school auditoriums, church basements, community centers, or hotel ballrooms—any place a group of voters could be brought together. The final meeting would end at 10 or 11 P.M., and then we would get up early on Sunday and begin the same routine in half a dozen other towns.

I would sing two or three songs to open those meetings or rallies, but we quickly figured out that I could be most useful traveling with the advance man who would arrive at a meeting hall an hour or so before Humphrey to check out the sound system, podium, campaign signs, and literature table to make sure everything was in place. Humphrey was always running behind schedule, and invariably there'd be a lull in the program while the crowd sat patiently, sometimes impatiently, and waited for him to arrive.

While the advance man checked out the hall, I would go on for twenty minutes, half an hour, or longer if necessary, warming up the audience with songs and stories of the campaign and building pace and enthusiasm. When word would come that Humphrey's bus had arrived in town and he would be in the hall in five minutes I would move quickly into sure-fire rally songs such as "We Shall Not Be Moved," with fresh lines made up for the campaign:

1. We're for Hubert Humphrey,
   We shall not be moved.
   We're for Hubert Humphrey,
   We shall not be moved.
   Just like a tree that's planted by the water,
   We shall not be moved.

2. Humphrey is our candidate . . .

3. We need Humphrey in the White House . . .

4. Humphrey will be president . . .

Another rousing number that provided good entry music was an adaptation of a Democratic Party song to the tune of "The Yellow Rose of Texas."

The man from Minnesota
Is for you and you and you
He fights for all the people
And not for just the few.

On the farm and in the city,
For the big man and the small,
The man from Minnesota
Is the very best one for all.

So let's all march together
And on election day
We'll vote for Hubert Humphrey
All over the U.S.A.

If our timing was right, he would move onto the platform as we were singing the last notes. The crowd would cheer and applaud, and the speech would begin on a high note, everyone feeling fine.

About ten minutes into the speech, I would sneak out with the advance man, and we would race to the next stop, perhaps an hour away. If the schedulers had done a good job I would have a typed list of the next meetings, the name of our contacts, and information about whether a meeting was for labor, farmers, teachers, Democratic Party activists, students, or interested citizens. Such details enabled me to review the appropriate songs for each group.

Of course, the labor groups were the easiest for me. I would quickly find out about the major issues in each plant and hit them hard in my songs. "Union Maid" was a good opener for large groups of women. If workers were worried about technological changes, "Automation" would be a hit. If there was a struggle for a decent pension, "Too Old to Work" would fit. If the employer was attacking the unions and there was a need for solidarity, songs like "Which Side Are You On?" "Hold the Fort," or "Solidarity Forever" would be just right.

I could have sung labor songs all night and into the next day without repeating one, although one reporter in Racine didn't know that. He wrote: "At a union rally here for Hubert Humphrey last night, folksinger Joe Glazer warmed up the crowd with labor songs. In a half hour Glazer ran out of songs and Senator Humphrey began his speech."

I was always on the lookout for simple, catchy songs that an audience could pick up instantly. To my surprise, there were many closet songwriters in the country, and Humphrey received a steady stream of campaign songs from friendly amateur composers. Those songs were turned over to me for a reply. Because the writers were all well-meaning supporters trying to help, we didn't want to discourage them with the painful truth about their earnest efforts. I would thank each for his or her "inspiring" song and state that we would make "every effort" to use it in the campaign.

It was usually necessary to put together my own campaign ditties, but I did run into one fine song written by Wisconsin's lieutenant governor, Philleo Nash, who was a guitar picker and avid supporter. He used the tune of "Davy Crockett," a song everyone knew at the time:

Hubert is a neighbor just across the line,
He's a good neighbor too; he's yours and mine
He's always been a help to us in Washington.
He's gonna be Wisconsin's favorite son.

    Hubert, Hubert Humphrey
    The president for you and me,
    Hubert, Hubert Humphrey,
    The president for you and me.

Although the verses were nothing special, audiences were able to bellow out the chorus the first time they heard it. It could fill a hall with enthusiastic noise. Years later, on a visit to the John F. Kennedy Library and Museum in Boston, I was pleasantly surprised to hear the bouncy chorus immortalized in the museum's film about Kennedy's life. In the portion dealing with his 1960 primary campaign against Humphrey in Wisconsin I heard my voice booming from the sound track: "Hubert, Hubert Humphrey / The president for you and me."

Meetings with Democratic activists were a snap. "The Giveaway Boys in Washington" was a favorite, as was "The Ballad of Richard Nixon," the man Democrats loved to hate. But I learned during the course of the campaign that the Nixon song was not everybody's favorite. I received a cool response when I sang it at a rural electric cooperative–sponsored dinner for farm families. Wisconsin was dotted with dozens of such co-ops, which had been organized by Franklin D. Roosevelt's Rural Electrification Agency (REA) in 1935 to bring low-cost power to areas long ignored by private power companies. Although co-op members were grateful for the REA, not all of them were Democrats. Many independents and quite a few Republicans attended these meetings, as I soon found out. Yet Wisconsin voters were permitted to cross over and vote for another party's candidates. It was important to win them over to vote for Humphrey.

Winning them over presented a bit of a challenge, but once I learned about the composition of such an audience I was able to come up with appropriate songs that touched the right nerve. One farmer's protest song almost a hundred years old still rang true, for example:

The Farmer Is the Man
Author Unknown

Oh, the farmer comes to town
With his wagon broken down,
But the farmer is the man who feeds them all.
If you'll only look and see
I think you will agree,
That the farmer is the man who feeds them all.

> The farmer is the man
> The farmer is the man
> Lives on credit till the fall.
> Then they take him by the hand
> And they lead him from the land
> And the banker is the man who gets it all.

When the banker says he's broke,
And the merchant's up in smoke,
They forget that it's the farmer feeds them all.
It would put them to the test,
If the farmer took a rest,
Then they'd know that it's the farmer feeds them all.

> The farmer is the man
> The farmer is the man
> Lives on credit till the fall.
> With the interest rate so high
> It's a wonder he don't die
> For the mortgage man's the one who gets it all.

At local REA co-op meetings I made a big hit with a song written in 1957 by Donna Schwarzrock, who lived on a farm near Hector, Minnesota. When the REA started in 1935 only 15 percent of U.S. farms had electricity. By the time of the Wisconsin primary, that number had reached well over 95 percent, with the help of the long-term, low-interest loans made available by the REA. It was difficult for a city boy like me to imagine the drudgery and back-breaking work that were part of a farm family's life before electrification. The REA meant power to run a water pump; it also made electric brooders and milking machines possible. It meant electric stoves, washing machines, refrigerators, sewing machines, irons, toasters, lights, furnaces, radio, and, eventually, television. You didn't have to be a partisan Democrat to appreciate the message in Donna Schwartzrock's song:

One Happy Swede
Words: Donna Schwartzrock
Tune: "Reuben and Rachel"

Aye ban a farmer in Minnesota,
Ban here mostly all my life,
Got myself some fancy contraptions
Mostly to please my purty wife.

The REA she's sure ban helpful,
Made our jobs here one big fun.
All we do is press the buttons,
Then our work, by gosh, she's done.

Now that woman doesn't nag me
For the water to go and get.
All she does is turn the faucet
And the whole darned place gets wet.

When she turns the 'lectric bulb on
For the neighbors all to see,
Then I tell you this old farmstead
Shines just like a Christmas tree.

All I need to make me happy
Is that thing they call TV.
With the money "our line" saves me
I can get one soon, by gee.

Now this REA is something;
With it you just can't go wrong
But I tell you and I mean it,
This old Swede helped things along.

Humphrey was having a hard time competing against the Kennedy glam-
our, the Kennedy money, the Kennedy organization, and the Kennedy family.
He summed up the situation with great humor at one meeting: "I went up to
Green Bay last week, and there was Bobby making a speech. I went to Eau
Claire, and Teddy was holding a meeting. I went to La Crosse, and Sarge Shriver
and the other brothers-in-law were campaigning. In Milwaukee, the three
Kennedy sisters—all lovely women—were giving a tea. In Madison, the mother,
a gracious lady indeed, was holding a reception for Jack. Sometimes I feel like
a corner grocer competing against a chain store."

Humphrey lost. But he did win convention delegates in four of ten congressional districts. He had become a national figure. He understood more clear-ly, he felt, how to stand up to the Kennedy machine. He would fight Kennedy in the next primary, which took place in West Virginia.

Humphrey thought that West Virginia was his kind of state. It was a low-income state with a strong labor movement. West Virginians worshiped Frank-lin D. Roosevelt, and there was no stronger Roosevelt-style Democrat than Hubert Humphrey. For those of us who campaigned in Wisconsin, it was on to West Virginia. I knew the coal miners' union version of the state song, "The West Virginia Hills":

The West Virginia Hills
Words: Walter Seacrist
Music: H. E. Engle

Oh, those West Virginia hills
So majestic and so grand,
With their miners standing loyal
As all union men should stand.
Is it any wonder then,
That my heart with rapture thrills,
For again we have a union
In the West Virginia hills.

Over the hills, beautiful hills
There's a union in the West Virginia hills.
Though over scab fields I should roam
Still I'll dream of happy home
And the rednecks in the West Virginia hills.

Oh, those West Virginia hills,
They're so beautiful and green
If they could only tell you
Of the awful sights they've seen.
Of their union sons and daughters
So noble and so brave
By a cruel gunman's bullet
Gone to fill an early grave.

Chorus

Although I had been singing this song for many years, it was not until 1960 when I crisscrossed West Virginia campaigning for Hubert Humphrey that I began to appreciate it. Beautiful, rolling hills were everywhere, except where they were covered with the ugly slag heaps of the coal mines.

West Virginia was a sad example of the failure of democratic society. The state had the largest concentration of rich, rich coalfields in the world, and there was enough wealth in that coal to provide a good living for every one of the hundred thousand miners who risked their lives to wrench the black gold from underneath those green hills. But that was not to be. I thought of the promise of the indomitable Mother Jones as I drove over the green hills and witnessed the poverty of the company coal towns of southern West Virginia: "West Virginia with its bleak hills, its miners' huts, its hungry children, the raggedy clothed women, the company police, the gun thugs, the law owned by the mine operators. By God, when I get to the other side I'm gonna tell God almighty about West Virginia."

The media constantly raised the issue of Kennedy's religion. After all, the United States had never had a Catholic president. True, Kennedy had won the primary in Wisconsin, but Wisconsin had a substantial number of Catholics, and Wisconsin primary laws permitted crossing over to another party. None of that was true in West Virginia, a heavily Protestant state.

Humphrey's staff knew he would not tolerate the slightest hint of anti-Catholic talk in the campaign, and I don't recall anyone ever crossing the line on that issue. I was involved, however, in one amusing aspect of the religious controversy. After the Wisconsin campaign, *Time* magazine carried the following story: "The Humphrey campaign is all set to exploit the religious issue in West Virginia with a song written to the tune of an old Protestant hymn, 'Give Me That Old-Time Religion.'" Religion, *Time* concluded, was being introduced. The hymn's original lyrics were:

Give me that old-time religion
Give me that old-time religion
Give me that old-time religion
It's good enough for me.

I was indignant at the suggestion that the Humphrey campaign was exploiting anti-Catholic feelings and sent the following telegram to *Time:* "You are 100 percent wrong in your reference to a Humphrey campaign song you state written especially for West Virginia. You imply song is anti-Catholic because it uses the tune of Protestant hymn, 'Give Me That Old-Time Religion.' Fact: This song written by me for the Wisconsin campaign. First performed by me from a sound track in a Milwaukee Polish neighborhood, probably 95 percent Catholic."

My lyrics had nothing to do with religion. I used the tune because it was easy to sing and easy to parody. This is the version we sang in Wisconsin:

I'm Gonna Vote for Hubert Humphrey
Words: Joe Glazer
Music: "Give Me That Old-Time Religion"

I'm gonna vote for Hubert Humphrey.
I'm gonna vote for Hubert Humphrey.
I'm gonna vote for Hubert Humphrey.
He's good enough for me.

He was good in Minnesota.
He was good in Minnesota.
He was good in Minnesota,
And he's good enough for me.

He'll be good here in Wisconsin.
He'll be good here in Wisconsin.
He'll be good here in Wisconsin,
And he's good enough for me.

We need Humphrey in the White House.
We need Humphrey in the White House.
We need Humphrey in the White House.
He's good enough for me.

I doubt if anyone associated the new lyrics with the religious theme of the original song and read anything sinister into them, but reporters were hungry for anything that would magnify a possible religious confrontation in West Virginia. Unfortunately for me and for the pursuit of truth, *Time* neither printed nor acknowledged my telegram.

I felt I could be of real help to Humphrey in West Virginia because the state was dotted with hundreds of union coal towns. I knew dozens of coal-mining songs, had sung at many coal miners' meetings, and could stir people with a mixture of mining and Humphrey election songs. I started by going on a one-week tour of the state's coal towns with Karl Rolvaag, the lieutenant-governor of Minnesota. When the campaign got underway, Rolvaag loaded his big Chrysler station wagon with Humphrey literature, installed a couple of loudspeakers on the roof, and drove a thousand miles to West Virginia to help his friend Hubert Humphrey.

We had a routine. We'd drive into an isolated coal town in Rolvaag's Chrysler, which was plastered with colorful Humphrey posters. We'd stop on a city square or in an open spot on Main Street, martial music blaring from the loudspeakers. If our advance man had done his job well, a respectable group of people would be waiting.

I'd open with a well-known song such as "This Land Is Your Land," say a few words about Humphrey and the coming election, and then sing a coal-mining song, perhaps "We Shall Not Be Moved," which thirty years earlier, there in the West Virginia coalfields, had been transformed from a gospel song into one of protest and solidarity. I would follow with several Humphrey campaign songs. Then I would introduce Rolvaag, slurring over the "lieutenant" portion of his title because West Virginia had no lieutenant-governor. While Rolvaag was delivering words of praise for Humphrey, our local supporters would hand out campaign literature. One day Rolvaag, son of the distinguished novelist Ole Rolvaag, author of *Giants in the Earth,* made me laugh when he pointed to the political pamphlets and leaflets and muttered, "When did we start calling this stuff literature?"

After stopping at four or five towns, we would end in a larger one that had a radio station where we'd try to get free radio time for our message. At some stations we had to buy fifteen minutes of time, which Rolvaag paid for out of his own pocket. At one station, we picked up Jimmy Wolford, who volunteered himself and his band of three or four men to sing at rallies. Wolford had a good country music voice and style. And his price was right, something even we could afford: $15 for the band. He turned out to be a real find, became caught up in Humphrey's politics, and, at the end, broke down and sobbed when Humphrey lost the primary.

Rolvaag and I were innocents when it came to the realities of money in West Virginia elections. In some towns we were given the names of key political leaders, usually the county sheriff, who had to be seen and talked to. "I'll give it to you straight, governor," one said (we didn't correct him when he said "governor"). "I like Hubert Humphrey, and I would love to vote for him. This county has only about 2 or 3 percent Catholics, so this should be good territory for Humphrey. But votes cost money here." He took out a little notebook and started going over the precincts, one by one. "Now, number 2, that's a pretty good-sized precinct. That'll cost about $12,000. Number 4 is not too big, we can do that for $7,000. Number 5 takes about $9,000."

"Is that money for expenses, for getting people to the polls?" we asked. He looked at us incredulously. "We have a tradition of paying the people $3, $4, $5, or a bottle of whiskey," he explained, "or a combination of all kinds." He came up with a total of $90,000—for the one county. Humphrey couldn't put up that kind of money. In the end, the county went overwhelmingly for Kennedy.

Much has been written about Kennedy money and the West Virginia election. There were times when all the loudspeakers had been rented by the

Kennedy campaign and all available cars for hire were committed to the Kennedy campaign. As Larry O'Brien, one of Kennedy's top men in West Virginia, recalled in his *No Final Victories:*

> I negotiated our payments for campaign expenses. Neither Jack nor Bob Kennedy knew what agreements I made—that was my responsibility. I had to have cash at hand and I usually left it with my secretary, Phyllis Maddock, for safekeeping. On one occasion . . . I completed agreements with the leaders of states in two extremely important counties, representing the largest single expenditure of the campaign. I called Phyllis on the house phone and whispered, "Bring me five." . . . she appeared in the lobby and slipped me five hundred dollars.
>
> "Not five hundred, Phyllis," I told her. "Five thousand."

Humphrey was becoming bitter about the Kennedy money flooding West Virginia, and on occasion he would vent his anger in public. I was present when one such exchange took place at a press conference near the close of the campaign:

> Reporter: Senator, I've got a quote here from the newspaper: "Senator Humphrey says, 'I'm not running around West Virginia with a little black bag handing out dollar bills." The Kennedys say that's a low blow accusing them of handing out money from a black bag.
> Humphrey: I didn't say that.
> Reporter [getting out the clipping and quoting directly]: "Humphrey says 'I'm not running around West Virginia with a black bag handing out money.'"
> Humphrey: That's just what I said, that I'm not doing it. You guys know I don't do it.
> Reporter: Oh, come on, senator. The Kennedy people say it means that you are accusing them of running around with a black bag handing out money. That's how they interpret it.
> Humphrey: If the shoe fits, let 'em wear it.

After the tour with Rolvaag I went to West Virginia several more times, flying in and out for rallies and special meetings. I was asked to the city of Huntington, where Humphrey people had taken over an amusement park. To involve an audience, I would sing old-time favorites such as "Working on the Railroad," "God Bless America," and "Let Me Call You Sweetheart" along with one Humphrey campaign song for every three older ones. Humphrey would greet the audience for two or three minutes and go back to shaking hands and meeting people. It was a good act, and we repeated it throughout the day. We closed the rally on a high note when Humphrey made one of his inspiring "vision" speeches, condensed to ten minutes. I led in a closing "Happy Days Are Here

Again," which is the greatest political song ever written and, ironically, doesn't mention politics, political parties, or a candidate:

Happy days are here again,
The skies above are clear again
Let us sing a song of cheer again—
Happy days are here again.

The final vote was 61 percent for Kennedy and 39 percent for Humphrey. That was enough to make everyone sad. Bitterness came with the knowledge that the West Virginia political system was made to order for the Kennedy bankroll. In retrospect, Humphrey never had a chance, no matter how brilliant a campaign he ran.

Many of Humphrey's staff did not want him to go to Kennedy headquarters and offer personal congratulations to the victor. Others wanted him to blast the Kennedy campaign about the money issue. But Humphrey was a wiser politician than they. He realized that Kennedy would likely be the Democratic Party candidate for president, and he would support him. It was no time for bitterness or recriminations. It was a time to close ranks, move ahead, and defeat Richard Nixon, the Republican nominee. Kennedy was nominated at the Democratic Party's Los Angeles convention. Even though I had preferred Humphrey, I was happy to support Kennedy, who was a liberal Democrat, a strong campaigner, and had a good chance to defeat Nixon.

Now that Kennedy was the Democratic Party's candidate, my guitar and voice were ready to campaign for him. I sang at John F. Kennedy's first big rally, which was held in a high school football stadium in Alexandria, Virginia, a suburb of Washington, D.C.

The stands were packed with enthusiastic, even rabid, Kennedy fans. A few thousand folding chairs filled the playing field, and every seat was taken. It was standing-room only. There must have been ten thousand charged-up Democrats in the stadium, waiting to wave their banners and placards and to cheer and yell as soon as Kennedy arrived. The smell of victory was in the air. It was a good time to sing a song I had written for the campaign:

Sweet Music in Washington
By Joe Glazer

There's gonna be
Sweet music in Washington
On Election Day.
Sweet music in Washington,
On that glorious day.

We're gonna get rid of
Those sour notes,
When the people cast their votes,
And they make Jack Kennedy the president
On Election Day.

The rally organizers had hired a good Dixieland band that backed me with exuberance. I was able to adapt some of the good Humphrey campaign songs of the primary battles with a simple switch of names. One, "The Democratic Victory Train," was sung to the country music tune of "The Crawdad Song." With the Dixieland band behind me, we did a rocking, swinging version of the song that night:

I've got a vote and you've got a vote, brother,
I've got a vote and you've got a vote, sister,
Let's put 'em together, what do you say—
Vote for JFK on election day
Ride on that Democratic train.
Ride on that Democratic train.
The workingman and the farmer too, brother,
The workingman and the farmer too, sister,
Workers, farmers, clerks and teachers,
Housewives, engineers, and preachers,
Riding on that Democratic train.
Straight to the White House.
Riding on Jack Kennedy's train.

The master of ceremonies announced that Kennedy would soon be entering the stadium and said, "While we're waiting for Senator Kennedy, volunteers will be passing around plastic buckets to raise money for the campaign. Please be as generous as you can." He then turned the microphone over to me for a campaign song. I was inspired and started to chant:

Put a buck in the bucket for Jack.
Help bring the Democrats back.
Put a buck in the bucket for Jack.
Help bring the Democrats back.

After repeating the chant a dozen times or more, I realized that the bucket brigade would take a while to reach everyone in the huge crowd. Then I started to make up additional verses to keep from boring the crowd—and myself—with the same two lines chanted over and over.

We need a buck from you and a buck from me
If we're gonna get rid of the G.O.P.
Put that train on the Democratic track
With a buck in the bucket for Jack.

To keep this campaign alive
Maybe you can drop in a five.
If you want to give Jack a thrill
Please drop in a ten dollar bill.

Hang on to your nickels and dimes
Because we want paper money this time.
So drop a buck in the bucket for Jack
Keep that train on the Democratic track.

People were clapping in rhythm and filling the buckets with paper money. Then a roar rumbled through the stadium. Kennedy and his entourage of a half-dozen cars had finally entered the field, and his big, red convertible was in the lead.

The crowd went crazy as Kennedy circled the playing field a couple of times, smiling and waving at everyone. I could see why Hubert Humphrey had trouble trying to beat the handsome Prince Charming of American politics. Everyone was on their feet, yelling, "Kennedy, Kennedy, Kennedy." Meanwhile, I kept chanting. The buckets were soon overflowing with campaign dollars.

Kennedy made his way to the platform, shook hands with all the local politicians, and gave me a particularly warm greeting, "That was great, Joe. You ought to sing at all the rallies." I was somewhat surprised that he remembered me, although I had introduced him at a Rubber Workers Union legislative institute in Washington and also met him at a Democratic Party dinner in Akron, where I sang. It was also likely that he had heard about my music on behalf of Humphrey in the Wisconsin and West Virginia primaries. A good politician remembers names.

What followed was one of the most exasperating episodes I have experienced at a political meeting. The local politician given the honor of introducing Kennedy took that duty seriously. A proper introduction would have been "ladies and gentlemen, it is my honor to present to you the next president of the United States—John F. Kennedy!" The introduction at the rally, however, began with Kennedy's birth in Brookline, Massachusetts; carried him through prep school at Choate and four years at Harvard University; and discussed his family at length, including several minutes of praise for Jacqueline Kennedy, who was not present. Next we swam and suffered with Kennedy through every yard of his heroic swim in the Pacific after his PT boat was torpedoed during World War II. The speaker was just beginning to get Kennedy elected to the House of Representatives and the Senate when a deafening roar from the crowd stopped him: "We want Kennedy! We want Kennedy! We want Kennedy!" He was driven from the stage—and just as well, too. Kennedy was fidgeting restlessly as his life story was reviewed year by year and almost month by month.

I heard Jack Kennedy speak many times over the years, and his speaking ability had never impressed me much. But during the campaigns in Wisconsin and West Virginia and in his travels across the country in search of the nomination he had honed his speaking skills and become effective on the platform. He never became a stem-winder, but he was direct and clear and had a sharp sense of humor. He also had the aid of excellent speech writers and could on occasion reach levels of eloquence.

Yet his New England accent—which eliminated the letter R where it belonged and stuck it where it didn't—was a problem although not a fatal one. Once in Montana he confused an audience of farmers when he talked about the production of "soda rash" (soda ash). I was also taken aback to hear him call Gamal Abdel Nasser, the president of Egypt, "Mr. Nassuh" and at the same time refer to the National Aeronautics and Space Agency (NASA) as "Nasser." I couldn't resist the temptation to write a song on the subject:

I'm Looking for the R in HAHVID
By Joe Glazer

I'm looking for the R in HAHVID.
I wonder where it can be.
There must be an R in HAHVID.
I checked it in the dictionary.

I must look with much more VIGAH.
I must look from evening till MAWN.
For the life of me I just cahn't FIGGAH
Where that R could have gone.

I've looked in Afriker, Ameriker, and Indiar too.
I've looked and looked all over the place.
Alabamer, Caroliner, South Dakoter—
The Rs have disappeared and haven't left a trace.

But I know there's an R in HAHVID.
It's gone forevUH I FEAH.
But I've got it, I have it, I've found it.
Here it is on the end of IDEAR.

After the rally, I met up with the person who had invited me to sing and said, "I'll send you a bill for my expenses, and you can send me a check." "Do you mind getting cash?" he asked. "No problem," I replied. "It'll be about 150 bucks for airfare, motel, and taxis." He opened a shoe box he was carrying that was stuffed with part of the take from the evening's bucket brigade collection and counted out 150 dollar bills. I felt like a high-roller who had just hit the jackpot. I shoved the wad of bills into my guitar case and headed for the motel.

I didn't get to sing at all the rallies as Kennedy had suggested, but I did sing at quite a few. I produced an LP album with nine of the campaign songs accompanied by a quickly organized six-piece band we called the Dynamic Democratic Dixielanders. Some of the songs were too long or too subtle for use in mass rallies, but they were just right for small fund-raising cocktail parties or luncheons. One of my favorites was "I'm an Old Republican":

I'm an Old Republican
Words: Joe Glazer
Music: "Ramblin' Wreck from Georgia Tech"

I'm an old Republican, bet your life I am
For all that's Democratic I do not give a damn.
I hated Thomas Jefferson and Woodrow Wilson too.
Couldn't stand That Man in the White House
And his wild-eyed New Deal crew.

Always thought that Truman was a no good such and such.
Never trusted Stevenson because he knowed so much.
I voted for McKinley and Warren Harding too
I loved old Calvin Coolidge; to Hoover I'll be true.

I hate your federal highways; dirt was good enough for me.
Hate your unemployment insurance and your Social Security.
I hate your public schooling—third grade should be enough.
I hate your public housing and all that socialist stuff.

If I ran the government I wouldn't spend a cent.
I wouldn't build a post office; I'd charge the Congress rent.
I wouldn't send a submarine beneath the deep blue sea,
For fighting wars there's nothing like the U.S. Cavalry. (Charge!)

Yes, I'm an old Republican, bet your life I am.
For all that's Democratic, I just don't give a damn.
I hated Thomas Jefferson and Franklin Roosevelt too.
I'm gonna hate Jack Kennedy before this campaign's through.

We developed a useful technique of adapting a good campaign song so it could be used for innumerable local and national candidates with minor modifications. We used our rendition of "Sweet Music in Washington," and when we came to the line "and they make Jack Kennedy the president on Election Day" we would substitute, through the magic of recording technology, the name of a candidate for the Senate or House. It was a neat way to get first-class radio spots or loudspeaker announcements for practically no cost.

The Democratic National Committee picked up the "Sweet Music" song and two others from my record, teamed them with Frank Sinatra's campaign version of the pop song "High Hopes," and put all four songs on an LP record. (In the 1960s Sinatra was a gung-ho Kennedy Democrat, although he supported Ronald Reagan in the 1980s.) On the other side of the LP were several one-minute spots featuring Kennedy on civil rights, education, care for the aged, and the New Frontier.

On one memorable occasion, I became Jacqueline Kennedy's escort. Just before Election Day, I sang at a luncheon for Democratic Party women activists. Seated on the dais were Jacqueline Kennedy, who was pregnant at the time, and Ladybird Johnson, wife of vice-presidential candidate Lyndon Johnson. This was at a time when only a handful of women were in Congress, so the wives of politicians were prominent. Other than the waiters, I was likely the only male in the room.

Bethune Church, who was married to Idaho's Sen. Frank Church, was in charge. She pulled me aside at the beginning of the luncheon to ask a favor:

> I'm nervous about Jackie. She is due to give birth any week now, and the doctor told her to avoid any kind of stress. The only way she can leave after the luncheon is right through the center of the ballroom, through the crowd of women who will be clamoring for her autograph, wanting to shake her hand, touch her, or hug her. Jackie is quite concerned.
>
> The maitre d' tells me the only other way out is through the kitchens, which you can reach through the back of the dais. Would you mind escorting her through the kitchens to her car after the luncheon? It'll be a big relief to me and to her.

It seems hard to believe, but in 1960 the presidential candidates and their families had no Secret Service protection. I knew that hotel kitchens, set up to serve thousands of meals at banquets, could be a labyrinth, so I checked out the path through the kitchens to the delivery dock where the Kennedy limousine and chauffeur would be waiting. Good thing, too, because the kitchens were a maze of stainless-steel refrigerators, counters, stoves, high carts piled with trays, slicing machines, and giant pots and pans. I mapped out the route—left at the cooler, right near crates of lettuce, then left again.

I thought that a good way to introduce myself would be to present one of the albums I made for the campaign. I inscribed it "for Jack Kennedy, next President of the United States." Jacqueline Kennedy thanked me and said in that breathless, childlike voice, "I hope it comes true." Meanwhile, Ladybird Johnson, who was seated next to her, was looking on curiously. I reacted quickly. "I've got one for you, too, Mrs. Johnson," I said as I grabbed another record, inscribed it, and presented it.

I sang two songs that were well received, but my mind was focused on the escape route through the kitchens. The guests were asked to remain seated when the luncheon was over while I escorted Jacqueline Kennedy. She slipped her arm in mine, and we walked through the door and past an army of kitchen helpers—chefs, salad makers, and dishwashers—who lined up and applauded as she passed them with a gracious smile. We reached the limousine without a mishap. On the way back, I made a wrong turn, so it was good I had mapped our route.

That was the Saturday before Election Day. Three days later, Kennedy defeated Richard Nixon. Three weeks after Election Day, Jacqueline Kennedy gave birth to John Fitzgerald Kennedy, Jr. I felt I had played a small part in that happy event.

9

Working for the Foreign Service

The election of John F. Kennedy stirred me to leave the labor movement after seventeen years and sign on with the United States Information Agency (USIA). Kennedy, young, handsome, and confident, set spines a-tingle with his idealistic rhetoric, "Let the word go forth from this time and place, to friend and foe alike, . . . we shall . . . bear every burden." And who can forget, "Ask not what your country can do for you—ask what can you do for your country"?

The Peace Corps captured the imagination of thousands of young Americans. The Alliance for Progress was launched to end poverty in Latin America. Many of my long-time friends and colleagues were attracted to the Kennedy administration and its ideals. Arthur Goldberg, the labor movement's most prominent lawyer, became secretary of labor. Esther Peterson, legislative representative for the Industrial Union Department of the AFL-CIO, was appointed consumer advisor. Ted Sorensen, who had spoken at several of my legislative institutes, was a top White House assistant. Arthur Schlesinger, Jr., with whom I had shared political platforms, was a key advisor. Hubert Humphrey, for whom I had campaigned in the primaries, became the Democratic whip in the Senate. I became caught up in the electric atmosphere.

During my seventeen years in the labor movement, first with the Textile Workers Union of America and then from 1950 to 1961 as education director for the United Rubber Workers, I had run hundreds of training schools for shop stewards and officers. I had also written dozens of leaflets and pamphlets on collective bargaining, worker safety, union history, politics, and labor legislation. In addition, I had spoken or sung at hundreds of meetings, rallies, conventions, and strikes. It was time to move on—and Washington was calling.

By September 1961 I was working for the United States Information Agency, training to be a labor information officer in Mexico and promote the Alliance for Progress. The Alliance was an ambitious Kennedy program to aid Latin American countries in developing their economies and democratic institutions. An important part of that plan's strategy was to reach people in the labor movement in those countries so Latin American workers would be able to share in the aid that would be available. That's where I came in.

In retrospect, there was nothing immodest about the goals of the Alliance for Progress. There was even talk of ending poverty in Latin America in ten years. Hey, we thought, we're Americans, and we have know-how and big shoulders. We are a can-do country. We'll go in and show "these little guys" how to do things our way. Then they'll become efficient and democratic like we are.

For four months I underwent intensive training in Spanish conducted by the Foreign Service Institute (FSI), located in Virginia across the Potomac from Washington. Despite three years of high school Spanish and two years in college, I was soon sweating to keep from falling behind. It was six hours a day, five days a week, with two hours of homework or practice every night. We had no more than four or five in a class, so there was no place to hide. I still shake my head in disbelief when I see commercial language schools advertise "master a language in a few short weeks." After sixteen weeks of Spanish and eight weeks of lectures on Mexico and Latin America and on USIA policies, procedures, and programs, I was off.

Before I left, I developed a song in talking-blues style that described the life of new foreign service officers (FSO) and their experiences with the FSI and the USIA. To understand the song, it is necessary to know that a foreign service officer, whether male or female, starts out as an FSO–8; they are then promoted to the rank of FSO–7, FSO–6, and on to FSO–1 (a senior officer). The song also mentions "JOTs" (a junior officer in training). I put the song on a tape, and it was played at overseas posts all over the world. For the next four years I would receive cries of recognition from people I had yet to meet.

Talking USIA
Words: Joe Glazer
(sung talking-blues style)

I remember the year when I got my degree
Every blue chip company was after me.
I got myself interviewed by U.S. Steel,
By Ford and GM Automobile.
I talked to Monsanto; I talked to Dow.
But I just couldn't get excited no-how.
I finally decided that I wanted to toil
For the public good—not for Standard Oil . . .

You know the Peace Corps
Helpin' the po' folks
Fighting discrimination and such-like

Well, I talked to every government agency
From the OEO to the FCC.
I talked to NASA and the DOD.
I had an interview with the NLRB.
I talked to J. Edgar at the FBI
But I guess I'm hard to satisfy
Because none of those agencies seemed quite right
Till finally I found the answer one night . . .

In a U.S. Government Printing Office publication.
It said—USIA—serve your country in Paris, Rome, London—
Tell America's story to the world.

Well, that seemed to make a lot of good sense to me
I felt I could be a good missionary.
I could talk to them foreigners in Paris and Rome
I could tell them all the things we're doing back home.

You know I'm a pretty good talker,
Placed second in the Cedar Rapids citywide elocution contest when I was a
sophomore in high school.

I talked to a man in Personnel
And without much ado I proceeded to tell
Him I was young and healthy and ready to go
To Paris or Rome or Tokyo . . .

To serve my country in its hour of need.
Languages? Well, I can say refrigerator in Eyetalian:
"Ice—a—box—a."

Well, I took me a test and I did right well
And they called me back to Personnel
And they said when I passed my security
I would be sworn in as a JOT . . .

FSO–8. Mighty nice of them to start me out
seven steps above a number 1.

They sent me 'cross the river to the FSI
To learn me some French so that by and by
I could talk to the natives face to face
As I walked down the Champs [hard *ch*] Eleezes or the Playce of the
Conquered

I studied that lingo day after day
For sixteen weeks till I could practically say
Everything in the book without hesitation,
Till I was ready to take on the whole French nation . . .

> Including Charles de Goalie;
> I could just see that first big interview for the *Voice of America:*
> "Monsieur Charles—pourquoi vous n'aimez pas
> Zee United States, eh?"

I spent so many months at the FSI
That I thought I would finally retire and die
And get buried nearby at Arlington
With a plaque listing all the things I had done . . .

> For my country:
> "Here lies a soldier of the foreign service . . .
> Known but to God and his personnel officer
> Who gave his life for his country while trying
> To pronounce a French 'Rrrr' correctly."

On graduation day I had ants in my pants
I could hardly wait to get to France.
I zoomed out to Dulles and was just about to leave
When a personnel man grabbed me by the sleeve,
"I beg your pardon but I must inform you
Your orders have been changed from Paris to Ouagadougou."

> . . . Ouagadougou?
> How could there be a place called Ouagadougou?
> . . . There was.

I was just about to ask where was this place
But I realized that would make me lose face.
So I murmured "Ouagadougou" with an all-knowing air
And said, "I'm prepared to go anywhere . . .

> . . . for my country."

Well, I checked every page in Rand McNally's book.
Ouagadougou, Ouagadougou—where should I look?
Was it Africa, Asia, or the Middle East?
Ouagadougou, Ouagadougou—was it man or beast?
When I finally found it it was quite a jolt-a
A country in Africa called Upper Volta . . .

> Upper Volta?
> Lower Slobovia!

Well, I hit that town one bright sunny day
Looked up and down Main Street and right away
I could tell it wasn't Paris or Tokyo
But that didn't stop me; I decided to show
The Agency I could do what had to be done
So they'd hear about it, all the way to Washington.

    . . . I was gonna put Ouagadougou on the map.

My output of materials was simply immense
All aimed at my target audience.
I talked to professors and comic-book readers.
I talked to reporters—and opinion leaders.
I spoke to workers at union meetings.
To the Chamber of Commerce I brought embassy greetings.
I talked to youth from five to fifty,
And my contacts with women were rather nifty . . .
I published a paper for farmers in the bush.
I gave the exchange program quite a push.
My tapes were played on every radio station.
I had English taught in every town in the nation.
I presented books and movie projectors.
I set up exhibits for stamp collectors.
I sang hymns in the churches, drank beer in the pubs,
Made speeches to the Ouagadougou Rotary Clubs.
I spread culture, music, love, and joy.
I was named the Ouagadougou All-American Boy . . .

    Of the year,
    Friend of Upper Volta,
    The people's ambassador,
    Hero of Ouagadougou.

When my tour was up I headed for home
And on the way back I spent an hour in Rome . . .
At the airport. I also managed to get a glance
From thirty thousand feet of the Republic of France.
But I wasn't worried because soon I knew
I'd be stationed for sure in one of these two
Places. Or maybe Rio or Athens or Mexico
Or Spain or Hong Kong or Tokyo.
Well, Personnel was waiting with arms open wide.
They said, "USIA is full of pride
At the magnificent job that you have done.
Even the president has heard about it in Washington.

You did so well as a matter of fact
The president himself wants you to go right back . . .

> For two more years.
> The prime minister loves you.
> The people love you. Ouagadougou loves you.
> And we love you so much we have made you an FSO–7
> . . . effective at the end of your next tour."

So if you happen to be passing through Ouagadougou,
It's on the road between Kinshasa and Timbuktu
You can't miss it, especially Saturday nights,
When Main Street is jumping. I'd love to show you the sights . . .

> We've got good eating and good music,
> Broad streets, tall trees, and a great big plaza,
> And right in the middle of the plaza a huge statue
> Dedicated to the Hero of Ouagadougou.
> That's right . . . me . . .
> FSO–8—USIA.

The song was even mentioned in the *New York Times*. Reporter Johnny Apple was doing a series of articles on the new countries in Africa, and when he mentioned Ouagadougou, the capitol of what was then called Upper Volta, he quoted several stanzas, crediting "an unknown bureaucrat." There went my opportunity for fame.

When I completed my training, I set out for Mexico with my family in the winter of 1962, making stops en route with friends as we drove south. At one stop, in Albuquerque, New Mexico, there was an urgent message. I was to fly to Washington to meet with Edward R. Murrow, director of the USIA, the next morning. A crisis had arisen. About what? Our furniture and all our worldly possessions were en route to Mexico. We had sold our house in Akron, Ohio, and I had quit my job in the labor movement. Could it be the not-very-funny joke I had made on a radio talk show about Murrow, a notorious chain-smoker, walking around in a cloud of smoke? The talk show host had asked about the Alliance for Progress and my job as labor information officer with the USIA. I had sung a few mild labor songs, certainly nothing inflammatory.

At 9 A.M. the next morning I walked into Murrow's office in the old USIA building two blocks from the White House. He had the inevitable cigarette in his hand, and three or four stubs were already in the ashtray. He smiled and was friendly, so I knew I was O.K. He laughed heartily when I told him of my concern about the smoking joke. A powerful member of Congress had telephoned after hearing the radio program. Murrow said, "This Congressman is worried that we are sending you down to Mexico to organize unions, foment strikes, and sing on picket lines. I assured him that was not your job. So I wanted you to be extra careful in Mexico. Don't make any unnecessary headlines when you're working with the unions there."

Murrow was surprised and annoyed when I told him I had flown in from New Mexico for our meeting. "I didn't know you were already on the road. We could have easily straightened this out on the phone," he said. I should have been angry at the over-zealous aide who had directed me to fly back to Washington unnecessarily. But if we had just talked on the telephone I would never have met Murrow in person. I had always admired him and his policy for the USIA: "We are obligated to present American society, warts and all."

Murrow survived the London blitz during World War II while broadcasting for CBS. Nightly, millions awaited his greeting: "This is London." He also flew on dangerous bombing missions over Germany with U.S. airmen and survived to broadcast the story. But he could not beat that old devil nicotine. In January 1964 one of his lungs was removed, and in 1965 he died of lung cancer at the age of fifty-seven. He had spent only a thousand days, fruitful ones, as USIA director.

A musical welcome on the harmonica at a union hall in New Delhi, 1969. (Photo by R. N. Khanna)

At a student assembly at the University of Indonesia in Jakarta, 1969.

At a concert at the U.S. Embassy in Manila, 1969. Amb. G. Mennen (Soapy) Williams is at right.

Singing for union members and their families at a rubber plantation in Malaysia, 1969.

Arlo Guthrie, David Carradine, Joe Glazer, and Pete Seeger at a benefit for the Farm Workers Union, Washington, D.C., 1975.

At an organizing rally of a thousand J. P. Stevens workers in Spartanburg, South Carolina, 1979. (Photo by Ed Snider)

At the White House with Jimmy and Rosalynn Carter, Labor Day 1980. (Official White House photo)

At a coal miners' rally near the White House, 1981. (Photo by Herald Grandstaff/UMWA Archives)

Joe Glazer sings "Solidarity Forever" to close the conference of the Great Labor Arts Exchange at the George Meany Center, Silver Spring, Maryland, 1992.

At a rally of striking teamsters, Washington, D.C., 1998.

The Labor Heritage Foundation presents Mildred and Joe Glazer with a giant guitar at a concert in honor of his eightieth birthday, Washington, D.C., 1998. (Photo by Murray Reich)

With family, 1998. Standing next to Glazer is son Daniel; seated (left to right) are Patti, Mildred, and Emily Glazer. (Photo by Victor Stekoll Photographers, Rockville, Md.)

In action, 1998. (Photo by Murray Reich)

10

Living and Working in Mexico

I was labor information officer in Mexico for the United States Information Agency (USIA) for three and a half years, beginning in early 1962. The USIA was an autonomous government agency that worked closely with the State Department. USIA's mission was to "tell America's story to the world."

It ran the Voice of America (VOA), which broadcasts in dozens of languages to countries around the world. It published magazines and pamphlets for overseas audiences and operated libraries and cultural centers in several hundred locations. The USIA brought opinion leaders from other countries to the United States and sent American lecturers and performing artists overseas—professors, writers, musicians, government experts, and labor leaders.

A feature article that appeared in the November 10, 1962, issue of *Business Week* described the work I did. The story was headed "Reaching the People in Latin America; New-Style Goodwill Ambassador to Mexico Is a Unionist Who Works with Local Labor Movement to Make Friends for U.S." The article described some of my activities in a typical week:

Glazer:
· Showed a U.S. union movie (*With These Hands*, the International Ladies' Garment Workers' Union story of its struggle from sweatshops to modern collective bargaining), [Dubbed in Spanish] at a Mexican union hall—and stood in the middle of a crowd for an hour afterward to answer questions.
· Lectured on the training of shop stewards at the Inter-American Regional Organization of Workers (ORIT)—following up with a party at his home for the ORIT students, young labor leaders from all over Latin America . . .
· Presented a USIA library (fifteen titles ranging from *Moby-Dick* to *How to Prevent Accidents*) to the Tampico local of the Labor Federation of the Women's Organization . . .

· Worked on . . . a twelve-page monthly magazine, *El Obrero* (The Worker), whose thirty thousand circulation covers union leaders and local unions throughout Mexico.

The article was very complimentary to me, but it ignored the work of the State Department's labor attachés with whom I worked closely not only in Mexico but also in other countries.

I worked at improving my Spanish and understanding the customs and culture of the Mexican people, especially their trade unions. I had thought my Spanish was adequate when I landed in Mexico but soon discovered that Mexicans spoke a lot faster and enunciated much less clearly than the experts on the tapes I had studied for sixteen weeks at the Foreign Service Institute. Every morning I would concentrate on one of the major daily newspapers, reading every story on the front page and looking up every word or expression I did not understand. In about six months I was able to make speeches at union meetings and carry on long discussions with union and political leaders.

My full-time assistant Francisco Villareal assisted me in translating some of the most popular American union songs into Spanish. I did not come across any Mexican union songs, even though hundreds of folk songs existed, as did many songs from the Mexican Revolution that began in 1910. Soon I had Mexican trade unionists belting out "Solidaridad por Siempre" ("Solidarity Forever") as if it were their very own:

Solidaridad por Siempre
Translation: Joe Glazer and Francisco Villareal

Llevaremos en la sangre la grandeza sindical
No tendrá poder más grande el laborismo mundial
Compañero si eres débil con tu fuerza individual
Busca la unidad gremial.

Solidaridad por siempre, solidaridad por siempre
Solidaridad por siempre
Con la fuerza sindical.

Más que el oro atesorado es el poder sindical
Es más fuerte que un armada y mejor que un arsenal
Crearemos nueva vida en el campo laboral
Con la fuerza sindical.

Chorus

My song "The Mill Was Made of Marble" was also a hit, and I sang the Spanish translation everywhere:

La Fábrica Era de Mármol
Translation: Joe Glazer and Francisco Villareal

Soñé que había muerto
Y hacia el cielo me fuí
Me dieron trabajo allí en el taller
De su gran fábrica textil.

> Las máquinas eran de oro
> De marmol era el taller
> Allí nadie se cansó nunca
> Y nadie llegó a envejecer.

Allá en el cielo lindo
Sin ruido para molestar
Se oye música angelical
Allá junto a mi tellar

> Chorus

Mi sueño fué dorado
Yo sé que no era verdad
Tal vez un día se convertirá
En una feliz realidad.

> Chorus

My music gave me entrée into Mexican unions. I was invited to sing at union meetings, picnics, dinners, and special occasions. To the labor songs I would add a Mexican folk song or two and also an African American spiritual. It made a good package. Before and after my performances I would chat with the members and leadership, answering questions about the United States—everything from collective bargaining to the civil rights movement to American politics. I also had a chance to ask questions of my own about Mexican unions, working conditions, and living standards. I knew I could expect a rosy spin on responses, so I sprinkled the replies with salt.

I had been warned that all Mexican unions were corrupt, but a progressive businessman, a friend of mine, said, "That's not true. Only 95 percent are corrupt." Another friend, the assistant to the head of the Mexican Packinghouse Workers Union, explained how things worked.

We had been invited to a party at the home of the union president, who lived in what turned out to be an expansive house in a posh Mexico City neighborhood. A luxurious car was in the driveway. How could he afford all this when the union had a small membership and union dues were low? My friend explained the financial picture. First, the official's union salary was only a minor part of his income. Second, he received a salary as an elected deputy to the Mexican National Congress as part of the labor bloc of the Partido Revolucionario Institucional (PRI), the party that had ruled Mexico since 1929. More important than his salary as a legislator was his right to import a car and appliances tax-free from the United States. The Mexican import tax was nearly 100 percent, so he could sell those imports at a fat profit. Third, he had a well-paying job as a supervisor in the *rastro* (packinghouse plant) in Mexico City, although it was understood that he never had to show up for the job. Fourth, the company had given him the exclusive concession to buy all the tripe the plant produced. The tripe was immediately sold to retail stores in Mexico City at a substantial profit. As it turned out, that concession was by far the biggest money-maker for the union head. One did not have to be a labor relations expert to realize that under the circumstances the union chief would not be the most effective representative of packinghouse workers.

Of course, American unions have their share of corruption, as does American politics and business and other areas of life. But the pervasiveness and the depth of corruption in all segments of Mexican society was something most Americans could never imagine, and I had trouble getting used to it.

The Mexico Folk Music Club

My most successful musical activity in Mexico started as a modest operation and exploded quickly into a huge undertaking. It all took place in the Mexican-American Cultural Center in a bustling section of Mexico City. It was one of several hundred centers run by the USIA all over the world to present concerts by American musicians; lectures by outstanding American authors, professors, and government leaders; and exhibits of paintings and sculpture by talented, young American artists. English classes were the most popular of the center's activities, however. In Mexico City, ten thousand students, young and old, studied English in classes that ran morning, noon, and night.

I had learned a lot of Mexican folk songs and in the process had improved my vocabulary and fluency in Spanish. Why could not students do the same with American folk and pop songs? Through the songs they would also learn something about the people, history, and background of the United States.

That was my plan as I began a folk song club in a small classroom at the center. Every Thursday evening, ten or twelve students would meet with me, and we would sing American folk songs. Each song was typed on a sheet with line-by-line translations in Spanish. Footnotes explained idioms, slang, or odd language constructions.

Each Thursday I would bring in two or three new songs, including "You Are My Sunshine," "I've Been Working on the Railroad," "Sixteen Tons," "Swing Low, Sweet Chariot," "The Battle Hymn of the Republic," "This Land Is Your Land," "He's Got the Whole World in His Hands," and "We Shall Overcome." It was a pleasant way for students to improve their English. They also learned something about America because I would give a short lecture on those songs that needed some historical background for proper appreciation.

The procedure was simple. I would sing a song through once or twice. I would then recite it with the group so they could master each phrase. Then we would sing the song together until the students controlled it thoroughly. At the end of four sessions we had ten good songs in our repertoire. At the end of four weeks our attendance had doubled to twenty-five or thirty, and we had to move to a larger classroom. We did little or no promotion, but word spread quickly that this was a great way to learn English. Soon we had fifty or sixty coming each Thursday evening. At the end of three months we had to move into the main auditorium at the Center. At first I was concerned that we would rattle around in the big hall that seated nearly two hundred, but to my surprise we filled it every time. When we had reviewed twenty-five or thirty songs, I had them bound in a notebook. That gave us a regular songbook of our own to work with.

We had some good voices in the group, and I encouraged them to come up front to the microphone and lead us in one of their favorite songs. We had occasional songs in Spanish, too, which everyone knew and would sing with gusto. The atmosphere was always festive. We had one big musical party every Thursday night, but I never lost sight of the goals—to improve the students' English and teach something about the United States.

After a while, I noticed American tourists in the hall. Someone had listed our activity in the English-language *Mexico City News* as one of the city's tourist attractions and a way to meet Mexicans socially. We must have been doing something right, because one evening an elderly tourist couple came up to me after the program to say how much they had enjoyed it. "We are going to recommend this to all our friends," they said. "This is better than the pyramids."

It was tourism and the prevalence of sightseers in Mexico that inspired me to write two songs that were always great hits at socials. They are still popular with groups that have been to Mexico. I recorded them on an album, *Your Vacation in Mexico* (1965):

Acapulco, Xochimilco
By Joe Glazer

For years we'd been dreaming 'bout
Going down to Mexico,
Crossing o'er the Rio Grande,
Meeting all the people there.
Talked to everybody
Who had ever made the trip before,
And this is what they told us to see:

Acapulco, Xochimilco,
Cuernavaca, Taxco,
Teotihuacan,
Puebla, Guanajuato,
Oaxaca, Ixtaccihuatl,
Popocatepetl too.

We got down to Mexico,
Checked into a big hotel,
Talked to all the people there,
Chatted with the manager,
Asked him where we ought to go
To see the best of Mexico,
And this is what he told us to see:

Chorus

We hired a tourist guide.
He took us everywhere,
Through the cities and the ruins
Up and down the countryside.
Didn't want to miss a thing,
Something different every day,
And this is what we managed to see:

Chorus

Soon we were home again,
Living with our memories,
Dreaming of the lovely time
We had in sunny Mexico,
Showing all the relatives
Color slides about the trip,
And this is what the relatives saw:

Chorus

Although that trip occurred
More than thirty years ago,
Friends insist on asking us
Before they go to Mexico,
"Tell us what we ought to see,
Tell us what we shouldn't miss,"
And this is where we tell them to go:

   Chorus

The second song, "Talking Mexico," describes the chief attractions of that country as well as the products and crafts for which it is famous:

Talking Mexico
By Joe Glazer
(sung talking-blues style)

Let me tell you 'bout an evening when it started to snow
And the temperature dropped to 'bout ten below.
My bones were frozen and my fingers were numb
And I said to myself a man must be dumb
To spend the whole darn winter in the cold, thin air
Just shaking the icicles out of his hair.

   Wearing gloves and galoshes
   Earmuffs and overcoats
   Praying for the sun to come out.

I got myself a copy of *Holiday Magazine*
And the sights I saw there made my eyes turn green.
I saw palm trees a-waving, señoritas full of smiles
In Jamaica, Tahiti, and the Virgin Isles.

I saw the beaches of Hawaii and the Mediterranean
And Nassau and Rio all drenched in the sun.
Well, I was wonderin' and a-ponderin' 'bout where I ought to go
When I turned the page—and there was—Mexico.

   Olé!—land of eternal spring
   The Aztecs and the Mayas.

I ran right down to the travel man
I said, "Mexico! On the economy plan."
So they put me in a group to save expense,
Cost me 680 dollars and 97 cents.

   Happiness Tours
   Not a bad group—

Twenty-two widows, fourteen retired schoolteachers,
Three old farmers, and me; kind of a peppy gang.

I got me a map and a great big book
And I studied that country, every cranny and nook.
Didn't want anybody to take me for a fool,
So I even took a course at the Berlitz school.

   Native instructors . . .
   Moochis grashis.
   Donde está el Hotel Hilton?
   Berlitz man says if I hide my camera I could almost slip by as a native.

We got into a jet and away we flew,
And before anyone could say, "Howdy do,"
The pilot announced, "You'll be happy to know
We have just landed in sunny Mexico."

   But it was raining.
   Rainy season was early that year.
   Good for the crops, the paper said.

But we wouldn't let a little thing like that spoil our day,
And we started right out with the Folklore Ballet,
Then we took a run down to the Zócalo,
Which used to be the heart of Old Mexico.
We saw the Palace, the Cathedral, and the Calendar Stone,
A leather goods factory—and glass—hand-blown.
Then the Lagunilla Market where they sell a lot of junk,
I bought two brass doorknobs, a sword, and a trunk . . .

   Full of old *National Geographic* magazines.

We floated through the gardens of Xochimilco,
But before I could find a flower we had to go.
We scooted out to the university,
Buildings full of colors like a Christmas tree.
Then Guadalupe Church was next on the list
And the Pyramids . . . that's a pile of rocks that shouldn't be missed.
Next, to the bullfights and before it got dark
We took a quick look at Chapultepec Park.
We climbed the Latin American Tower for a view of the city,
They say the view's great—but it was foggy—what a pity.
So we rode up the Reforma—that's a beautiful street—
And the nightclub tour was a musical treat.

Mariachis and marimbas; fiddles and guitars
Maracas and cucarachas,
Man, that first day was a busy one.

We got up bright and early on the very next day,
Had to go to Acapulco, but on the way
We stopped at Cuernavaca and Taxco too.
Bought a fistful of silver, for that's the thing to do—

In Taxco.
Bought me a silver tea set,
Bought me a silver eatin' set,
Bought me a bunch of silver earrings and bracelets,
Bought me a silver necklace,
Bought me silver cuff links and tie pins,
Bought me a set of silver candlesticks,
All bargains . . .
Man, I saved me a fortune.

We're back on the bus and away we go
And over the hill—is Acapulco.
Ah, the blue, blue water and the lovely bay,
And the green, green mountains and the ocean spray,
And the air as clear as a crystal bell,
And the sand and the palm trees and the Hilton Hotel.
We lay on the beach from ten to five,
Saw the Jai-lai games and the famous high dive.
We skied and we sailed and we swam in the bay,
And we watched the sunset on Pie de la Cuesta way.
Took a leisurely trip in a glass-bottomed boat,
Eating grapes which were served by the mermaids floating by.

. . . Planters Punch
Gin and tonic . . . papaya and coconut juice.

It was cold in Chicago and snow in D.C.
New York had a blizzard but that didn't bother me
'Cause it was warm in Acapulco and I felt like a king,
Just lying on the beach, not doing a thing . . .

Except buying stuff . . .
Watermelon, huaraches, belts, sombreros,
Chiclets, candy, newspapers,
Tacos, tamales, Pepsi Cola, Coca Cola, Orange Crush,
Sea shells, baskets . . . free enterprise.

Well, after Acapulco it was one big blur
I'm not sure exactly what did occur.
Bought a lot more bargains in a thousand different places
Till I was cleaned out like a bad day at the races.
I bought chess sets of bone and idols of stone,
Rebozos of wool, and the horns of a bull,
Mantillas of lace, and a leather briefcase,
And baskets of straw for my mother-in-law.

  I bought sweaters in Toluca,
  Pottery in Oaxaca,
  Lacquerware in Pátzcuaro,
  Plates in Puebla,
  Guitars in Paracho,
  Mayan gods in Yucatan,
  Tequila in Jalisco,
  And Kaluah at the airport.

Had three hats on my head, two baskets under my arms
Loaded with the products of the workshops and farms
From Guadalajara to Veracruz,
And when that plane took off I had the blues.

When I finally got home I shoved the snow from my door.
I piled a mountain of stuff all over the floor.
I took a shot of tequila and Kaluá too,
Collapsed on a serape colored orange and blue
And I dreamed I was back in Old Mexico,
A long, long way from the ice and snow.

  Goodbye, lovely señoritas,
  Goodbye, palm trees and papaya,
  Goodbye, beautiful warm sunshine.

Man, I'll never forget those four days I spent in Mexico!

A Visit from the Kennedys

The highlight of my stay in Mexico was the two-day visit by President and Mrs. Kennedy in June of 1962. The entire embassy staff of more than a hundred was mobilized as if we were preparing for a war. Every minute of Kennedy's schedule was detailed, reviewed, pondered, studied, and worried over. Where should he go? How much time should he spend there? Whom should he see? What should he say? Who should be invited to the various lunches and dinners? The battle plan was laid out in a seventy-five-page memorandum that we studied for weeks.

And then there was Jacqueline Kennedy! Traditionally, a first lady would present no problem on presidential state visits. She would leave the president's entourage once or twice to visit a nursery or kindergarten, say something nice to the children for the benefit of the handful of reporters following her, smile at the camera, and quickly rejoin the president.

But the State Department had warned us that on the president's recent trip to Venezuela, Jacqueline Kennedy had been mobbed by a mass of reporters and photographers. She was getting almost as much attention as the president himself and had come close to being knocked down several times as the media surged around her. The White House insisted that the embassy provide a special Spanish-speaking escort to control the press when she was touring separately from the president. Because the USIA was in charge of the entire press operation, the ambassador asked us to handle the problem.

My boss at the USIA didn't waste time. "Glazer," he said, "take care of Jackie. See that she doesn't get hurt." I think he picked me for two reasons: I was the largest male on the staff, and I had once escorted Jacqueline Kennedy through the kitchen of Washington's Shoreham Hotel and to her limousine after we both had attended a political luncheon. Finally, every spot that Kennedy would visit had to be checked out by the Secret Service, and they ordered a number of changes in our proposed schedule. At the time, many on the staff were annoyed at such "interference." But as I write these words I recall the assassination of Kennedy a year later and the attempted assassinations of Gerald Ford and Ronald Reagan. It is hard to disagree with the super-cautious procedures of the Secret Service.

The Secret Service had a special advantage in Mexico. The Mexican government did not appreciate criticism or dissent. The police had rounded up potential troublemakers—agitators, dissidents, radicals, or what-have-you—and shipped them out of town until after the Kennedys' visit. There was no Mexican Civil Liberties Union to complain, sue, or turn out news releases. It was a minus for the ideal of democracy but a plus for the U.S. Secret Service and the president's safety.

From the moment the Kennedys walked out the door of Air Force One into the glorious sunshine at the Mexico City airport, people went crazy. They cheered, they screamed, they applauded, and they smiled at each other and at every American they ran into. It didn't stop until the Kennedys left two days later.

The president was a confident, handsome, charming prince. He never looked better. The Mexicans even forgave his butchering of their language when he tried to say a word or two in Spanish. Jacqueline Kennedy was a princess and breathtakingly lovely. Her clothes were eye-catching pastels: light greens, yellows, and blues. In the evening, she seemed to be Cinderella at the ball, beautiful, gracious, aristocratic yet friendly, and bedecked with gorgeous gowns and sparkling jewels.

A million or more people lined the streets to catch a glimpse of the Kennedys. One photographer told me he panicked when he saw nothing but a white blur in his lens. He was relieved when he realized that he was looking at a solid wall of confetti and torn paper pouring from the windows of nearby office buildings.

I wasn't paying much attention to the parades and activities surrounding the Kennedys because I was concentrating on my role as Jacqueline Kennedy's press escort. It's hard to believe now, but I don't recall any Secret Service agents being assigned specifically to her. I was particularly concerned with her visit to the headquarters of the huge government agency that turned barrels of powdered milk supplied by the United States into millions of cartons of milk for Mexico's poor children.

Her tour of the building went from the lobby to the director's office; then to the various departments, where the powdered milk was processed; and finally to the shipping department, where individual milk cartons were placed on trucks for shipment to schools. It was up and down and all around, with a horde of news-hungry reporters, photographers, and television crews yapping at her heels. I had rehearsed a string of orders in Spanish in my most authoritative voice: "In back of the line, please"; "wait here"; "please give Mrs. Kennedy some room"; and "nobody cross this line." Occasionally I had to shove an overly aggressive photographer out of her face. Reporters who couldn't get close enough to hear her comments were shouting, "What did she say? I need a quote." We were on a tight schedule because the First Lady had to meet the president at his next stop. I had to keep everyone moving along.

We ended with some frayed nerves but no bloody noses. I was sweating and my stomach churned, but I had survived. Jacqueline Kennedy had survived. The Mexicans were happy because they could showcase an operation they were proud of, and the American embassy was happy because an intelligent USAID program was getting good publicity. All in all, the Kennedy visit created good feeling that would be hard to duplicate. As is the custom after historic events, many songs were written to celebrate the visit.

Seventeen months later the balladeers who made up *corridos*, the traditional sagas about generals and bandits, heroes, and martyrs, were singing a different tune. On November 23, 1963, I was on the Avenida Reforma on my way to lunch when suddenly everyone around me seemed to know that President Kennedy had been shot in Dallas. Soon the radio was reporting that, to our horror, the president was dead.

All of Mexico was in shock. Thousands lined up to sign the condolence book at the American embassy. All activity in Mexico seemed to stop as millions watched every detail of the funeral on television. I published a special edition of my magazine, *El Obrero*, with a photograph of Kennedy surrounded by a black border. It was full of pictures and quotations from the Kennedys' triumphal visit of the year before. Songs and poems poured from the hearts of the Mexican people.

Ballad of the Death of John F. Kennedy
By Marina Casanova de M.
(translated from Spanish)

The world trembles, frightened, over the terrible event
Because a great and good president has been assassinated.
He always insisted with zeal and profound love
That the good of democracy should exist in the world.
He never backed down, he was truly energetic,
He was an apostle of peace and a light of liberty.
He steered through difficulties,
Always searching for justice.
He said that blacks and whites are equal before God.
They buried Kennedy, and a votive lamp
Shall be an everlasting reminder
for those that loved him.
With this I take my leave, this will become history.
I only ask of my God that Kennedy be in heaven.

John F. Kennedy was a mythical figure, beloved by the Mexicans. It would be many years before the pain of his death would be eased.

11

Labor Advisor to the U.S. Information Agency

In the summer of 1965 I was transferred out of Mexico to become labor advisor to the USIA at its headquarters in Washington, D.C. I had spent three and a half good years in Mexico and was not quite ready to leave. My Spanish had become quite strong, I had excellent contacts with many of the key Mexican labor leaders, and I had made some good friends for the United States. I had knocked down some prejudices, and through my activities many people had received their first balanced picture of the United States.

I had a good hold on bits of Mexican culture and customs, and that made for more relaxed living. I came to understand the "mañana syndrome." When the shoemaker told me shoe repairs would be ready next Tuesday, for example, I understood, and he knew I understood, that Tuesday was a goal he would not reach. I wouldn't bother him about the shoes until the following Saturday or Monday. Once you knew the rules, the system worked fine.

I would miss the color and excitement of Mexico, a country struggling to build a modern society on the ruins of ancient Indian civilizations and four hundred years of colonial rule and misrule. I was probably at the height of my effectiveness as a labor information officer, and I would have loved to remain in Mexico for another year or two. But the offer to go to Washington was one I could not refuse.

The labor advisor's job was made for me. I had worked in the American labor movement for seventeen years and gotten to know firsthand most of its key leaders and how their unions operated. I also met thousands of rank-and-file workers in their homes, in union halls, and on picket lines. My labor songs had given me entrée almost everywhere in the labor movement.

The USIA put out a vast panoply of magazines and pamphlets, news reports and news releases, radio and television programs, and films. A labor advisor had to keep an eye on any item dealing with labor to make sure that the USIA writer had not tangled the facts and that the writer's interpretations made sense. Another part of the job was to assist editors and writers and television and radio producers in finding good stories about labor. In one case, for example, a telephone call came in from the Voice of America (VOA):

VOA: Do you know George Shultz, the secretary of labor?

Glazer: I met him years ago when I was education director of the United Rubber Workers, but I doubt if he'll remember me.

VOA: Well, he has agreed to be interviewed on VOA next Friday at 1:30 P.M. by a panel of journalists. It would be nice if you could meet him at the entrance to the VOA offices, brief him, and escort him to the studio.

At 1:15 P.M. on Friday I waited for Secretary Shultz. He didn't show until 2. He hustled out of his limousine, full of apologies. "A call from the White House delayed me," he explained. No one can argue with that.

I introduced myself, "I'm Joe Glazer. We met about fifteen years ago in Pittsburgh when you spoke at a meeting of the United Rubber Workers. I'm sure you don't remember it." He took a good look at me. "Aren't you the fellow who plays the guitar and sings labor songs? I remember you very well. I even remember the song you wrote about the Kohler strike."

I was floored. Kohler, the giant manufacturer of plumbing equipment, had experienced a bitter, historic strike in the early 1950s. I recalled the strike but had no memory of a song about it. When Shultz saw my look of disbelief, he said, "It went like this: 'No matter how much you may rub and scrub / You can't get clean in a Kohler tub.'" It all came back to me. I marveled at his memory and thanked him for reminding me of one of my own jingles. I explained briefly what he could expect from the panel and delivered him to the VOA producer in good spirits.

On another occasion, the editor of *Amerika,* the USIA magazine published in Russian for distribution in the Soviet Union, came down to my office. He was planning a major feature on a U.S. steelworker with a Slavic family background. Could I help him find a proper subject? I promised to get back to him in a day or so. *Amerika* was a USIA showpiece. It was large in size and printed on glossy paper, with well-edited articles on American life, culture, politics, and literature. Its illustrations were of the highest quality.

I made a few calls to friends at the Steelworkers' headquarters in Pittsburgh and soon located the worker I needed. His grandfather had come from the Ukraine to work in a U.S. steel mill in Homestead, Pennsylvania. Our subject was a third-generation steelworker, a shop steward in the plant and proud of his union and its accomplishments. He earned high wages and had paid holidays and an excellent health insurance plan for himself and his family. The family's eldest child was in college. Two younger children were active in high school sports and delivered newspapers before school. His wife worked part time as a clerk in a local department store. The couple owned their modest home, which had a small backyard where the family grew vegetables. It was a real Norman Rockwell story, and it was true. There were tens of thousands of steelworker families like that one.

I connected the reporter doing the story to the union representative who would be shepherding him and a photographer around town, helping to get the interviews and photographs. I also checked the completed article before it was translated into Russian. It was good. The deed was done.

In 1970 I was assigned to help a Finnish producer do a one-hour program, *A Day in the Life of a U.S. Auto Worker.* When I telephoned the producer I learned that he had a clear idea of what he wanted to shoot. "In Finland," he explained, "we see a lot of American TV programs, but they are mostly sitcoms or westerns or police crime shows. It's the same with the Hollywood films that are so popular here. We never see how an average worker lives. I just want an average guy—not a big talker or leader—I want to film him at home with his family and on the job with his buddies."

I lined up a worker in one of the blue-collar suburbs that ring Detroit. He was neither a leader nor a "big talker." In fact, I was concerned that we might not be able to coax him to talk at all. He ran a punch press at a large Chrysler plant in Detroit, and the plant manager was happy to cooperate with the Finnish television crew.

I met the crew in Detroit and stayed with them for the three days of shooting. We filmed the autoworker at 5 A.M. when he got up and didn't stop until he got ready for bed early in the evening. In between, we filmed his wife making breakfast and packing his lunch pail, their youngsters going off to school, his long freeway commute to the plant, his work on the job, his time shooting the breeze with buddies during the lunch break, and then his return trip home through heavy freeway traffic. At home, he was shown playing with the children, eating dinner, watching television, then going to bed.

We discussed collective bargaining with the local officers at a big union hall near the plant and interviewed the plant manager for the company's perspective on industrial relations. That seems like dull viewing fare—no car chases, no one killed, and no buildings blown up—but the finished program was honest, straightforward, and heartwarming. I thought that a lot of people in the United States could benefit from watching such a program.

I recall a special spot in the film. The producer was up-to-date on the U.S. women's liberation movement and asked the autoworker's wife whether she resented getting up at 5 A.M. each day to make her husband's breakfast and pack his lunch. If he made his own, surely she could sleep a couple of extra hours before the children got up. "Why should I resent it?" she asked. "He does his job, and I do my job." She was a from a small town in Kentucky, in love with her husband and happy with her life. The question didn't seem to make much sense to her.

One exciting aspect of the labor advisor job was that my territory included the entire globe. I was developing a reputation as an interpreter of American life and labor through my music, and soon I was receiving invitations from USIA posts all over the world for my musical lectures. I performed at USIA cultural centers, at ambassadors' residences, in union halls, on radio and television, at universities, and in concert halls.

Sometimes I appeared in unusual places. In India, for example, I performed a concert at a seventh-century Mogul ruin where the outdoor auditorium was illuminated by thousands of candles. In Iceland I sang to workers in a huge fish-packing plant during their lunch hour, and in a Tokyo geisha house I sang to a group of Japanese labor leaders who boomed out the chorus of "Solidarity Forever" in Japanese.

The majority of my programs dealt with labor and industrial relations, but I also talked and sang about the civil rights movement, equality for women, ethnicity and immigration, and politics and American history. In addition to the labor groups, I performed for government officials, employers, academics, journalists, and university students. By the time I retired from the USIA in 1980 I had appeared in sixty countries. It was quite a trip.

I have been asked how I deliver a lecture to someone who doesn't understand my language. That's easy—I use a good interpreter. The next question usually is, How do you reach someone with songs that tell a story if that person doesn't understand your language? The answer to that is not so easy. Even though people say that music is an international language, I can relate a story that indicates otherwise.

It was one o'clock in the morning in the city of Rangoon in Burma. I was sitting on a mat on the floor of a huge hall with two thousand local residents, listening to a four-hour program of Burmese folk music. It must have been terrific because people all around me were laughing, applauding, and thoroughly enjoying themselves. I had no idea what they found so funny because the interpreter who was with me kept whispering, "Too complicated to translate." After a couple of hours I managed to slip out a side door.

Is music an "international language"? It could be if you're talking about a symphony orchestra, a concert pianist, a jazz band, or rock music. The beat counts, not the words. Of course, it is possible to become accustomed to, or learn to appreciate, music that hasn't been part of your heritage. But singing-folk music is a camel of a different color.

Tourists who visit Mexico and don't understand a word of Spanish can watch a musical show with great enjoyment. There is usually a great deal of "show biz": lighting effects, colorful costumes, foot-stomping, and arm-swinging. The audiences of my USIA programs were not tourists, and I had no show-biz support. I had to help audiences get the maximum benefit from a serious and worthwhile artistic effort. Based on some tough overseas experiences, I developed "Glazer's laws"—the basics for communicating musically with audiences who don't understand your language.

1. Keep songs short: Stay away from long ballads. If you have to include them, cut verses. The audience isn't following your English anyway.

2. Variety is the key: Good performers know their programs must have a change of pace, but variety is even more important when there is a language barrier. If there are a lot of rhythm and mood changes, the audience will feel what you are doing even if they don't understand it.

3. Learn a song in the local language: The audience will love it regardless of your accent. On a tour through Northern Italy, for example, my pièce de résistance was a lovely little Alpine mountain song I learned from an Italian trade unionist. Everyone knew and loved it. It always won them over.

4. Translate an American song into the local language: Good singing translations are hard, but I could generally work out a simple chorus or repetitive phrase with the help of USIA local employees. On one tour of Asia I learned the chorus of "Solidarity Forever" in Japanese, Tagalog, Tamil, and several other languages. My accents could have been better, but local audiences loved it.

5. Keep introductions short and sweet: Your brief introductions and explanations should be interpreted phrase by phrase. Skip introductions now and then to keep the program moving.

6. Sing along: Do you want people to sing along on some of your choruses? It's easier for them if the words are printed in the program.

But enough of that. Let's go to Paris!

12

Singing Overseas

France

My first trip overseas with guitar in hand was to Paris in 1951, ten years before I went to work for the USIA. The European community had been devastated during World War II, and the United States was providing hundreds of millions of dollars to rebuild the shattered infrastructures of France, Italy, Great Britain, and even Germany. This was all done through the Marshall Plan, an inspired and generous scheme to help both allies and enemies get back on their feet.

The Marshall Plan's staff included economists, planners, and financial experts as well as labor specialists who worked with the trade unions that were trying to reestablish themselves after the disruptions of the war. The theory was that it was not possible to build democratic, viable societies in Europe without a strong, free labor movement.

The labor specialist for the Marshall Plan's mission to France was Kenneth Douty, an old colleague from my Textile Workers Union days. He had seen me and my guitar in action many times and knew what I could do. He believed that a labor music program adapted to the needs of French unions would help promote the aims of the Marshall aid program and invited me to do a three-week singing and speaking tour of industrial centers in France.

French unions were very weak. They were split into three federations, the strongest of which was controlled by the Communist Party. The communists, of course, were strongly anti-American. They parroted the Soviet line that the Marshall Plan was an imperialistic scheme to enslave French workers. They also attacked American unions as weak and in the pockets of capitalist bosses. That was the kind of propaganda Douty was trying to counter.

Like the trips of other American trade unionists, my visit had two principal purposes: to help free French unions with information, ideas, and techniques to build a more effective organization and to help create a more realistic understanding among French workers of the American trade union movement and America itself.

Douty devised an interesting package for my tour. He supplied me with a quartet, two women and two men, from a workers' youth group. They made fine harmony and had a good repertoire of French folk and protest songs that complemented the American labor songs I planned to sing. I taught them the choruses of "Union Maid," "Solidarity Forever," "Roll the Union On," "Too Old to Work," "The Mill Was Made of Marble," and several others. I even taught them a couple of old French songs I had learned from French-Canadian textile workers in New England.

The young workers—they couldn't have been more than twenty—got into the spirit of the songs. They sounded as militant and determined as any group of American strikers on a picket line. I had a hard time trying to get them to pronounce an "American" r in songs like "Roll the Union On." But they kept singing with a French r that came from deep in their throats. We finally compromised. They sang it their way. No harm done.

Between us, we put together a well-paced, varied program that stirred audiences. We would open with three or four driving American union songs, the quartet joining me on the choruses. I would then step off-stage, and the quartet would sing a set of three powerful French workers' songs. I followed with some solos: union songs and spirituals, a favorite with French audiences. We would close with rousing songs such as "We Shall Not Be Moved" and "Solidarity Forever."

Before going to France I took intensive French lessons in Akron, Ohio, where I was working as education director of the United Rubber Workers. Every morning before reporting to my office, I would spend an hour with a professional French teacher. I wrote out short English introductions of the songs I was planning to sing in France, and my instructor translated my remarks into French. I reviewed the French introductions over and over until I mastered them. Much of my three years of high school French came back to me, and I became able to introduce the songs effectively by glancing at a few notes.

One number the quartet sang kept running through my head, and I decided to add it to my regular repertoire. It was an old song called "Les canuts" (The Weavers), and it came out of a historic strike in Lyons when it was the silk capital of France. The song has a haunting melody in a minor key, and when the young workers sang it in the union hall in Lyons their beautiful harmonies sent chills down my spine. The lyrics were a simple, eloquent cry against injustice, with a demand for change:

Les Canuts (The Weavers)

Pour chanter *veni creator*
Il faut avoir chasuble d'or.
Nous en tissons pour vous
Grands de l'église.
Mais nous pauvres canuts
N'avons pas de chemises.

Nous sommes les canuts
Nous allons tout nus.
Nous sommes les canuts
Nous allons tout nus.

Pour gouverner il faut avoir
Manteaux et rubans en sautoir
Pour gouverner il faut avoir
Manteaux et rubans en sautoir.
Nous en tissons pour vous
Grands de la terre.
Mais nous pauvre canuts
Sans drap on nous enterre.

Chorus

Mais notre règne arrivera
Quand votre règne finira.
Mais notre règne arrivera
Quand votre règne finira.
Alors nous tisserons le linceul
Du vieux monde
Car on entends déjà
La révolte qui gronde

Nous sommes les canuts
Nous n'irons plus tout nus.
Nous sommes les canuts
Nous n'irons plus tout nus.

This is the English translation:

In order to lead the mass at church
One must wear a cloak of gold.
We are the ones who weave these
Beautiful garments for you, great men of the church.
But we poor weavers do not have a shirt of our own.

We are the weavers;
We always go naked.
We are the weavers;
We always go naked.

In order to govern
One must wear fine cloaks
With fancy ribbons.
We weave these clothes
For the great men of the earth
But we are buried without a shroud.

Chorus

But our reign will arrive
When your reign is over.
We are now weaving
The shroud of the old world
Because we hear the revolt
That is now growing.

We are the weavers
No longer will we go naked!
We are the weavers
No longer will we go naked!

The day before we were to leave on our tour I had an urgent call from the man who handled public relations for the Marshall Plan mission in Paris. "I've got an interview for you this afternoon with Art Buchwald. I told him about your program and he wants to do a full column about you." He was really excited. "Who is this Buchwald?" I asked innocently. "I never heard of him."

It was some years later that Buchwald would become a top humor columnist for the *Washington Post,* renowned throughout the country. At that time in Paris, the PR man was stunned by such ignorance. "Buchwald's column in the Paris edition of the *New York Herald-Tribune* is read by every important English-speaking person in Europe," he explained patiently. "Yesterday he featured President Truman's daughter Margaret. Before that he had Sugar Ray Robinson. You are in high-class company. This is the first time in six months he has agreed to do an interview for me."

I was properly impressed. I scooted over to Buchwald's office at the *Herald-Tribune* to meet a short, roly-poly, friendly man whose impish eyes twinkled behind heavy glasses. I couldn't help but notice a big toy truck on the wall next to his desk. It looked as if it was ready to travel up the wall to the ceiling. Buchwald explained, "Yesterday I interviewed Mr. Schwarz, the head of F.A.O. Schwarz toy company, and he gave me that trick truck."

I didn't have any trick toys for Buchwald, but I did have a copy of the CIO songbook I had edited, and I left that with him. I also gave him a pretty good idea of what I was doing in France. He asked a few questions, we chatted for a while, and that was that. Or so I thought. The next day, the quartet and I were on the train, on our way to one-night stands in places like St. Etienne, Clermont-Ferrand, Lyons, and Marseilles.

We traveled with an interpreter because I was scheduled to answer questions at each stop, and my French was not good enough to handle that job. Questions about unions, collective bargaining, strikes, and working conditions in the United States were easy, but occasionally I was thrown a curve. In the coal-mining and textile town of St. Etienne, for example, a worker poured out an emotional question in rapid-fire French. I couldn't follow it well, but I heard clearly the phrase "Willie McGee, père de quatre enfants" (Willie McGee, father of four children). I was only too well acquainted with the case of McGee, who had been lynched in Mississippi for a supposed violation of the state's Jim Crow laws and customs. But how in the world did a coal miner in the middle of France know about Willie McGee? I later found out that the communists had made his case a cause célèbre and were using it against the United States. The questioner wanted to know how I could be running around France singing and preaching about democracy while blacks were being lynched in Mississippi.

I acknowledged the heinousness of these acts. I then went on to describe how discrimination and segregation reached into churches, schools, means of transportation, stores, and restrooms in many states. I explained that unlike France, which was strictly centralized, the United States was a collection of independent states, each of which had its own domestic laws. Even a president could not interfere. I cited an example that Frenchmen would find dramatic: "A train crossing the country will have to stop selling wines and liquor when it passes through a dry state."

I explained that the labor movement, civil rights organizations, and others were pushing for legislation that would give the federal government the power to intervene in cases like that of Willie McGee. I am certain that the answer did not satisfy anyone, but it was the best I could do. We would have to wait until the mid-1960s for Congress to pass legislation giving the federal government authority to deal with civil rights. That was also before an influx of immigrants to France from Africa brought out overt negative racial attitudes there.

In Marseilles, I received a worried telephone call from Ken Douty in Paris. Buchwald's column had appeared on May 29 and created a stir in diplomatic circles and among the officials of the Marshall Plan. Douty explained the problem: "The column was not bad. He included a photo of you with the guitar and made some offbeat humorous comments in his typical lighthearted style. But he never explained our purpose in touring you. He made it seem like Uncle Sam is spending taxpayer money for a folksinger to travel around entertaining union workers with songs about strikes. He barely mentioned your qualifications as a serious union educator."

I was upset because I knew our program had been effective in promoting the Marshall Plan's goals. Douty, however, had worked out a plan to turn it all around. He arranged for the director of the Marshall Plan Mission to host a concert of our group in his magnificent residence in Paris. The diplomatic community, French trade unionists, and journalists were invited to see for themselves what the program was all about. Douty said, "The show will take place the day after you get back."

We put on a stirring show in the huge, ballroom-sized living room of the mission director's mansion. The elegantly appointed room was jammed to overflowing. More than a hundred guests filled every seat and spilled out through French doors into the garden. We had honed our act in the provinces, and we performed in high style without a glitch. I selected the best of our numbers for this abbreviated concert, songs where the introduction made important policy points. When I introduced "Too Old to Work," for example, I said, "This song was inspired by a one-hundred day old strike of autoworkers fighting to win company-paid pensions to supplement the government Social Security benefits to retired workers. The Social Security law was passed in 1935 as part of President Roosevelt's New Deal program of social legislation. But the benefits had not kept up with the times. So workers used the power of their unions to improve their pension." That made two important points: American unions are tough, militant, and willing to strike for long periods of time to achieve their demands, and the United States has a system of social legislation in place, even though it has to be updated from time to time.

I could feel the good vibes. Even skeptics and naysayers were caught up in the spirit of the evening as our message of songs and commentary in French and English unfolded. The standing ovation after our closing chorus of "Solidarity Forever" was warm-hearted, sustained, and enthusiastic. The potential disaster of the Buchwald column had been turned into a triumph. I was floating on cloud nine as I prepared to leave for my next stop—England.

England

When my tour of France was over in June 1951, I stopped in England for four or five days before heading home to the United States. Pat Knight, an old friend and former colleague who was in England on a Fulbright grant, worked with the U.S. Embassy to set up programs at labor schools and various union gatherings.

I had enjoyed my three-week tour of France and felt I had scored points for the United States, but I looked forward to performing for an English-speaking audience. After introducing my songs in carefully phrased, well-rehearsed French and having to answer questions through an interpreter, I planned to fly free in England.

My first engagement was a full-fledged concert at a training school for fifty leaders of the giant Transport and General Workers Union (TGWU). I was disturbed by the strong strain of anti-Americanism I found in England, even among the union members for whom I was performing. To counter that feeling, I worked into my program songs and commentary dealing with racial relations, the U.S. economy, the American labor movement, and American politics—all topics on which I had received many questions and comments, most of them antagonistic. I tried to tell the U.S. side of the story honestly but with a light touch, admitting frankly the weaknesses of American society and gently correcting the misinformation and ignorance I knew was prevalent. I must have hit the right notes because at the end of the concert Ellen Mc-Cullough, the union's education director who was running the training program, shook my hand and with a friendly smile said, "That was a very effective piece of musical propaganda." I smiled back and said, "I just sing songs and tell stories." She was a sturdy, no-nonsense woman who held an important post in a million-member union made up mostly of men.

We had a good talk over tea, and I raised a question: "The United States is giving Great Britain hundreds of millions of dollars in loans and grants under the Marshall Plan and yet there is so much antagonism toward America. Why is that?" I'll never forget her answer: "I hope your country will never be in a position where you must accept help from a friend in order to survive."

"Hold the Fort," which is listed in American labor songbooks as a "British Transport Workers' Song," was part of my program. What could be more appropriate? I was surprised, however, to learn that in the Transport Workers' Union songbook "Hold the Fort" was listed as a "British Transport Workers' song sung in the United States." Did that mean it was no longer sung in Great Britain?

It turned out that "Hold the Fort" has had a colorful history. It began in the United States in 1870 as a gospel hymn written by Philip H. Bliss, a well-known singing evangelist:

Hold the fort for I am coming
Jesus signals still
Wave the answer back to heaven
By thy Grace we will.

It was introduced in Britain in 1873 by Ira Sankey, a great American evangelist and gospel singer, during a revival tour. Toward the end of the nineteenth century it was parodied by the British Transport Workers. Then, somehow, it recrossed the Atlantic, where the Industrial Workers of the World (the Wobblies) took it up and put it into their *Little Red Songbook*. It became one of the best known American union songs. I have sung it scores of times at rallies and on picket lines. It is a rousing, powerful piece of music. I was happy to bring the song back across the ocean to reintroduce it to the union that gave birth to it many years earlier.

Hold the Fort
Words: Anonymous
Music: Philip H. Bliss

We meet today in freedom's cause
And raise our voices high
We'll join our hands in union strong
To battle or to die.

   Hold the fort for we are coming—
   Union men be strong.
   Side by side we battle onward
   Victory will come.

See our numbers still increasing
Hear the bugle blow.
By our union we shall triumph
Over every foe.

   Chorus

Fierce and long the battle rages
But we will not fear
Help will come whene'er it's needed
Cheer, my comrades, cheer.

   Chorus

While singing for other labor audiences in Britain, I came across another important labor song that had crossed the Atlantic and was known in both Britain and the United States: "The Red Flag," written in England in 1887. It became popular with Wobblies, socialists, and other radical groups in the United States although it was not sung by more traditional labor unions:

The Red Flag
Words: Jim Connell
Music: "Tannenbaum"

The people's flag is deepest red
It shrouded oft our martyred dead.
And ere their limbs grew stiff and cold
Their hearts' blood dyed its ev'ry fold.

  Then raise the scarlet standard high
  Within its shade we'll live or die.
  Though cowards flinch, and traitors sneer
  We'll keep the red flag flying here.

With heads uncovered swear we all
To bear it onward till we fall.
Come dungeon dark or gallows grim
This song shall be our parting hymn.

  Chorus

Most Americans associate the symbol of the red flag exclusively with communism. But years before the communists adopted the symbol and the song, a red flag had been the banner of the working classes and democratic socialists of Europe and elsewhere. In the United States, "The Red Flag" was adopted by radical groups but never caught on with mainstream unions. In Great Britain, however, it became the official anthem of the Labour Party and was sung regularly at its conventions.

On August 1, 1945, "The Red Flag" was sung in the House of Commons. The Labour Party had just defeated the government of Winston Churchill's Conservative Party. Parliament assembled after the election, and when Churchill entered the House the Conservative Members of Parliament, in a show of support for the defeated leader, greeted him with "For He's a Jolly Good Fellow." Labour's M.P.s immediately responded with a rousing rendition of "The Red Flag." For the first time in history, "The people's flag is deepest red" rang out in the House of Commons.

The *Daily Herald*, a British labor newspaper, recorded the emotion felt by T. G. Thomas, a young M.P. from a Welsh mining district: "He sang the socialist anthem which had heartened so many in the dark days, and which he had learned from the pioneers in his childhood. 'How they sang it in the coalfields after the election!' he said. 'How the crowds cheered and the old people wept with joy! I little dreamed I should live to be an M.P. on a day like this!'"

The Labour Party created a minor social and economic revolution with its universal health program, broadened educational initiatives, and other social programs. Yet even the most dedicated idealists can tire of the never-ending struggle to build a better world, and old revolutionary songs no longer have the power to stir their souls. One anonymous, weary radical wrote an irreverent version of "The Red Flag":

> The working class can kiss my ass
> I've got the foreman's job at last.
> The system I'll no more resist,
> I'm going to be a capitalist.
> Now you can raise the standard high.
> Beneath its shade to fight and die.
> But, brother, please don't count on me—
> I've up and joined the bourgeoisie.

In 1965, some fourteen years after my Marshall Plan visit to England, I became labor advisor to the USIA. In that capacity I found myself acting as host to the very same Ellen McCullough who had been my host at the training school of the Transport Workers' Union. She was visiting the United States on a study grant from the USIA, and I arranged some of her program. I made sure she visited key trade union leaders, labor department officers, some outstanding local unions, the more innovative labor educators, and leaders and members of U.S. transport workers' unions. I was puzzled that someone in the State or Labor Department had scheduled her to have lunch with a chapter of the Daughters of the American Revolution in Baltimore—not exactly a labor crowd.

Ellen knew about the conservative reputation of the D.A.R. and was somewhat apprehensive when I put her on the train to Baltimore. She returned later that day with a story:

> When I entered the hall all of these properly dressed, elderly ladies were waiting for me. Then I heard the piano. No mistake about it—it was "The Red Flag"! I said to myself, "Lord, they are welcoming me with the anthem of the British Labour Party. Maybe the D.A.R. is not as conservative as I've been told." I was quickly brought down to earth when the women started singing "Maryland, My Maryland," which uses the same tune, "Tannenbaum," as does "The Red Flag." I was tempted to sing

a few lines from "The Red Flag" to shake them up a bit, but I didn't have the nerve. I made a few pleasant, bland remarks and got out of there as quickly as I could.

As labor advisor to the USIA I traveled and performed in some sixty countries. Ironically, my most memorable trip to England took place several years after my retirement in 1981 from the USIA. In May 1984 I had a call from Roger Schrader, the labor counselor at the U.S. Embassy in London. He got to the point right away:

> Joe, our ambassador [Charles Price] hosts an annual American-style barbecue at his residence for all the senior British trade union leaders and their spouses. The entertainment usually consists of some American-style country music. But this year the ambassador wants to try something different. He asked me if there is any such thing as "labor music." He's a Republican businessman from Kansas and doesn't know much about labor and even less about labor music. But he's a good ambassador and wants to put on an effective program for these union leaders. When I told him about your work and gave him one of your records to listen to, he said, "You know, it's not my kind of music but I think the union leaders here will like it. See if you can get him over here." So that's why I'm calling you.

I was delighted at a possible opportunity to touch base again with British trade unionists but felt I had to level with Schrader. During the paranoiac Nixon administration I found myself on Richard Nixon's "Enemies List" as well as on a blacklist of potential speakers drawn up by the USIA. This, after twenty years of service for the USIA! I was in good company, however—Walter Cronkite, David Brinkley, Tom Wicker, Betty Friedan, Coretta Scott King, Ralph Nader, John Kenneth Galbraith, Sen. Edmund Muskie, Sen. George McGovern, and many other distinguished citizens. Roger got back to me that very same day. "The ambassador doesn't give a hoot about those lists. If you're okay with me that's all he wants to know."

The program was scheduled for July 22. I have seen many fancy ambassadors' residences in my travels for the USIA, but Winfield House, the London residence of the American ambassador, was in a class by itself. It had been donated to the United States by Barbara Hutton, heiress to the Woolworth five and dime store millions. The mansion, in the upscale Regent's Park neighborhood, was in the midst of a huge manicured estate and peacefully protected from the hustle and bustle of London.

Nearly 150 union leaders and their spouses were at the residence, and there was no problem feeding them all, comfortably seated, in the various living rooms, sitting rooms, drawing rooms, and garden rooms that popped out in every direction. When I was ready to do my act in the main living room, everybody moved in around me, creating an intimate auditorium.

I have always liked to connect with an audience in some special way right from the beginning of a performance. That evening I said:

> I want to dedicate this program to a person who was born a few short miles from this spot, in the East End of London. He was the son of a struggling cigar maker. In the 1860s when unemployment was high among the London cigar makers, the union provided a special fund for unemployed members who wanted to emigrate to the United States. This struggling cigar maker took advantage of the union's offer and sailed from London with his family on June 10, 1863, arriving in New York City after a seven-week journey. His son, Samuel, to whom I dedicate this program, was thirteen years old. He went to work immediately at the trade of cigar maker. This young lad, Samuel Gompers, grew to become the founder of the modern American labor movement.

From then on I was home free. The audience sang out on the choruses, listened intently to my union stories, and laughed heartily at all the jokes. It was a most satisfying response. Roger Schrader did tell me, however, that he thought the ambassador's wife was rather uncomfortable hearing militant songs like "Roll the Union On" and "Hold the Fort" ring out in her home.

One piece of material was a guaranteed winner. It involved politics inside the Labour Party some years back when the right wing of the party was headed by Herbert Morrison and the left wing was headed by Aneurin ("Nye") Bevan. Neither side had much use for the other. Someone in Britain had written a brilliant takeoff on my song "Too Old to Work, Too Young to Die":

> Who will take care of you
> How'll you get by
> When you're too left for Herbie
> And too right for Nye?

Before I closed the program with "Solidarity Forever" I was moved to give credit to Ambassador Price, who, although from an entirely different background, appreciated the vital role the British trade union movement played in life and politics. I said, "He will readily admit that this is not the kind of music he is used to hearing."

While saying goodbye to the union leaders, one shared a further version of "The Red Flag." It was a two-line revision that noted the shift of the British Labour Party from the left toward the center of the political spectrum: "The people's flag is palest pink. / It's not as red as you might think."

Israel

One of my early foreign tours, even before my work overseas with the USIA, was to Israel in 1956, just after the war in which the Israelis captured the Sinai Desert from Egypt.

I was invited to join a small group of U.S. labor leaders as guests of the Histadrut, the then-powerful Israeli labor federation. The five members of our group represented important segments of the American labor movement, so we were treated as VIPs. We had lengthy interviews with key officials of the Histadrut and the Israeli government. That included the redoubtable Golda Meir, the former Milwaukee teacher who had migrated to Israel in 1921 and worked her way up to the post of prime minister in 1969. When we visited with her in 1956 she was minister of labor.

She disarmed us immediately with an opening challenge: "Well, tell me what you found wrong in Israel?" The American labor leaders included veteran negotiators who peppered her with penetrating questions. Meir was more than equal to responding. Her concluding remarks included her often-repeated comment about the Arabs: "We can forgive them for killing our sons, but how can we forgive them for making our sons kill theirs?"

I would see the savvy Golda Meir once more conquer an audience—this time at an AFL-CIO convention in Atlantic City sixteen years later. When AFL-CIO president George Meany introduced her, she called out the names on the big union signs at the various tables: "'Machinists,' 'autoworkers,' plumbers.' Where are the carpenters?" A yell went up from the carpenters on the right side of the hall. "Good to see you," she called out. "You know, my father was a union carpenter in Milwaukee." The convention went wild; delegates whooped and cheered and pounded on the tables. After that opener she could do no wrong.

I had been asked to bring my guitar on the 1956 trip to Israel because several concerts had been arranged for me. My first performance was in the dining-hall-turned-auditorium of a kibbutz, one of Israel's communal farming settlements. Several hundred "kibbutzniks," young and old, were in the audience. Before singing to non-English-speaking audiences I always ask my host, "Do they understand English? Will I need an interpreter to translate my introductions to the songs?" My host, the secretary of the kibbutz, assured me that most of the group understood English. Songs in Yiddish, he added, would be appreciated by the older members of the audience.

I had trouble with the audience from my first song. There seemed to be a steady buzzing in the hall. I sang a couple of songs in Yiddish to change the mood, but the murmurs continued so I switched back to English. There was a strong round of applause at the end of the concert, but I was not happy. If I cannot control an audience I consider my performance a failure. When I complained to my host about the murmuring, he assured me, "That's not your fault. When you were singing in English the young people who study the language in school were explaining the song to their mothers and fathers, and when you were singing in Yiddish the old folks were explaining the song to their kids." The mystery was solved. I felt a lot better.

I kept in mind the advice of the Israeli labor attaché in Washington, who advised, "It's okay to see the Roman ruins, the Wailing Wall, the desert turned to productive farms, but if you want to learn what Israel is all about meet the people." One weather-beaten old woman with whom I visited lived on a well-tended farm in northern Israel and had come to Israel from Poland in the 1930s with other Zionist pioneers. "We had no machinery," she told me. "To clear the land, we had to dig up two hundred wagonloads of stones with a pick, a shovel, and our bare hands." I also talked to a laboratory technician who had come to Israel from Russia via Shanghai. "Stalin drove our family out of Russia and we landed up in China," he told me. "Then Mao chased us out of China." In the market of the ancient city of Acre, I stopped at the stall of a leather worker "por los caballos" (for the horses). His ancestors had been expelled from Spain in 1492 and had gone first to Bulgaria and then Israel. Four hundred fifty years later he was still speaking Ladino, a variation of Spanish.

Israeli soldiers were everywhere, many on leave, traveling between their homes and their military camps. I exchanged songs with several and quickly learned one or two to add to my programs, much to the delight of the audiences.

One evening I had an especially memorable experience in the beautiful city of Haifa at an officers' training school on Mount Carmel. The army would send in a trained musician and song leader once a week, and I was asked to sing for them on one of those musical evenings. I was a little late, and as I ascended the hill I was moved to hear "Let My People Go" being sung in Hebrew.

This story of pharaoh and the children of Israel had made an extraordinary journey. White Christians brought the story of the Bible to the New World from ancestral homes in Europe. Their slaves, transported thousands of miles across the ocean from Africa, learned the ancient story of the children of Israel's bondage in Egypt. They shaped it into a song reflecting their own hopes for freedom. Several hundred years later the song traveled back across the ocean to the land of the Bible itself. It was translated into the Hebrew of the Old Testament and sung by Jews who had gathered from the four corners of the earth to the land of their forebears. They taught me the Hebrew words to the song:

Sh'lach-na et ami

Ma-her Moshe tza-veh par-oh:
Sh'lach-na et ami!
Mitz-vat a-el e-mor na lo:
Sh'lach-na et ami!
Koo-ma lech na
El ke-vad ha-lev ha-rah
Tzav lo bish-mi:
Sh'lach-na et ami!

In turn, I taught them the English words:

Let My People Go

When Israel was in Egypt land.
Let my people go.
Oppressed so hard they could not stand.
Let my people go.

Go down, Moses,
Way down in Egypt land,
Tell old pharaoh, "Let my people go."

No more shall they in bondage toil.
Let my people go.
Let them come out with Egypt's spoil.
Let my people go.

Chorus

The last verse was especially apt just then because Israeli soldiers had recently returned with "Egypt's spoil": tanks, guns, and ammunition taken from General Nasser's army in the Sinai campaign of 1956. One additional and unusual spoil of war, they told me, were hundreds of officers' boots. That perplexed me—why officers' boots? They answered that the Egyptian officers had retreated in droves—and could run faster in the desert without their boots.

I taught the officers-in-training the English words of several other spirituals. Music, I explained, had helped make a hard and bitter life more bearable for slaves and given them the hope of some day "crossing the River Jordan into the Promised Land." The audience laughed when I sang the verse of "Swing Low, Sweet Chariot" that went "the Jordan River is wide and deep / I've got to cross it before I sleep." The real Jordan River is neither wide nor deep, and these men knew it.

I taught them "Joshua Fit the Battle of Jericho," "Rock-a-My Soul in the Bosom of Abraham," and several others based on Old Testament stories. They quickly caught the mood and tempo of the songs, and by the time we finished singing the room was rocking like a country church on a Sunday morning. When I reached my hotel that evening I was still flying high.

My next trip to Israel was in 1967 while working for the USIA. It was immediately after the war in which the Israelis repulsed simultaneous attacks by five Arab nations. It was a spectacular victory, and it was all over in a week, thus the designation the "Six Day War."

The war produced many heroes, but none more popular than Naomi Shemer, a young singer-composer. Just before the war, she had written "Yerushalayim shel zahav" (Jerusalem of Gold). Shemer's poetic musical tribute to the city of King David and King Solomon evoked overwhelming emotion in every Israeli. For them, Jerusalem was the holy city of the Old Testament.

> Jerusalem of gold
> Of copper and of light
> For all of your songs
> I am the violin.

Israeli leaders appreciated the power of music to move souls. The evening before the assault on the Jordanian-controlled East Jerusalem (Israel controlled West Jerusalem), the army helicoptered Naomi Shemer to every frontline position, and at each one she played her guitar and sang the song. The attack took place at dawn. It was a highly charged, tense time. After a few hours of fierce fighting, the entire city of Jerusalem was united under Israeli rule for the first time since biblical days. There were tears and cheers, and Naomi Shemer's song, sung by triumphant Israeli paratroopers, reverberated against the golden stones of the city.

I had one more major involvement with music and the state of Israel. It was July 4, 1976, the bicentennial anniversary of the signing of the Declaration of Independence, a glorious Fourth. Dozens of triple-masted schooners sailed majestically up the Hudson River, and there were fireworks, television specials, patriotic music, and speeches.

At the same time, at Entebbe Airport in Uganda, some ninety-one Israelis whose airplane had been hijacked on June 27 were being held hostage by Gen. Idi Amin, the dictator of the country. Amin came across as a comic book character full of bluster and bombast with dozens of medals on his resplendent uniforms. But he was a brutal megalomaniac capable of killing those hostages in cold blood.

I was in Washington, D.C., on my way to a meeting of a group called Friends of Histadrut when the news came over the car radio. Every one of the ninety-one Israeli passengers as well as the crew of twelve had been rescued by the Israeli air force. There was only one Israeli casualty, Yehonatan Netanyahu, who headed the rescue operations and was the brother of the future Prime Minister Binyamin Netanyahu. It was one of the most spectacular rescue missions in modern history.

I felt I had to write a song about the incredible feat and began to scribble as soon as I heard the report. An hour later I sang it at the meeting:

Goodbye Uganda, Israel Shalom
By Joe Glazer

It was early Sunday morning
Without a word of warning
Those big Israeli planes swooped from the sky.
A hundred years from now
They'll still be telling how
That deed was done the fourth day of July.

My friends, you should have seen
The face of General Amin
When he heard those hostages were flying home.
He ranted and he roared
But they were safe aboard.
Goodbye Uganda, Israel Shalom
(Hey! Hey!)
Goodbye Uganda, Israel Shalom.

They were lying on the ground
Guerrillas all around,
Praying for some miracle to come
They heard shooting; they heard noise
'Twas those brave Israeli boys,
Flew 2,500 miles to bring them home.

Chorus

There was dancing, there was singing,
Folks were yelling, bells were ringing,
When those airplanes hit the ground in Tel Aviv.
Some were laughing, some were crying,

Bands were playing, flags were flying
A July fourth you never would believe.

Chorus

I recorded the song and sent it at once to Israel, where it was played on the air, picked up by musicians, and printed in a number of newspapers. I continue to sing it, and its miraculous story of triumph over evil still stirs audiences.

Scandinavia

Although I sang and spoke in sixty countries for the USIA, the Scandinavian countries were among my favorites. I toured Sweden, Norway, Finland, and Denmark three or four times and made two trips to Iceland. With each visit I looked for some kind of thread, a connection that would ring a bell with my audience.

It was easy to make a connection in Scandinavia because two million Swedes, Norwegians, Finns, and Danes had migrated to the United States to seek their fortunes during the second half of the nineteenth century, a time when those countries were among the poorest in Europe. Almost everyone I met had a story about ancestors who had crossed the ocean and trekked across the United States to Minnesota, Wisconsin, the Dakotas, or Nebraska. They had cleared the land and built log cabins or sod shanties. Along with raising farm crops they had also raised a crop of Petersons, Andersens, Johnsons, and Swensons who became governors, senators, businesspeople, successful farmers, university professors, and labor leaders. Who hadn't heard of Charles Lindburgh, Carl Sandburg, and Hubert Humphrey? I liked to tell audiences that I was bringing them greetings from twenty million Americans of Scandinavian descent.

When I performed to labor groups I never failed to mention Andrew Furuseth and Harry Lundberg, important leaders of the U.S. Seamen's Union and both born in Norway. My prize Scandinavian connection was invariably Joe Hill, maker of dozens of labor songs. Hill was a Swedish American who became a world-famous martyr when he was executed in Utah in 1915.

Joe Hill was born Joel Hagglund in the town of Gavle, about a hundred miles north of Stockholm. He came from a musical family, had a good ear, and quickly learned idiomatic English when he arrived in the United States at the age of twenty-three. He joined the Industrial Workers of the World, a radical labor organization founded in 1905 to compete with the craft-oriented American Federation of Labor.

The Wobblies developed the use of labor songs into a fine art. They sold tens of thousands of copies of their *Little Red Songbook,* which was widely used by their members. It cost 10 cents and could easily fit into a back pocket. On the cover of every edition was a slogan: "IWW Songs—To Fan the Flames of Discontent." By contrast, when I edited the first AFL-CIO songbook in 1956 we used the following slogan on the back cover: "Songs for Union Halls, Rallies and Picket Lines."

Joe Hill was the chief songwriter for the Wobblies; a dozen or more of his songs were always in the *Little Red Songbook.* He had a knack for turning out easy-to-sing verses for a strike or some other Wobbly cause. He usually set the verses to a popular tune of the time or to a well-known hymn. Soon Wobblies were singing them at street-corner meetings and rallies. Even while awaiting execution in Salt Lake City in 1915, at the request of fellow Wobblies in San Francisco Hill wrote a first-class song on unemployment and soup lines to the tune of the British army marching song "Tipperary":

> It's a long way down to the soup line.
> It's a long way to go.
> It's a long, long way down to the soup line
> And the soup is thin I know.
> Goodbye good old pork chops;
> Farewell beefsteak rare.
> It's a long, long way down to the soup line
> But my soup is there.

Early in 1974 on one of my tours of Sweden, my guide, a staff member of the Swedish Labor Federation, said, "Joe, tomorrow morning we have something special for you. We are going to Gavle where Joe Hill was born, and we will visit his home, which is now a museum."

On the two-hour drive up to Gavle I was as excited as a young lad going out on his first date. I thought about the ironies of Joe Hill's life in Sweden and the United States. He was from a family of orthodox Lutherans who regularly attended Salvation Army meetings. In the United States, upset at the poverty and injustice he saw around him and embittered at religious leaders who preached about salvation and heaven, Joe Hill became vigorously antireligious. He wrote some of his most effective songs attacking these "pie-in-the-sky" preachers, using the tunes of Salvation Army hymns he had learned in Sweden and heard again in the United States. Thus, the hymn that begins "In the Sweet Bye and Bye, we will meet on that beautiful shore" became:

You will eat bye and bye
In the beautiful land in the sky.
Work and pray, live on hay,
You'll get pie in the sky when you die.

He even took a pointed crack at the Salvation Army in one verse:

And the *Starvation* Army they play
And they sing and they clap and they pray
Till they get all your coin on the drum
Then they tell you when you're on the bum.

You will eat bye and bye . . .

The Hagglund family home at 28 Nedra Bergsgatan in Gavle turned out to be a pleasant little museum, with furniture from the period and exhibits, posters, photographs, and other artifacts about Joe Hill. It had all been preserved by the government as a Swedish national historical landmark.

The labor leaders running the museum were obviously expecting me and my guitar. They had invited the press, the radio station, and labor leaders from the area. I soon found myself giving a mini-concert of Joe Hill songs and telling the story of his short life and tragic death in the United States. I sang Joe Hill's great song "Casey Jones," which he wrote during a strike on the Southern Pacific Railroad in 1911. I told them that the song was printed on small cards that were sold to raise money for the strikers and their families. I had sung Joe Hill's songs at a hundred meetings in the United States and other countries, but singing them there in the very home where Hill was born almost a century earlier was thrilling. Did I only imagine I heard his voice coming from the old wooden beams and singing along on the choruses?

I told the audience that Joe Hill was arrested on a murder charge in Salt Lake City in January 1914 while visiting Swedish friends there. Despite the intervention of President Woodrow Wilson and the Swedish government, despite the condemnation of the trial as unfair by the American Federation of Labor, and despite numerous protests from public meetings throughout the country and around the world, Joe Hill was finally executed by a five-man firing squad on November 19, 1915.

The citizens assembled in Gavle could not get enough of the adventures of their hometown celebrity. Joe Hill's story had inspired novels and plays. I told them that Joe Hill's body was brought to Chicago, where thirty thousand mourners marched in one of the greatest funeral processions ever seen in that or any other city. Joe Hill's songs were sung all the way to the cemetery. As soon as a song would die out in one place, the same one or others would be taken up along the line. Eulogies were delivered in nine languages, including, of course, Swedish.

Even the disposition of his ashes was dramatic. They were placed into envelopes and scattered throughout the United States and on every continent. "So," I summed up, "there's a little bit of Joe Hill in Sweden, Norway, in England, in every state of the United States, except Utah because Joe had emphatically said, 'I don't want to be found dead there.'"

The night before Joe died, a speaker at a protest meeting cried, "Joe Hill will never die!" In a way he never did die, I explained, because he has become a symbol of the hundreds of men and women who have been killed while battling for labor's rights.

The museum presented me with a colorful Joe Hill poster in Swedish, and I, in turn, gave them an autographed copy of my album *Songs of the Wobblies*.

In closing, I sang "The Ballad of Joe Hill" written by Earl Robinson and Alfred Hayes some twenty years after Hill's death. I think that the song is the most important factor perpetuating the memory and the legend of Joe Hill.

Joe Hill
Words: Alfred Hayes
Music: Earl Robinson

I dreamed I saw Joe Hill last night
Alive as you and me.
Says I, "But Joe, you're ten years dead."
"I never died," says he.
"I never died," says he.

"In Salt Lake City, Joe, by God," says I,
Him standing on my bed,
"They framed you on a murder charge."
Says Joe, "But I ain't dead."
Says Joe, "But I ain't dead."

"The copper bosses killed you, Joe,
They shot you, Joe," says I.
"Takes more than guns to kill a man,"
Says Joe, "I didn't die."
Says Joe, "I didn't die."

And standing there as big as life
And smiling with his eyes,
Joe says, "What they forgot to kill

Went on to organize.
Went on to organize."

"Joe Hill ain't dead," he says to me,
"Joe Hill ain't never died.
Where working men are out on strike
Joe Hill is at their side.
Joe Hill is at their side."

"From San Diego up to Maine
In every mine and mill,
Where workers strike and organize,"
Says he, "You'll find Joe Hill."
Says he, "You'll find Joe Hill."

(Repeat first verse.)

Hayes had written "Joe Hill" as a poem some ten years after Hill died. Ten years later, Robinson put the words to music. The song was known primarily to limited labor circles and never earned much money, but thirty years after it was written Joan Baez sang it at the Woodstock festival in New York state. I would guess that 99 percent of the audience had no clue about who Joe Hill was, but that didn't matter.

Joan Baez's rendition of the song was included in the LP album made up of some of the songs sung at Woodstock. The album sold millions of copies, and Earl Robinson received thousands of dollars in royalties—some fifty years after the event memorialized in the song. Robinson facetiously told me that his family gives a prayer of thanks to Joan Baez every night at dinner.

On Labor Day 1990, the Utah labor movement and others organized a colorful outdoor festival in Salt Lake City to pay tribute to Joe Hill on the seventy-fifth anniversary of his death. The prison where Joe Hill had been locked up for twenty-two months and where he was executed in 1915 had been demolished. In its place was a lovely park where the festival was held. Union families and friends picnicked on the grass on a beautiful day under blue skies and warm sunshine and listened to the songs of Joe Hill.

Earl Robinson was there to sing his famous ballad. Pete Seeger played his banjo and sang several Joe Hill favorites. Utah Phillips, a self-professed modern-day Wobbly, sang "There Is Power in the Union," one of Hill's finest compositions. I decided to sing "Rebel Girl," which Hill wrote in prison after he was visited by Elizabeth Gurley Flynn. Hill was quite taken with the beautiful, blue-eyed, black-haired Flynn, who was a key Wobbly agitator and organizer. When he finished writing "Rebel Girl" he sent it to Flynn with a note: "You have been an inspiration and when I composed the 'Rebel Girl,' you was right there and helped me all the time. As you furnished the idea I will . . . give you all the credit for that song . . . I would like to kiss you goodbye, Gurley, not because you are a girl but because you are the original 'Rebel Girl.' Goodbye."

I picked up on Joe Hill's salute to activist women by dedicating the song "to the modern rebel 'girls,' union women everywhere, to union wives, mothers and daughters who have helped make the labor movement an instrument for justice."

The Rebel Girl
By Joe Hill

There are women of many descriptions,
In this queer world as everyone knows.
Some are living in beautiful mansions,
And are wearing the finest of clothes.
There are blue-blooded queens and princesses,
Who have charms made of diamonds and pearl.
But the only and thoroughbred lady
Is the rebel girl.

That's the rebel girl.
That's the rebel girl.
To the working class
She's a precious pearl.
She brings courage, pride, and joy
To the fighting rebel boy.

We've had girls before,
But we need some more
In the Industrial Workers of the World.
For it's great to fight for freedom
With a rebel girl.

Yes, her hands may be hardened from labor,
And her dress may not be very fine,
But a heart in her bosom is beating,
That is true to her class and her kind.
And the grafters in terror are trembling,
When her spite and defiance she'll hurl.
For the only and thoroughbred lady
Is the rebel girl.

Chorus

Just as Joe Hill was my connection to Swedish workers, Andrew Furuseth was my connection to Norwegian workers. Although unknown to most Americans, he had been a colorful and important leader of the American labor movement, and his dramatic life story quickly captured the imagination of the Norwegian workers to whom I spoke and sang.

Andrew Furuseth sailed the seas for many years in the days when seamen were little more than slaves, completely at the mercy of the ship's captain. In the 1870s and 1880s, he made many trips carrying cargo, mostly timber, down the Pacific coast of the United States. Because most of his fellow sailors were Scandinavian, he was able to talk with them and organize them into a loyal following. He helped found the Sailors Union of the Pacific in 1885, becoming secretary in 1887 and then president in 1908 of the broader-based International Seamen's Union, a position he held until his death in 1938. Fittingly, when he died his ashes were spread across the oceans.

Furuseth devoted his life to breaking the chains that bound every sailor, hand and foot. He was ascetic, even aloof and melancholic. He never married. The sailors on the ships were his family, and his home was the sea, the docks, the ports, and the union hall.

During World War I, when Furuseth threatened to pull his sailors out on strike if working conditions were not improved, the government threatened to throw him in jail. "Put me in jail," he responded, "but you cannot put me in quarters more cramped than I knew as a seaman. You cannot give me worse food than I have always eaten. You cannot make me more lonely than I have always been." Those words are carved into a granite base on which sits a magnificent bust of Furuseth, overlooking San Francisco harbor.

In 1974 I told Furuseth's story to a labor group in the town of Hamar, which is a short drive from Oslo, Norway's capital. I was dramatically reciting, with the aid of my interpreter, his famous put-me-in-jail speech when a labor leader jumped up excitedly and said, "Furuseth was born right near here in the town of Romedal, and we have a huge bust of him with these same words carved in the stone!"

I had to see that memorial, and the next morning U.S. embassy personnel drove me to it. There, on a great block of granite guarding the main highway into the town of his birth, was Andrew Furuseth. His gaunt, rugged face was gazing into the distance as might have his Viking ancestors when they were searching for a hint of land. As we approached the impressive bust, one local official, Eiolf Paul Berg, told us the story of how the monument came to be erected. "We heard about the memorial to Furuseth when it was put up in San Francisco and some of us thought he should be honored in the same way here in his home town. We collected the funds with the aid of the Norwegian Seamen's Union and the Norwegian Labor Federation (L.O.). Even some businesses and the local bank helped out."

Berg took us into the tiny municipal building where the town's records were stored and showed us old family histories, including the one of the Furuseth family. There it was, written in a dusty, oversized ledger. Andrew Furuseth was born the fifth child of a poor tenant farmer. He left home when he was sixteen and in 1873, at the age of nineteen, sailed for the United States aboard the *Marie*.

On the drive back to Oslo, the story of Andrew Furuseth kept buzzing around in my head. I was scheduled to do a concert that evening at the residence of the U.S. ambassador, and a hundred top leaders of the Norwegian labor movement and the ruling Labor Party had been invited. Wouldn't it be great to do a song that told the saga of this poor Norwegian lad who made his mark thousands of miles across the sea in the United States?

By the time the concert was to begin, I had sweated out eight verses that told the story of Furuseth, from his birth in Romedal to his death eighty-four years later in the United States. I set the lyrics to the music of "The Buffalo Skinners," one of America's epic folk ballads, and the job was done. I was especially happy that I was able to work the put-me-in-jail speech into the verse.

The Ballad of Andrew Furuseth
Words: Joe Glazer
Music: "The Buffalo Skinners"

In the little town of Romedal, back in 1854,
Andrew Furuseth was born, the poorest of the poor.
He left his home in Norway to sail upon the sea.
Those were the days when a sailor's life was a life of misery.

He slept in a filthy hole in the ship with bedbugs all around.
Conditions were not fit for a dog, the worse that could be found.
The captain was a tyrant; the sailors were his slaves;
And many's the time they wished that they had died in a watery grave.

After many years of sailing the whole wide world around,
Andrew Furuseth set foot in San Francisco town.
He gathered up his comrades on every dock and pier.
He said, "We'll build a union and we're going to start right here."

He crossed the land from coast to coast, to every seaport town.
He said, "We've got to stand like men. Don't let them grind you down.
We'll build a seaman's union, for every man that sails.
We'll build a seaman's union if they put us all in jail.

"You can lock me in that dungeon, throw me in that cell,
But no prison that you put me in can be worse than the sailors' hell.
You can lock me in that dungeon and throw away the key,
But I'll never be as lonely as the sailor on the sea."

This grand old sailor left this earth in 1938.
Sailors mourned his passing from New York to the Golden Gate.
His ashes were all scattered across the ocean deep.
This restless son of Norway was finally asleep.
There's a little bit of Furuseth on Norway's rocky shore
And on the coasts of the U.S.A. where the mighty oceans roar,
But I believe his restless soul still sails the seven seas,
Till Justice rules in every land, his soul won't rest in peace.

The head of the Norwegian Labor Party was so moved by the song that he insisted I record it for him the next morning before I left Norway. Some years later, Haakon Lie, an old friend and former secretary of the Norwegian Labor Party, wrote a biography of Furuseth that was featured on a television special. I was honored to be asked to record the song on videotape, parts of which were incorporated into the special.

India

In 1968 I attended a debriefing at the State Department by Chester Bowles, the U.S. ambassador to India. Bowles, a former governor of Connecticut and a Democratic Party activist, had heard me sing at a number of political dinners and rallies during the period before I became a government employee and had to eschew politics. He greeted me warmly and invited me to come and sing in India. "You know," he said, "we've got a lot of unions there." I told him I'd come if invited.

Sure enough, in about ten days my boss received a long cable from Bowles and the USIA chief in New Delhi requesting my presence in India for one month for a lecture and singing tour targeted at unions, labor relations institutes, universities, journalists, management associations, labor ministry officials, and other groups interested in learning about the American labor movement and the U.S. industrial relations system.

To prepare myself I read all the State Department reports plus a fat file of newspaper clippings, but reading is not seeing or smelling or feeling or being there. The New Delhi airport where I arrived in January 1968 provided a taste of what I was to encounter in much of India. Swarms of travelers were clustered around the gates and counters, clutching their tickets, waving them aloft, calling out their destinations, and trying frantically to catch the attention of the harried clerks. That afternoon when I was driven around the ancient city of Delhi I began to appreciate for the first time the meaning of the word *teeming*. The narrow streets were clogged with loaded carts, some pulled by hand, some by burro or bullock, as far as the eye could see. There were bicycles, motor bikes, and scooters, all competing with scores of small, three-wheeled taxis and cars and trucks of every description. Merchandise from stalls and stores overflowed into the thronged streets where shoppers in both traditional and western dress vied for space with tourists, beggars, scurrying businessmen, clerks, messengers, and the occasional cow.

My first performance was at a dinner and reception hosted by Ambassador and Mrs. Bowles at their residence, an elegant structure designed by the eminent American architect Edward Durell Stone. There were a hundred guests— labor and political leaders, government officials, diplomats, journalists, assorted opinion-makers and intellectuals, and senior embassy staff members.

It was uppermost in my mind that I was there not merely as an entertainer. I wanted to leave the audience with some kind of message, building my points naturally into songs of struggle and accomplishment. In addition to a large stock of labor songs, I included spirituals, songs of the American pioneers and immigrants, and folk songs with a humorous twist.

It was made plain that the pluralistic nature of U.S. political democracy was not understood, even by sophisticated Indians, when a government official cornered me after the concert. What agitated him was "Solidarity Forever," especially its last verse:

> In our hands is placed a power
> Greater than their hoarded gold,
> Greater than the might of armies
> Magnified a thousand fold.
> We can bring to birth a new world
> From the ashes of the old
> For the union makes us strong.

"That is a very militant song, almost revolutionary," the Indian official admonished. "I can't understand a diplomat like yourself singing such a song here in the American embassy. Aren't you concerned that your government will fire you?" I assured him that there was no danger of that. I tried to explain that the U.S. Information Agency, which I represented, tries to present a broad cross-section of the United States. The labor movement was an important part of that picture. I told him that I had sung "Solidarity Forever" in U.S. embassies around the world. The embassies were all still standing, and not a single ambassador had suffered a heart attack. He exited shaking his head in wonder.

The very able labor attaché Morris Weisz, whom I knew, and his expert Indian assistant P. K. V. Krishnan organized an extensive program for me across India. My experiences varied; some were very successful, and others were surprising and unexpected. My appearances ranged from intensive question-and-answer sessions with small groups of journalists who wanted to know about American politics, race relations, and foreign policy to a major concert before five hundred railroad workers in their union hall. There were lectures and songs to university economics classes, visits to steel mills and textile plants, one-on-one discussions with labor leaders in their union offices, dinner programs with personnel directors and labor relations specialists, and abbreviated labor concerts at factories and plant gates before hundreds of sweaty, tired workers.

Language could be a problem because India has a myriad of regional and local languages and dialects. English was no problem when I appeared before university students or leadership groups. Programs before rank-and-file workers were another matter. In one large industrial city in central India I knew I was in trouble when the committee was discussing which language I should be translated into. Normally, the local language would be the one most widely understood, but in this particular plant there had recently been a large influx of Tamil speakers who didn't understand the local language. Whatever was decided led to a complete fiasco. The interpreter spoke with such a thick accent that no one knew what he was saying.

As if that weren't bad enough, the union cultural committee had decided to go all out and put me in the company soccer field instead of in the company auditorium or cafeteria as was usually done. They must have thought that if the Beatles could fill Yankee Stadium in New York, Joe Glazer could fill ten thousand seats in the middle of India. We drew some two thousand, but those eight thousand empty seats were a depressing sight.

Sometimes a performance brings out an unexpected reaction. In the city of Madras, a major port on the East India coast and an important textile manufacturing center, I found myself performing at a mill that seemed to be literally built in a garden. Instead of the usual grim, gray, industrial landscape, the textile mill was surrounded by trees, grass, and flowers—a pleasant surprise. I thought it was the perfect spot to sing "The Mill Was Made of Marble," my song about the dream of a textile worker.

I dreamed that I had died
And gone to my reward—

A job in Heaven's textile plant
On a golden boulevard.

> The mill was made of marble,
> The machines were made out of gold,
> And nobody ever got tired,
> And nobody ever grew old.

This mill was built in a garden—
No dust or lint could be found.
And the air was so fresh and so fragrant
With flowers and trees all around.

I thought my performance was well received by the textile workers, but the head of the union, a plain-spoken man with strong opinions, was scowling. "I did not like that song," he said. "I know my workers. If the machines are made out of gold they'll break the machines and take the gold home. And then the plant will close, and we'll have no work." I looked at him. He was not smiling.

Five hundred miles up the coast from Madras, in Calcutta, another memorable experience took place. My only major performance there was in the afternoon at the Longshoremen's union hall in the port district. About fifty bone-weary longshoremen in work clothes sat on backless benches in the beat-up union hall. A few tired-looking posters clung to walls that needed a good paint job. The wooden desk up front was scarred and marked from years of use and abuse. This was quite a contrast from the luncheon I had just attended in a well-appointed, plush private club, but I felt at home here for I had been in a hundred union halls just like it in the United States.

In my quick morning tour of Calcutta I had explored the docks, where sacks of American grain were being unloaded, one sack at a time on the backs of the longshoremen. This was a period of a serious grain shortage in India, and the United States was providing shiploads of grain during the crisis. That was my hook, my connection.

After some foot-stomping union songs, I moved into my main theme: "Brothers of the Longshoremen's Union—this morning I visited the docks of this great port city. I saw the big ships coming from America loaded with grain grown by the farmers in my country. I saw your brother longshoremen—maybe some of you were among them—unloading the bags of grain, getting them ready for shipment to help your countrymen feed their families."

I proceeded to extend warm, fraternal greetings from the longshoremen of the United States who had loaded those bags of grain onto the ships ten thousand miles across the seas. I told them I would tell American longshoremen about the work in India to help finish the job the Americans began on the other side of the world. "In honor of this great joint effort," I continued, "I want to sing for you the anthem of the American labor movement. It is called 'Solidarity Forever,' and it describes, better than anything I can say, what workers can accomplish when they practice true solidarity." I began to recite the first verse of "Solidarity Forever":

> When the union's inspiration through the workers' blood shall run,
> There can be no power greater anywhere beneath the sun.
> Yet what force on earth is weaker than the feeble strength of one?
> But the union makes us strong.

The interpreter picked up my rhythm, my intonation, and even my pauses as he translated line by line. I could feel the emotion mounting in the hall when he repeated the chorus as if he were singing it:

> Solidarity forever!
> Solidarity forever!
> Solidarity forever!
> For the union makes us strong.

When I finished, there were cheers and applause. Suddenly one worker leaped to his feet and began leading a kind of hip, hip, hooray in Bengali. He would yell out a phrase, and the audience would roar back its approval.

After the first cheer the interpreter whispered a quick translation: "Long live the friendship between Indian and American workers!" The second cheer was louder and more intense: "Long live international solidarity among all workers of the world!" The third cheer was ear-splitting. Everyone was on their feet. "What was that all about?" I asked. The interpreter told me, "That cheer was 'Long live the Revolution!'" I said, "I think it's time for me to go."

My most rewarding musical experience in India occurred in a New Delhi radio studio before a live audience of one. Presumably several hundred thousand, or perhaps several million, were tuned in; it was an important nationwide program. The man who interviewed me was stiff and proper, even supercilious in manner. I had the feeling—maybe I was being overly sensitive—that he had no use for "uncultured" Americans, especially one who talked and sang about labor unions. I answered his questions and sang several songs, using all the wiles and charm I could muster. He never bent. Then I closed with this:

My final song is called "This Land is Your Land." It is a very popular American song by the folk composer Woody Guthrie that tells about the breadth, the variety, and the color of America "from California to the New York Island." I have an Indian version of this song that I made up after watching the impressive National Day Parade on January 26. When I saw the great variety of India going past me—the elephants and the Indian-made jet planes, the people of many colors and languages from every corner of India, the dancers and their costumes, it reminded me of my own country, which is also a vast land with people of many colors, religions, and customs. So I changed some of the words of the song, and this is how the new Indian version sounds:

This Land Is Your Land (Indian version)
Words: Joe Glazer
Music: Woody Guthrie

> This land is your land, this land is my land
> From Himalayas mountains to Kanyakumari
> From the streets of Bombay to the hills of Assam
> This land was made for you and me.

I walked through the markets of ancient Delhi
I strolled through the gardens of the Taj at Agra
And all about me a voice was singing,
"This land was made for you and me."

> Chorus

I saw the dam at Bhakra and Tanjore's rice fields
The docks and steel mills and the tea plantations
I gazed at the temples of a thousand cities
And I said, "This land was made for you and me."

> Chorus

I saw the Sikhs and the Hindus, the Christians and Muslims
From the plains of the Punjab to the Indian Ocean
I gazed at the faces of a million people
And I knew this land was made for you and me.

> Chorus

As I sang, I could see from the corner of my eye that my frozen-faced Indian friend had completely thawed. From the look on his face, I had just sung the greatest song ever sung on the All-India Radio Network. When I finished, he gave me such a warm embrace that I almost dropped my guitar. "Come back anytime, Mr. Glazuh," he told me in a British-Indian accent. "Anytime. That was a beautiful song."

Unfortunately, the last verse rings false in view of the continuing bloody conflicts between Hindus and Muslims and Hindus and Sikhs. I like to imagine that somehow the power of song will triumph and goodwill will ultimately prevail over fear and hatred.

I made three more trips to India for the USIA and never stopped being fascinated with that ancient land.

Foreign Travel: Bits and Pieces

I sang and spoke for the USIA in dozens of countries and on every continent except Australia. I consider myself a pretty good lecturer but am convinced that my music had a bigger impact on audiences than my best lectures.

Certain songs, such as "This Land Is Your Land" and the civil rights anthem "We Shall Overcome," were sure-fire winners in English-speaking countries. I would often adapt the words of "This Land Is Your Land" to local geography, as I had done in India. It was always a resounding success. It was easy to follow Woody Guthrie's pattern where English was widely used. All I needed was an hour or two with a USIA staffer who knew the geography of the country and a song would be born.

Malaysia was a perfect spot for a "This Land." The country had three major ethnic groups, the majority Malays and the minority Chinese and Indians, each with its own language, culture, and traditions. The Malays had the political power, but the Chinese controlled most of the economy and enjoyed a much higher standard of living. The Indians included large numbers of workers on rubber plantations as well as small shopkeepers. There was no love lost among the various groups.

The government was trying hard to build a united nation from the three disparate groups. In my lyrics I tried to emphasize the positive—yes, each group dressed differently and did its own thing, but they all worked together. Of course it was a "feel-good" song reflecting more idealism than realism, but it struck a note many citizens wanted to hear—a goal many hoped the country would reach.

This Land Is Your Land (Malaysian version)
Words: Joe Glazer and Jim Elliot
Music: Woody Guthrie

This land is your land
This land is my land
From the Thailand border

To the Singapore causeway.
From Borneo's mountains
To the straits of Malacca.
I tell you, this land was made for you and me.

I walked through the rice fields
And the rubber plantations,
I visited the Ops Room
And called on the Tunku,
Saw the famous tin mines
And the LBJ Kampong.
This land was made for you and me.

Chorus

I roamed and I rambled
Through the Cameron Highlands,
I strolled on the beaches
Of sunny Port Dickens,
I swam with the sea snakes
In Penang's waters.
This land was made for you and me.

Chorus

Saw the Malay beauties
In their colorful batiks,
Saw the Indian maidens
In their beautiful saris,
Saw the Chinese ladies
In their shapely cheongsams.
This land was made for you and me.

Chorus

I gazed at the faces
Of ten million people
In the fields and factories
And the Parliament building.
Saw them working together
To build a nation.
This land was made for you and me.

Chorus

The minute the concert was over, I was surrounded by a group of Malaysian government officials. One, to whom the others deferred, insisted, "You must sing that song at our big annual Unity Day Rally next Tuesday. We will have ten thousand people at this rally. Your song will be the highlight of the program."

I could barely squeeze in a sentence to the effect that I was scheduled to be in Indonesia that Tuesday. He insisted, "You must change your schedule." He grabbed the American ambassador by the arm and urged that I stay for the Unity Day Rally. The ambassador said that the insistent man was an important minister in the government and in charge of the Unity Day Program. "We must do what we can to accommodate him," he said. But I was fully scheduled and advertised, and no change could be made.

That Tuesday, as I was going through my paces in Jakarta and other Indonesian cities, I could not get my mind off Unity Day in Malaysia. Several weeks after I returned to Washington, I learned about hair-raising events taking place in Malaysia. A vicious ethnic riot had broken out in Kuala Lumpur and other cities in Malaysia not long after the Unity Day celebration. Malaysian mobs attacked Chinese on the streets, pulled Chinese out of cars and buses, beat them, stabbed them, and slit their throats. It was a brutal, bloody, no-holds-barred attack.

Would ten thousand voices singing the Malaysia version of "This Land Is Your Land" have made a difference? I doubt it. A song is a song. It can make you laugh or cry, and it can make you feel romantic or proud or patriotic. But it is no match for poisonous hatreds with deep roots.

There were times when I overrated the power of music and had to be brought down to earth. I sang a Philippine version of "This Land" at a large dinner that the Philippine labor minister hosted in my honor. The audience of trade union leaders and government officials was fluent in English, and I was able to present a full-scale program of American labor songs without the usual translations to slow me down.

Filipinos love to sing, and they joined every chorus with enthusiasm and spirited abandonment. They banged tables and hit glasses with silverware in perfect rhythm to the music. They were overflowing with solidarity and goodwill toward the United States.

The labor minister, who had a well-deserved reputation as a spellbinder, praised the good relations between the Philippines and the United States. He talked about the crucial role the trade union movement played in raising the living standards of workers. Then he really poured it on. He turned to me and the U.S. ambassador, G. Mennen (Soapy) Williams, the former Democratic governor of Michigan. Williams had heard me sing at many political rallies during my former life in the labor movement. The minister declared, "Mr.

Ambassador, I want you to know that Joe Glazer is the best export from the United States since the Declaration of Independence!"

I was feeling good about those comments until the ambassador whispered, "That's not the first time I heard him use that line." That sobered me, but later, when he accompanied me to my hotel, Williams said, "While I wouldn't rank you with Thomas Jefferson, still it was a very good show. It reminded me of the old days on the campaign trail."

In India, however, I could have started a diplomatic uproar with an adaptation of "This Land." The local employee providing me with the geographic boundaries of India wanted me to include Kashmir as the most northern boundary. The area is in a bitter dispute with Pakistan, and the United States is not taking sides. Fortunately, an American USIA employee squashed the suggestion immediately.

"We Shall Overcome" was another song I frequently included in overseas programs. The civil rights revolution led by Martin Luther King and others received constant and widespread publicity all over the world. Scenes of police dogs attacking blacks marching to get the vote and of blacks being hauled off to jail were potent ammunition for the nation's enemies. Even allies experienced perverse pleasure from the difficulties and embarrassment of big, rich Uncle Sam who professed to be a democracy for all.

The music of "We Shall Overcome" was powerful but uncomplicated. The lyrics were simple and repetitive, and even where English was not well known I could always get audiences singing with me. But I never sang "We Shall Overcome" without introducing it:

> Many of you know this next song, "We Shall Overcome," that has become the anthem of the civil rights revolution in the United States. The revolution aims to complete the unfinished business of the American Civil War of the 1860s. That war freed the slaves, but they never did win complete equality and freedom. That is what this current civil rights revolution is about.
>
> I wish to dedicate this song, first to all of the brave young black college students who defied the local laws that forbade them from eating in a restaurant or from using public swimming pools. Many were beaten and jailed, and some were killed. And we must salute the white students who marched and sang and fought side by side with these black students even though they had nothing personal to gain.
>
> Second, I dedicate this song to Lyndon B. Johnson, president of the United States, a white southerner who stood before the United States Congress and deplored racial inequality, concluding with the ringing words "we shall overcome."
>
> Finally, I dedicate this song to people all over the world fighting against discrimination, poverty, and tyranny who have adopted those words in their struggles. And

I especially dedicate this song to people in those countries where they are not even allowed to sing it.

Normally, I had no problem getting an audience to sing with me. I would even get them to stand up, link arms, and sway to the music. In Burma in the late 1960s, however, I could not get the audience to sing a note of "We Shall Overcome." They had joined in easily on earlier songs, so I knew they could sing, but on this one they clammed up. Dead! The mystery was solved when my embassy guide whispered, "This is one of those countries where they are not allowed to sing this song. You better move on to the next one."

In Finland there was no problem with the audience. Finnish labor leaders had been invited to the ambassador's residence for a Joe Glazer concert. Despite the Finns' reputation for being reserved, they enjoyed every minute of the program, singing along and clapping. But "We Shall Overcome" was too much for the ambassador. He was very conservative and had no use for trade unions or for those who sang labor songs. He stalked out, I later learned, convinced it was a "communist song." When the concert was over I skipped my usual presentation of one of my LP records to the ambassador. I thought it would not be properly appreciated.

Then there was the time in Japan when I found myself using an unusual song to good advantage in a geisha house. Lou Silverberg, the veteran labor attaché at the U.S. embassy, told me that leaders of the Japanese autoworkers union were planning to honor me with a party at an elegant geisha house in downtown Tokyo.

The party took place in a private room reserved for us—six or eight leaders from the autoworkers and three or four representatives from the embassy. The only women present were geisha dressed in traditional kimonos and smiling and bowing constantly.

Silverberg and I didn't speak their language, and they didn't speak ours. Yet at one point I observed Silverberg carrying on what seemed to be a pleasant conversation with one of the geisha. That surprised me because I knew he had given up on the difficult Japanese language years earlier and worked with an interpreter. I moved closer to eavesdrop and couldn't believe my ears. He was speaking Yiddish, smiling all the time, while the geisha answered in rapid-fire Japanese, also with a big smile. His Yiddish was an interesting mixture of nonsense, wise sayings, and an occasional colorful cuss word. When the geisha moved on, he explained, "This is the only way I can keep sane at these affairs. It doesn't matter what you say or in what language you say it as long as you keep smiling."

We were seated on the floor around a low table. It was hard for six-footers like Silverberg and me to find space for our long legs. The geisha brought us saki and various Japanese delicacies. They smiled. We smiled back. We ate and drank some more, all the while trying to get comfortable while sitting on the floor.

The Japanese labor leaders toasted us. We toasted them. A geisha came into the room and sang a couple of songs accompanying herself on the samisen— something like a guitar. Of course, we didn't understand a word. Then I pulled out my guitar, which Silverberg had asked me to bring.

It was obviously not the time or place for a proper labor concert, so I sang some abbreviated versions of songs that had rhythm and drive. I had worked out a singing Japanese version of the chorus of "Solidarity Forever." That brought the entire group together, including the geisha, who got into the spirit of the song.

The party was bouncing along quite nicely, and I wracked my brain for an appropriate song that would need no translation and would close the program on a high note. Suddenly, a song I hadn't sung for twenty-five years popped into my head. It was "Minnie the Moocher," made famous by Cab Calloway in the 1930s. Its singing chorus had nonsense syllables that the audience could echo—just the thing. I used all kinds of nonsense-syllable variations to avoid monotony. I would throw in a Japanese word like *sayonara* occasionally, and that would bring squeals of delight from the geisha.

As the song developed and the volume of the singing pouring from the room increased, geisha from nearby rooms stuck their heads in the doorway to see what was going on. Soon a dozen or more were clapping to the rhythm and singing "hi de hi de hi de hi." It was a sight to behold. Finally, an older woman, undoubtedly a supervisor, ordered them back to their duties.

I would hazard a guess that the official State Department report of my tour of Japan never mentioned geisha singing "Minnie the Moocher," but there is no doubt in my mind that it was the most memorable part of the trip.

13

New Voices, Part 1

"They don't sing anymore. The labor movement has become fat and soft and today you don't hear the old militant labor songs. In the old days when the labor movement was a fighting movement workers marched and sang. But no more." You hear this spouted all the time—in newspaper editorials, in magazine articles, and by nostalgic old-timers or pseudo-radicals. But it's nonsense. There is more labor singing now than ever before. Many people have never heard of Larry Penn, a Milwaukee trucker who has written dozens of labor songs and sung at scores of rallies and picket lines. They have never heard of Eddie Starr, a third-generation steelworker who composes and sings about workers and their problems, songs based on years of hacking out a living in a steel mill in Granite City, Illinois. They have never heard of Anne Feeney, the granddaughter of a Pennsylvania coal miner who has stirred workers in strikes from California to Virginia with her rousing songs excoriating scabs and union-busting bosses. In fact, there are dozens of men and women like them all across the country. Given the occasion or the cause, more labor singing occurred during the 1990s than ever before.

Labor songs have always come in cycles. The best have emerged from struggle. Many songs were topical responses to special conditions that no longer prevail and so are no longer sung. In the early days, battles for the eight-hour day culminated in strikes and demonstrations on May 1, 1886, when they sang:

We are summoning our forces
From the shipyard, shop, and mill
Eight hours for work,
Eight hours for rest,
Eight hours for what we will.

The bloody Homestead strike of 1892, when the union was crushed by the Carnegie Steel Corporation, inspired much verse and song:

Now the troubles down at Homestead
Were brought about this way
When a grasping corporation
Had the audacity to say
You must all renounce your union
And forswear your liberty
And we will give you a chance
To live and die in slavery.

The Industrial Workers of the World, established in 1905, was America's great singing union. Had the Wobblies been as effective in union-building as in writing songs they would not have disappeared after the 1920s. They left a body of radical labor songs rarely sung now, although one, "Solidarity Forever," endures as the anthem of the American labor movement.

The Great Depression of 1929 and the birth of the Congress of Industrial Organizations (CIO), which struggled to organize mass-production industries during the 1930s, popularized "We Shall Not Be Moved" and "Roll the Union On." But the relative prosperity labor enjoyed during the 1950s and 1960s (union membership reached 35 percent of the work force in 1955, for example) did not develop many militant labor songs. No union poet has been inspired to write a song about "we've just signed a good union contract and everything is okay at our plant today."

During the 1970s and 1980s, twenty years of Republican presidents combined with increased automation, computerization, and low-cost overseas competition to produce hard times for the trade union movement. By 1994, union membership had dropped to 15 percent of the eligible work force. There were demonstrations against wage cuts and against antilabor policies by state and national governments. There were strike rallies, solidarity rallies, and rallies for jobs and justice. There were many opportunities for labor songs about union busters, jobs, scabs, solidarity, plant safety, automation, and cheap imports. I flew to Washington state for a solidarity rally at the state capitol. I flew to Columbus, Ohio for a statewide protest rally of 1,500 union bricklayers. I sang in Texas at the state AFL-CIO convention. I sang in Washington, D.C., at a coal miners' rally protesting Ronald Reagan's cuts in payments to black lung victims.

One day in 1978, my friend Archie Green, the nation's leading expert on labor folklore and music, talked with me about the future of labor union music. Archie's background is unique. After twenty years as a union carpenter in

San Francisco shipyards, Archie got a Ph.D. in folklore and joined academia. This was his pitch:

> Joe, it's great that you and your music are in demand all over the country. But you are only one person, and you can't do this forever. There must be lots of young people, and some not so young, who can write and sing labor songs. We must find them. We must encourage the seasoned ones and help them get better known among the unions. We must nurture the inexperienced singers so they can perform with confidence before the biggest rallies and conventions. In a few years we will have a whole stable of union singers who will be available all across the country.

Archie's arguments made sense. The result was the establishment in 1978 of the Labor Heritage Foundation (LHF), a nonprofit organization to promote labor music, art, and culture in the labor movement and among the general public. Working closely with me was Joe Uehlein, a young trade union organizer and labor singer. Joe came from a strong union family in Pennsylvania and first heard me sing at a steelworkers' rally in Cleveland when he was only six. I became chair, and Uehlein became president of the LHF. Our secretary was Saul Schniderman, a labor history buff and an active officer of the American Federation of State, County and Municipal Workers Employees. After several years we were able to hire a part-time director, Laurel Blaydes, who worked for the LHF for twelve years and performed invaluable work in developing its programs.

We began with a three-day Great Labor Song Exchange at the George Meany Center, the AFL-CIO staff training school in Silver Spring, Maryland. The event attracted a dozen singers and would-be singers who had read our announcement in a labor newspaper. Whenever I would get word about some guitar-picker leading "Solidarity Forever" at a union rally I would track that person down, call their union, and urge the union president to send the singer to the song exchange. Soon we had twenty and then forty; in a few years we had a hundred participants each year from dozens of unions from Maine to California. The program included such topics as "How to Sing at Union Rallies," "Songs for Picket Lines," "The History of Labor in Song and Story," "How to Produce a Labor Song Cassette," "Songs about Current Labor Issues," and "How to Incorporate Labor Music into Union Programs."

No doubt the most useful part of the program was the song exchange periods, when each and every participant had the opportunity to present a favorite labor song or an original song. The best were copied, taped, learned, and brought back home to Minneapolis, Pittsburgh, Atlanta, or wherever. We discovered many talented singers and songwriters who had been performing in their local communities. We encouraged newcomers so nervous they could barely hold their guitars. We also attracted polished protest sing-ers and urged them to add more labor songs to their repertoires.

Soon we had a cadre of labor singers who were available to perform at con-ventions, rallies, banquets, picnics, and strikes. What follows is the story of some of the new voices of labor. Many more singers deserve to be included, but those I discuss in this chapter and the next are a representative sample.

Paul McKenna

Paul McKenna is not only an exceptionally able writer of union songs, but he also brings to his songs a knowledge of the day-to-day problems of the union: organizing, handling grievances, economic strategy and analysis, and negoti-ating. He is research director of a twenty-thousand-member statewide local of the Service Employees International Union (SEIU) in Oregon.

I knew nothing about his talents when I was first asked to do a record al-bum for the 1980 convention of the SEIU. In addition to the traditional labor songs, I planned to include some that were associated with service employees (hospital workers, health-care workers, building service employees, and state and local government employees). I couldn't find any songs about such work-ers, however. I wrote one useful song about the history of the SEIU, but I des-perately needed more material.

Just at that time Archie Green mailed me a song McKenna had written specifically for an SEIU organizing drive. Almost every week someone sends me a political or labor song. They are generally amateurish, written with an axe and a rhyming dictionary. But not this song. Right away, I recognized a talented songwriter.

The song was "MCA," to the tune of "MTA" as sung by the Kingston Trio. Like so many labor songs, it was written for a specific situation and describes special working conditions. It doesn't lend itself to other situations, but what a song it is. In the mid–1970s, the SEIU was trying to organize service workers in Yosemite Park who worked for a subsidiary of Music Corporation of Amer-ica (MCA). When he first heard *MCA* he immediately thought of "MTA":

The MCA Song (excerpts)
Words: Paul McKenna
Music: "MTA" by Jacqueline Steiner and Bess Hawes

Let me tell you the story about a man named Charley.
He was camping in the mountains last May.

And he fell in love with the Yosemite Valley
So he got a job with MCA.

But he rapidly found it's a company town
And the workers are kept way down.
Yes, the land is pretty but the work is kind of shitty,
And there ain't no union around.

Charley's first night working he was waiting on tables
At the classy Ahwanee Hotel.
Well, the food was flyin' and the customers were cryin'
And the manager was giving him hell.

After work Charley headed to his new living quarters
To lay down and rest his head,
But the walls were peeling, there were holes in the ceiling,
And his roommates were hogging the bed.

In a company town with no union around
Better keep your voices down.
If you start in bitchin', they'll stick you in the kitchen,
Or run your backside out of town.

Now you workers in Yosemite take a lesson from Charley
Start working for a change today.
Organize yourselves! Vote for Local 250!
Take the power away from MCA!

Yes there's hope to be found, 'cause the union's in town
And the time for a change is due.
MCA will cower when they feel our power.
Organize! Join SEIU!

I invited McKenna to attend the Great Labor Song Exchange (later called the Great Labor Arts Exchange) at the George Meany Center in 1980. He turned up, only twenty-eight, slim, and of average height, with a shy smile, a full head of curly hair, and impish brown eyes behind his glasses. The Song Exchange was an eye-opening experience for McKenna. He met other fine union song-writers and labor music veterans. "I was in awe," he said. "It was fantastic. I was inspired to move ahead with my song writing."

Nothing in his family background could have foretold McKenna's move to the labor movement. His parents were Republicans, particularly his father. But, McKenna said, "Growing up in the sixties moved me politically to the Left—Vietnam, the civil rights movement, etc. By the time I had graduated from college in 1974 with a major in economics I very definitely wanted to 'do something meaningful' with my life."

McKenna found a job as a research specialist for the Service Employees International Union by answering a classified advertisement in the *Philadelphia Inquirer*:

> I knew very little about the labor movement and less about labor research. I don't believe I had ever heard of the Service Employees, which turned out to be one of the AFL-CIO's largest unions, with hundreds of thousands of members . . .
>
> I was assigned to the Northern California Joint Council of SEIU which had a large membership in the San Francisco Bay area. I did research for the union on collective bargaining issues, union contracts, and comparative wages. I took to union work like a fish to water. It was during this period that I wrote the "MCA" song.

After McKenna's exposure to other union songwriters in 1980, his song-writing took off, and he produced nearly a dozen first-rate union songs. One was a big union hit despite the misgivings he had while working on it. "I remember sitting at my kitchen table in San Francisco working on the song and thinking, 'This is ridiculous. Nobody will ever sing this song,'" he recalled. "Contrary to my kitchen table musings, it has ended up being one of my most widely circulated songs, which, as Chuck Berry said, 'Goes to show you can never tell.'"

Hospital Workers on Strike for Higher Pay
Words: Paul McKenna
Music: "Stars and Stripes Forever" by John Philip Sousa

Hospital workers on strike for higher pay!
We're hospital workers out on strike.
Struggling to make a decent living,
Fighting the bosses and the scabs
And we are not about to give in.
We're demanding higher wages.
We've gotta get a raise.
We've gotta get a raise.
Our wages are outrageous.
We've gotta get a good raise.

Oh, we're out walking on the picket line
And we're ready to keep on walking.
And to carry around a picket sign
Till the management sits down
To do some talking.
Let's all sing "Solidarity Forever."
Yes, the union makes us strong.
Raise our voices in harmony together
People sing this union song.

We shall overcome the opposition of the hospital employers.
We shall not be moved by their injunctions
And their high-priced, downtown lawyers.
Our enthusiasm won't diminish
We are in this battle till the finish
Till the bosses hear what we are saying
Realize that we're not playing.

We'll stay out in the heat and the cold
In the rain and the wind and the weather.
The union is going to prevail.
Stick together and we won't fail.
We will stand hand in hand organized
And we won't let the scabs or bosses bust us.
With spirit and courage and pride
We will unite to win the fight
For bread and justice. Hey!

When I first heard McKenna sing this song, I thought, "This is crazy. A union song sung to 'Stars and Stripes Forever'? Impossible!" But the incongruity worked. People laughed—in fact, they howled. During the last few lines they clapped and stomped in rhythm as though marching in a parade. And they all yelled "Hey!" at the end.

The song is now a regular part of my repertoire. I have a recurrent dream about singing it at the White House, backed by a hundred-piece marine band in full-dress uniform. It hasn't happened, but as Chuck Berry said, "Goes to show you can never tell."

Another McKenna hit is "Union Buster," which is aimed at the highly paid consultants who advise employers how to maintain a "union-free environment":

The Union Buster
Words: Paul McKenna
Music: "Oh, Susanna" by Stephen Foster

Let me introduce myself—Jack Gypper is my name.
I'm a management consultant, union-busting is my game.
I'm a master of the con job, I'm an expert at the hoax,
And I make my living stealing bread from the mouths of working folks.

I'm a union buster, the bosses' trusty aide;
I help keep their employees overworked and underpaid.

In the old days we had gun thugs, we had ginks and finks and goons;
Nowadays we use fancy words but sing the same old tunes.

Pitting folks against each other, spreading hatred, fear, and lies;
Cutting down the hopes of workers who are trying to organize.

Chorus

There's no tactic I won't stoop to, there's no trick I haven't tried,
To intimidate and infiltrate, to conquer and divide
I'll wear the union down with litigation and delay
And all the while I'm raking in a thousand bucks a day.

Chorus

When I was young I used to fight with kids one-half my size;
Pull the legs off bugs and spiders, and the wings off butterflies.
Now I've grown to be a man, I haven't changed at all,
I still step on the underdog, the humble, and the small.

Chorus

Jack London tells the story—God was working in his lab,
And from some hateful substance He made my good friend the scab.
He gave some of that awful stuff a graduate degree,
Put it in a three-piece suit and that's how he made me.

Chorus

Joe Uehlein effectively used "Union Buster" in an organizing campaign in rural southern Georgia. The management of a factory had hired a union-busting consultant to snoop on workers and intimidate them. Employees had been allowed to play personal cassettes over the plant's public address system while on the job. They usually favored country music, but Joe gave the workers a cassette of "Union Buster," which they played the next time the labor consultant came to the plant. He ran to the personnel director's office to demand that the "damn song" be turned off. Workers were then notified that they would no longer be allowed to play cassettes over the factory's speakers. As a result, when the union buster next came around the workers sang, hummed, or whistled "Union Buster." He got their message and gave up. The union won the election, and the workers have a contract.

McKenna estimates that he has written 150 songs, many of them for specific union campaigns in which he has been involved. He has described his philosophy of writing union songs:

Over the years, my speciality has been writing songs that are hard-hitting but fun, using humor to knock bosses and other powerful people down a few notches. That kind of song can be very empowering for workers and very effective for organizing and union-building. Lately though I've been trying to write more serious songs—

songs that move and inspire and uplift people. This kind of song is much harder to write and not as much fun, but I think has a greater and more lasting impact on people in the long run.

I hope to continue writing and singing for another thirty or forty years, as long as I'm around. Writing labor songs has given me a vehicle to express myself musically, which I value enormously. What keeps me writing is my love for music and the challenge of taking an idea and working it through to a song more than any desire to change the world through music, although I think that's possible too.

McKenna has already demonstrated that his songwriting is so effective that it is capable of producing change.

Jon Fromer

When Jon Fromer was laid off in 1993 after twenty-three years as a producer at KRON, the NBC-TV station in San Francisco, he wrote a song:

Middle of the Night
By Jon Fromer

I did my job for many years when they showed me the door
Wind up with a handshake, not needed anymore
Say hello to memories, goodbye to the friends I made
Wonder how we're gonna get by when I'm not getting paid.

In the middle of the night I look over at you
Knowing you're there helps me make it through
Don't know what I'd do if I didn't have you
In the middle of the night.

Too many around me losing jobs and homes and lives
I've got a lot of friends looking after me, I know that I'll survive
Still I can't help but wonder if I've got what it may take
The world looks big when you're feeling small and lying here awake.

Chorus

Seems you give the company the best years of your life
I wonder how many millions cannot sleep tonight
How many hearts are aching? How many dreams are breaking?
How many have someone they love always on their side?

Chorus

Fromer is an active officer of the American Federation of Television and Radio Artists and also belongs to the American Federation of Musicians and the Communications Workers of America. He has written songs for years to pep up organizing drives, strikes, civil rights rallies, and other protest meetings, but "Middle of the Night" was one of the first he wrote for himself and from his experience. Most of his songs are fighting, defiant, militant messages: "Stand Up for Your Union," "Solidarity Is the Answer," and "We Need a Union to Have Power." Such themes are just right for his booming voice and the powerful, driving beat of his guitar.

Fromer is not a huge, raucous, working stiff who seems intimidating on a picket line. An inspiring leader, he is of medium but powerful build. He has both a music and pro-labor background. His grandmother was an organizer and founding member of the International Ladies' Garment Workers' Union (ILGWU). His father was born during an organizing drive in Kentucky. His parents were artists and musicians who understood how labor music, art, and drama could inspire the labor movement.

Fromer makes his living as a busy television producer in San Francisco, but he always takes the time to bring his guitar and music to struggles for social and economic justice. He is a key member of a unique organization, the Freedom Song Network, a Bay-area coalition of musicians who contribute time and talent to bring about social change. Their 250 active dues-paying members are available on short notice to help on picket lines and demonstrations. Fromer describes an incident that occurred in 1984 when the Longshoremen's Union was boycotting South African ships during the historic battle against apartheid:

> We supplied singers and pickets every morning at 7 to march and sing on the waterfront. One morning a small group of over-zealous supporters wanted to jump the fence. This would have led to a violent confrontation that the union did not want. The music kept everyone together and prevented the development of what could have been a nasty situation.
>
> On another occasion, a hot argument was getting out of hand, and we started singing and circling, and everybody present followed suit and got into the spirit. It was militant and loud enough for everyone. It made you move and warmed up the cold mornings on the waterfront. The music gave focus to the gathering and helped make a successful demonstration.

Fromer can belt out a mean song on a picket line, but he is also a soft-spoken, generous artist with a warm smile and a twinkle in his eye, always ready to help workers in need of moral support. In 1982 the teaching assistants at the University of California at Berkeley called upon him and his group for help. They were trying to win a contract to improve their working conditions, although the university's administration refused to meet or talk with their union. Every day for two months Fromer led the singing outside the administration office. One day, a frazzled university spokesperson emerged and said, "Okay, if you'll stop all that noise we'll meet with the union." A contract containing many job improvements was signed. Fromer's music turned out to be a "joyful noise" indeed. Here's an excerpt from one of his union songs:

We Need a Union to Have Power
By Jon Fromer

We need a union to have power.
We need a union to survive.
We need a union to stand together.
We need a union for a better life.

Alone you've got nothin', take whatever's comin';
When we unite, we've got strength to fight.

Chorus

Union sisters are here to say
For equal work they want equal pay.

Chorus

Finding himself with more time to devote to good causes when he was laid off in 1993, Fromer permitted his enthusiasm and musical generosity to get him into trouble. Before latching on to another job on the local PBS station he responded to numerous calls for help in the Bay area and would play into the night at parties and meetings. As a result, he developed carpal tunnel syndrome, a painful affliction in his right hand and arm, caused by excessive repetitive motion.

Fromer was fitted with a protective device that limited his hand and wrist movements, and he also made a serious attempt to cut down on engagements. One night while playing for a rally to save California's Occupational Safety and Health Administration (CALOSHA), he found himself joined by three or four other guitar-pickers, each of them wearing a carpal tunnel support too. You can't keep a good union musician down.

Fromer's most popular song is "We Do the Work," the theme of a television labor show seen regularly across the country:

We Do the Work
By Jon Fromer

We plant the food. We drive the cab.
We load the ship. We run the lab.

We build the bridges. We fly the plane.
We do the work. This is our day.

> We do the work. We do the work.
> We do the work. This is our day.

We type the page. We clean the streets.
We sew the clothes. We change the sheets.
We sell the goods. We lay the stone.
We do the work. This is our home.

> We do the work. We do the work.
> We do the work. This is our home.

We dig the ditch. We serve the meal.
We give the care. We mold the steel.
We teach the kids. We lend a hand.
We do the work. This is our land.

> We do the work. We do the work.
> We do the work. This is our land.

Whenever Jon Fromer sings at a strike or a union rally, he keeps in mind his father's counsel, repeated over the years: "Always remember that a singing movement is a winning movement; a singing movement cannot be beaten." "Maybe I'm just a hopeless romantic," he says, "but I really believe in the power of music to move people. That'll keep me going until I'm a hundred."

Charlie King

If Charlie King's beard were white and he wore a red suit he could easily pass as Santa Claus. Instead of dropping toys through chimneys on Christmas Eve, however, he drops songs throughout the year in union halls, on picket lines, and at protest meetings and rallies. He earns most of his living performing at coffeehouses and giving concerts at churches and schools.

Charlie is big and jovial, always ready to puncture the guardians of the status quo with a new song. He is also a master at showing how difficult life in an industrial society can be despite technological advances:

Bring Back the Eight Hour Day
By Charlie King

Say, you work at a white collar job
You get paid at a fixed monthly rate.
But you come in for meetings a half hour early;

You're working a full hour late.
Then you sit for an hour in traffic
With the rest of the overtime drones.
There's a latchkey kid you must chase off the bed
Then you eat a cold supper alone.

So, bring back the eight hour day.
When did we give it away?
There's so much to do
When the work day is through.
Bring back the eight hour day.

They've got cellular phones for your car,
They've got notebook PCs for your lap.
If you crawl off to sleep you stay close to your beeper.
Now why do we stand for this crap?
They tell you, "You gotta compete."
No, we're tired from footing the bill.
Eight hours for work, eight hours for rest
Eight hours for what we will.

Chorus

Charlie's father was a member of the Steamfitter's Union in Quincy, Massachusetts, but Charlie didn't learn his union or protest songs from him. His father, a political conservative, endorsed the ideas of Wisconsin's Sen. Joseph McCarthy, and Charlie grew up absorbing ideas from the John Birch Society. The Vietnam War politicized him, however, and he became a conscientious objector. Father and son were alienated for many years: "We didn't see eye to eye politically, but nevertheless our closest bond came through the singing of old songs together. He taught me a lot of 'Heart of My Heart' vintage songs."

King became active in the farm workers' struggle in 1971. In New York City he picketed supermarkets ("don't buy grapes") and liquor stores ("don't buy Gallo wine"). It was during this period that he learned his first labor songs.

From 1971 to 1976 he lived in a commune in New York City, contributing $12 a week toward his food and board. He survived by doing odd jobs—short-order cook, messenger, anything. He did find one singing job at an Upper East Side bar patronized by yuppies looking for dates. "I got by singing the old songs my father had taught me," he recalls, "some Hank Williams, some 1950s', 1960s' pop ballads, and some young John Prine, who was a big influence on me. I also threw in an occasional picket-line song, which the boss didn't appreciate and neither did the patrons. It would make a good story to say I was fired because

I sang those labor songs, but the painful truth was the boss decided to spend the money instead for a free sandwich bar."

The most memorable time of his labor singing career was the long, bitter packinghouse workers' strike in Austin, Minnesota, during the 1980s. "The strike changed their lives," he remembers. "Their whole world changed. But the strike didn't have the support of the international union, and it was lost."

A more rewarding experience occurred at Wesleyan University in Connecticut in 1978. "I was singing to university clerical workers, all women, who were earning less in a year than students paid in annual tuition. I sang Woody Guthrie's 'Union Maid,' and they loved it. I had to sing it over and over again":

Union Maid (excerpts)
Words: Woody Guthrie
Music: "Red Wing" by Frederick Allen Mills

There once was a union maid,
She never was afraid.
Of the goons and ginks
And company finks
And the deputy sheriffs
Who made the raid.
She went to the union hall
When a meeting it was called.
And when the company boys came 'round
She always stood her ground.

Oh, you can't scare me,
I'm stickin' to the union,
I'm stickin' to the union,
I'm stickin' to the union.
Oh, you can't scare me,
I'm stickin' to the union,
I'm stickin' to the union
Till the day I die.

"The women learned the song, and they sang it as they marched down to the union hall. The three union organizers at the front of the hall, all in suits, all somewhat traditional, were taken aback. What was this all about? These 'gals' were really on fire. They ended up getting a pretty good contract."

My favorite Charlie King song is a rare gem, "The Dancing Boilerman." It has nothing to do with strikes or solidarity or fighting the boss, but it does touch on working conditions. It is one worker's imaginative response to boredom on the job:

The Dancing Boilerman
By Charlie King

Hear me whistle a tune in the boiler room
At the golf ball factory.
There once was a time I worked out on the line
But that ain't the life for me.
Not since I got the call at the square dance ball
And it's changed my life in a way—
While they're all manufacturing I'm down here practicing
Dancing the day shift away.

> It's allemande left round the boiler
> And a grand right and left round the stack.
> A quick do-si-do to those dials in a row,
> Check the pressure and promenade back.
> Got a few more years left as a toiler
> Till I make my retirement pay,
> Then I'll just roll away with half a sashay
> And get my chance to square dance
> My whole life away.

There used to be gloom in the boiler room.
I'd just stare at those gauges all day.
Then me and my wife put some juice in our life,
Learned to dance at the YMCA.
Now the record I play, it reminds me each day:
"Don't let the good life pass you by."
'Neath the steam pipes so hot, I'm so hot to trot.
Gonna dance till the day that I die.

> Chorus

"Charlie," I asked, "how did you come to write such an offbeat song?" He explained:

In 1977 my wife, Joanne McGloin, had a part-time research job interviewing workers at a golf ball factory, the Acushnet Sporting Goods Company in Fall River, Massachusetts. They were asked about the quality of their worklife. Most workers came to the cafeteria to be interviewed. But the lone worker in the boiler room could not leave his post, so she went down to see him. A worker all alone with no one to look at. She was sure he must be terribly bored and lonely. But no, he had a phonograph hidden there that he played so he could practice square dance steps that he had marked out on the floor with footprints.

Charlie immediately saw the possibilities for a song in this story and quickly put together "The Dancing Boilerman," setting it to a lovely waltz tune. I recorded it and have sung it many times to audiences of all kinds, who relate to it and enjoy it. Charlie sent a copy of the song to Stanley Kozera, the man in the boiler room. At Christmas he received a box of a dozen golf balls from Kozera with "The Dancing Boilerman" printed on each ball.

One of Charlie's well-known songs is "Two Good Arms," the moving story of Nicola Sacco and Bartolomeo Vanzetti, the Italian anarchists who were executed in Massachusetts in 1927. Although King occasionally writes a historical song such as "Two Good Arms," he normally concentrates on current, pressing issues. Here are excerpts from a song, "America Needs a Raise," he wrote for a 1996 AFL-CIO campaign to raise wages:

America Needs a Raise
By Charlie King

Part-time, temporary, underage. America needs a raise.
Full-time, poverty, minimum wage. America needs a raise.
Layoffs, sweatshops, union busters. America needs a raise.
Don't want handouts. Give us justice! America needs a raise . . .

Shut-downs, mergers, deep down-size. America needs a raise.
NAFTA [North American Free Trade Agreement] runaway, profits rise. America needs a raise.
Outsource, cutback, privatize. America needs a raise.

Stand up! Fight back! Organize! America needs a raise . . .
We want fewer jails and better schools. America needs a raise.
Fewer guns, more learning tools. America needs a raise.
Less greed, less grind, more holidays. America needs a raise.
Forget the flowers. Howaboutaraise?!? America needs a raise.

Charlie works full-time at being a musical agitator. He has sung at benefits for the homeless, for oppressed peasants in Latin America, and for groups supporting Native Americans. Working with labor unions is special to him: "They are fighting, striking to help themselves, to control their own lives. There's a power to it you can't find anywhere else."

Bobby Cumberland

"Joe, without your help and encouragement, I would still be in my closet, instead of having the time of my life. Thank you," Bobby Cumberland said to me.

The Great Labor Arts Exchange in the Washington area was so successful that we decided to develop regional exchanges around the country. In 1986 we held one in Chicago for union members from the Midwest. While the forty-some participants gathered for the opening session I worked the room like a good politician needing to "connect" with my audience. I was scheduled to open the conference with "Songs and Stories of Labor History" and wanted to know as much as I could about the participants.

"What union are you with?" I asked. "Where is your plant located?" "What product do you make?" "What is your job in the plant?" "What is your position in the union?" Then, during my presentation I would use examples that had special meaning to someone in the audience.

While making my rounds I spied a handsome young couple sitting quietly by themselves in the back of the room: Bobby and Vickie Cumberland. He worked in a can-making factory in Kansas City and was a member of Steelworkers Local Union 8907. This is how our conversation went:

Glazer: How did you hear about the conference?
Cumberland: I saw a small notice in a labor paper. I wanted to see what this was all about, and my wife and I drove all night to get here.
Glazer: Do you sing or play an instrument?
Cumberland: I play the guitar and write and sing songs about safety on the job.
Glazer: How do your members like your songs?
Cumberland [in horror]: Oh, I never sing at the union hall. I never sing for people. I practice and sing in my basement garage.
Glazer: Well, I'd like to hear some of your songs, and I'm sure people here would, too. Maybe you'll sing for us.
Cumberland: I don't know about that. I think I'll just watch and listen.

Cumberland, a tall, slim, good-looking man in his thirties, was well-spoken but terrified to sing before a crowd. By the second day, after watching, listening, and chatting with the participants, he was relaxed enough to sing a few of his safety songs. I was moved and impressed by "The Finger Song":

The Finger Song
By Bobby Cumberland

One, two, three, four, five, six, seven,
Eight, nine, ten reasons to be careful.
Two, four, six, eight, ten: two hands.
Twelve reasons to pay attention: Oh yeah.
It's every little thing they do.

That makes life so pleasant for you.
Like, scratching your nose,
Filling up bowling ball holes,
That's why I say—

> Please be careful
> I'm sure you're gonna miss them.
> Please be careful
> You'll be sorry when they're gone.
> Please be careful
> I'm sure you're gonna miss them.
> It only takes a second and they're gone.

It's every little thing they touch
That shows you need them so much.
Like, tying your shoes,
Unwrapping candy bars, too,
Zipping your pants,
Think of romance.

> Chorus

When Bobby started counting out "one, two, three," he stopped playing the guitar and jabbed his fingers in the air, one by one. Any worker watching that performance would not likely be careless on the job.

I asked him how he got started singing about safety. "There was a terrible accident at work in 1982," he replied. "My friend and co-worker lost his hand, and to this day I say, 'But for the grace of God, there go I.' Shortly after this happened I noticed my lyrics changed. There was less about love and more about work and especially workplace safety and health. I didn't plan it that way. For the next four years until now I kept this music to myself because I thought it so odd."

After much persuasion he agreed to sing at the show, which was open to the public, on the last evening of the conference. Although he tried to back out when he saw nearly two hundred union members and their families filling the hall of the Amalgamated Clothing Workers' Union, I persisted. He brought the house down with his moving songs. This is one:

That's Why (Eye Wear)
By Bobby Cumberland

I love to watch baseball; see that curve ball break,
I like to see the catches those fielders make.

That's why I wear these glasses. That's why I keep them on.
It's radio games when your eyesight's gone.

I love to see the sunset and the sun rise
And the twinkle in my sweetheart's eyes.

That's why I wear these glasses. That's why I keep them on.
It's a real blind date when your eyesight's gone.

I don't want a dog to lead me all around,
I don't want a cane to have to find the ground.
Like to see the color of the food I eat,
And smiles of faces of friends I meet.

That's why I wear these glasses. That's why I keep them on.
You stay in the dark when your eyesight's gone.

Once he broke the barrier of shyness, Bobby's union singing and songwriting career took off. He sang at his own union meetings in Kansas City. He sang and talked regularly on a union radio program. He also became an expert on plant safety and Occupational Safety and Health Administration (OSHA) rules. He used statistics and simple props effectively and sang his songs and lectured about safety at regional and national conferences. He became a polished performer, socking points home briskly and clearly, sometimes with humor and sometimes with sadness or anger. No one would have guessed that a few years earlier he had been so frightened of an audience that he had to be bullied onto the stage.

On April 28, 1987, twenty-eight workers were killed when an office building under construction in Bridgeport, Connecticut, collapsed. When the AFL-CIO designated April 28 as Workers' Memorial Day to commemorate the tens of thousands who had been killed, injured, or permanently disabled each year, Bobby Cumberland wrote a song for the rallies held across the country on that date:

Workers' Memorial Day
By Bobby Cumberland

A Workers' Memorial Day
On April 28 the unions say
Maybe we can save a life this way
With a Workers' Memorial Day.

A hundred thousand fall each year,
That's what the figures show.

If we don't rise and take a stand
That number is sure to grow.

Chorus

Take the time to care.
Please, please, please be there.
Take the time to care.
Please, please be there.
On Workers' Memorial Day.

Chorus

One of Cumberland's most moving songs was inspired by a fire in 1991 at a non-union chicken processing plant in North Carolina, where twenty-five workers were burned to death. The plant had never been inspected by any state, federal, or local authority in the eleven years of its existence. There were no automatic fire extinguishers, illuminated exit signs, or fire drill procedures as required by state law. Doorways were blocked and exits were locked, reminiscent of the Triangle Shirtwaist fire of 1911, in which 146 young workers died.

Carolina Sadness (excerpts)
By Bobby Cumberland

Carolina sadness, Carolina blue,
Carolina sadness, we have paid more dues.

Why did you lock the doors, Roe? [the plant owner]
Why did you lock them tight?
Why did you lock the doors, Roe?
Do you think it right?

Chorus

Mothers without daughters,
Daughters without dads,
Brokenhearted lovers,
Roe, we are so sad.

Chorus

"It was so rewarding to sing about safety, health and the environment for my union brothers and sisters," Cumberland wrote upon returning from a Steelworkers Union conference in Cleveland in 1995. "To look into their faces and to know they are with me on these issues is a feeling that money can't buy. I guess those tunes weren't so odd after all."

Si Kahn

During the 1970s, friends in the Textile Workers Union kept telling me about Si Kahn, a guitar-picking organizer in the South who made up great songs about southern workers.

Kahn was a college graduate from the North who had never worked in a textile mill, but he was a good listener and a sensitive observer. Textile workers liked and trusted him. He quickly absorbed the folklore, culture, and customs of southern mill hands and was soon making up songs that graphically reflected conditions in the mills.

Textile workers who had breathed in cotton dust over the years would develop byssinosis—"brown lung disease" they called it. Kahn saw workers who could barely walk up a short flight of stairs. One, a textile worker at the J. P. Stevens mill in Roanoke Rapids, related, "You know, back before we heard what was wrong with us, people thought they just had asthma or something":

Brown Lung Blues
By Si Kahn

When the wind blows each morning
See them coming down the hill
Women walking with each other
Going to that cotton mill.

    Cotton mill I hear you calling
    Through the years that have passed on
    Now to work I am not able
    Where have all the pay days gone?

I would go to work each Monday
With that tightness in my chest
Now to work I am not able
When I sleep I get no rest.

    Chorus

Now I watch them from my window
Think about this old mill town
Forty years I was a spinner
Till the brown lung laid me down.

    Chorus

Now I listen to my children
Begging for a pair of shoes

Got no way to make a living
All I got's those brown lung blues.

Chorus

I finally met Kahn in 1979 in Spartanburg, South Carolina, where we were both singing at a large rally in the campaign to organize J. P. Stevens workers. He was thirty-five at the time, a tall, trim, curly-headed man with glasses and a ready smile. I was expecting a singer with a big, booming, picket-line voice. But that wasn't Si Kahn. Although he had led singing at many a union rally, his style worked best in a living room or an intimate setting. He was a story-teller with a guitar, not a cheerleader.

Kahn had grown up in what he calls the "Deep North" in the town of State College, home of Pennsylvania State University, where his father, a rabbi, worked. He anticipated my first question:

I'm sure you want to know, What is a nice Jewish boy doing singing in a place like this? The story starts with my parents. They had a sharp sense of the difference be-tween right and wrong, and of one's personal responsibility to do something about injustice, the outsider, the oppressed, the refugee. And our house became a refuge for all of them.

When the first black football players were recruited by Penn State and all the bar-bers in town claimed they "could not cut Negro hair," our kitchen became a barber shop. When the first refugees from the failed Hungarian uprising in 1956 came to town, our study became a hotel.

When Kahn graduated from Harvard University in 1966, he didn't know what he wanted to work at but he knew it wasn't medieval history and litera-ture, his major field of study. "The lessons I had learned at home proved more powerful than the lessons I had learned at Harvard," he said.

In the summer of 1965 he had gone south to work for the Student Nonvio-lent Coordinating Committee (SNCC), the student wing of the southern civ-il rights movement. There he helped blacks in Forrest City, Arkansas, register to vote. Except for a final year at Harvard, he has lived and worked in the South ever since.

While working in the civil rights movement in the South, Kahn could see the vital role old gospel songs and new freedom songs, many of them based on the old gospel tunes, played in daily life. He also saw how music brought people together, how it made them feel strong, and how it sustained them in adversity.

He remembered all that when he went to work in Kentucky with the Unit-ed Mine Workers of America (UMWA) in 1973 and in 1975 in North Carolina for the merged Amalgamated Clothing and Textile Workers Union. (Called ACTWU at the time, this union subsequently joined with the International Ladies' Garment Workers' Union and is now called UNITE!—the United Needletrades, Industrial and Textile Employees.) He wrote songs about working conditions, about the mill hands' lives, and about building a union. Kahn is good at working a meaningful, poetic phrase into a simple, folklike tune and developing a song that is easy to sing and remember. When a worker thrown out of work by a mill shut-down lamented, "It's so quiet, I can't sleep," Kahn was inspired to write his best-known song, "Aragon Mill":

Aragon Mill
By Si Kahn

At the east end of town, at the foot of the hill,
Stands a chimney so tall that says Aragon Mill.
But there's no smoke at all coming out of the stack,
For the mill has pulled out and it ain't coming back.

Now I'm too old to change and I'm too young to die,
And there's no place to go for my old man and I.
There's no children at all in the narrow, empty streets.
Now the looms have all gone, it's so quiet I can't sleep.

And the only tune I hear is the sound of the wind,
As it blows through the town, weave and spin, weave and spin.

Now the mill has shut down. It's the only life I know.
Tell me, where will I go? Tell me, where will I go?
And the only tune I hear is the sound of the wind,
As it blows through the town, weave and spin, weave and spin.

In 1980 Kahn left the labor movement to found and direct Grassroots Leadership, headquartered in Charlotte, North Carolina. The group helps communities and local groups across the South organize on issues such as civil rights, voting rights, literacy, health care, job discrimination, and the environment. In "People Like You," Kahn pays a moving tribute to those who have worked for such causes over the years:

People Like You
By Si Kahn

Old fighter,
You sure took it on the chin.
Where'd you ever get the strength to stand,

Never giving up or giving in?
You know, I just want to shake your hand—because . . .

People like you
Help people like me go on, go on,
Because people like you
Help people like me go on, go on.

Old battler,
With a scar for every town.
You thought you were no better than the rest;
You wore your colors every way but down,
And all you ever gave us was your best—but you know that.

Chorus

Old dreamer,
With a world in every thought,
Where'd you get the vision to keep on?
You sure gave back as good as what you got.
I hope that when my time is almost gone . . . they'll say that . . .

People like me
Helped people like you go on, go on.
Because people like you
Helped people like me go on, go on, go on.

Kahn still works closely with unions and has been voted the poet laureate
of the North Carolina AFL-CIO. He responds quickly to requests for a song
needed for an important union struggle. In 1987 he wrote a song for AFL-CIO
unions conducting a national Jobs with Justice campaign:

Jobs with Justice (excerpts)
By Si Kahn

Who owns the future, who owns the earth
Who owns our labor, who says what it's worth
Who owns our children, who owns our lives
Who decides if we get jobs with justice?

Justice, justice, justice
We want jobs with justice, justice, justice
We want jobs with . . .

Good union wages, the right to organize
Safety conditions, we're fighting for our lives
Health care and pensions, that's what we mean
When we say that we want jobs with justice.

Si Kahn has performed at hundreds of concerts all over the United States and in Canada and Europe and has also recorded many albums, yet he doesn't consider himself a performer-musician. He does acknowledge being a songwriter because he has written more than five hundred songs. He calls the music a "hobby that got out of hand. Organizing is the work I do, and music is one way I do it. I am an organizer who sings." Kahn is an excellent organizer and has made Grassroots Leadership an effective organization in many southern communities. But my guess is that more people will remember him for the "hobby that got out of hand" than for his organizing talents.

Elise Bryant

Elise Bryant introduced rap and dramatic chants into the folk song–style repertoire. She is a regal, imposingly handsome woman of African American descent and has a powerful, resonant voice and commanding stage presence. She sings and does dramatic performances, alone or with a group, at union rallies and meetings and for community groups. I met her in 1985 when she attended her first Labor Arts Exchange at the George Meany Center.

She electrified the other participants with her strength and drama and brought a new, stirring quality to our program, not only because she was black but also because her performance projected urgency and excitement. Until that time we had not been successful in recruiting African American trade unionists to the Arts Exchange. Almost all participants were white, and they sang primarily in the folk music tradition of Woody Guthrie and Pete Seeger. Later performers played electric guitars and sang union songs with a rock and roll beat, attracting younger trade unionists.

Born in Detroit in 1951, Elise was the sixth of seven children. Her father worked on the line at Ford's huge River Rouge complex and was a member of United Auto Workers Local 600. Her mother cleaned the homes of the wealthy. When I asked about music in the family's home, she said: "My father was a great dancer and enjoyed all the big band music of Duke Ellington and Count Basie. My mother couldn't carry a tune in a bucket. We mostly listened to Motown and sang gospel music."

After high school, Elise attended the University of Michigan in 1968, but she wasn't ready for college and dropped out. Twenty-three years went by before she graduated with a bachelor of fine arts in theater.

She worked at a student-run university bookstore, where she helped found a union. Labor music and labor drama came later. "I don't think I heard a labor song until I attended my first summer school for union workers back in

```
          B & G
       RECEIPT #6785
 me  to George Meany Center
 ok Store and Gift Shop.

  Jennifer
 02 15:08:34/15:09:21

 : angel w/ union      12.00
 rs Troubadour         23.00
 o: Working for v        5.00
                      _____
 Total                  40.00
                         2.00
                      _____
 al                     42.00
 By:VISA                42.00

 k You Please Come Again.
```

1979 when I was twenty-eight years old," she said. A turning point came in 1982, when Hy Kornbluh, director of the Labor Study Center at the University of Michigan, saw Elise act in a community theater and hired her to put together a labor theater troupe using music and drama.

"I loved the old union songs like 'Union Maid' and 'Solidarity Forever,'" she said, "but I felt that we needed music that was contemporary and reflected the cultural style of the day. At that time rap was becoming popular so our group decided we would write a labor rap song and thus 'The Work Rap Song' was born":

The Work Rap Song
By Elise Bryant and Friends

We work!
Jump out the bed at 7 A.M.
Wash your face and get to The Place
By 8 A.M. boss is on my case,
Says to me, "You'd better pick up the pace!"

We work!
Now it's 9 A.M. I'm working on time
Double time, triple time, overtime!
Working nine hours a day—six days a week
While my friends are still on the street.

We work!
10:15, the rat race is on.
Your break's so short you miss using the phone,
Lunch time comes and goes real quick,
Gulp it down and then back on the stick.

We work!
1 o'clock, four hours to go.
You're working hard, but the time goes slow.
5 o'clock! Time to stop!
Thank God it's over, 'cause I'm 'bout to drop.

We work!
Home by 6, too tired to cook,
Pick up the kids, drop off a book,
Keeping busy, no time for the blues,
Fall asleep while watching the news (zzzzzz).

We work!
Midnights, afternoons or 9 to 5,
All God's children got to work to survive.

We're the muscle and brains that help America thrive,
We're the backbone of the nation and that's no jive!
We work!

[At this point, each member of the troupe calls out his or her name and occupation. After each name the group chants "We work!" in unison.]

We work!—Elise Bryant, theatre director
We work!—Kinda Frederick, programmer
We work!—Roger Kerson, journalist
We work!—Yvonne Lockwood, folklorist
We work!—Majidah Muhammed, childcare worker
We work!—Dock Riley, truck driver
We work!—Shirley Poling, high-low driver
We work!—Pat Skrobe, assembler
We work!—Rae Sovereign, painter
We work!—Jamie Crawford, autoworker

We're the muscle and brains that help America thrive,
We're the backbone of the nation and that's no jive!
We work!

Bryant and her troupe chant the song, rapping it out while performing a tightly choreographed pantomime that complements the lyrics. The performance is charged with the energy Bryant has infused into the performers. It is dynamite, labor show business, and worthy of a Broadway production. The audience goes crazy.

The troupe Bryant organized is called Workers' Lives/Workers' Stories—Theatre by Workers, for Workers, about Workers. The group consists of factory workers, service and white-collar workers, and professionals. Six to eight regulars perform with Bryant in union halls and community centers and at strikes and rallies. Most had little or no musical or stage training, but under Bryant's no-nonsense direction they have been whipped into a highly effective dramatic musical team that portrays workers' lives on the shop floor with strong realism. "The Workin' for a Livin' Chant" is a favorite:

The Workin' for a Livin' Chant
By Dwight Peterson

All: Beat, beatin'! Work, workin'!
      Beat, beatin'! Work, workin'!

Leads: Beat, beatin' to the rhythm of the daily grind,
        Work, workin' to the groan of the assembly line.

Beat, beatin' to the rhythm of the daily grind.
Work, workin' to the groan of the assembly line.

Lead 1:   Waste your body and rot your mind!
Lead 2:   Give it up for the almighty dollar sign!
Lead 3:   You get what's yours and I'll get what's mine!
Lead 4:   Give your soul to the company time!
Lead 5:   Workin' for a livin' to feed my kids!
Lead 6:   Doin' what my father did!

Group A: Groan and work and body rot
           And beat and sweat and awful hot!

Group B: Beat, beatin' to the rhythm of the daily grind,
           Work, workin' to the groan of the assembly line.

Elise Bryant can sing all kinds of labor songs with the best of them but says, "Now I mostly stick to writing plays and poems, but more often I find myself writing chants for labor rallies and strikes." Her colleagues also contribute chants:

Let's Get Organized
By Crystal Harding
(echo response in parentheses)

Brother (Brother) there's no time to fight.
Sister (Sister) together we'll make it right.
People (People) we can all share the prize.
So we gotta—

    Get it together, hold that line,
    And let's get organized!

I know (I know) we can make them see.
I know (I know) good things come from unity.
I know (I know) some day they'll hear our cries.
So we gotta—

    Chorus

I know it won't be easy,
I know it takes some time.
There's a mountain in the pathway,
But it's a mountain we can climb!
We'll all be better off in the end,
And you'll be glad you're in it, friend!

So—let's get organized.
Let's get organized.
Let's get organized.
Get it together, hold that line,
And let's get—organ—ized!

Chorus

People (People) there's no time to fight.
People (People) together we'll make it right.
People (People) we can all share the prize.
So we gotta—

Chorus

I know it won't be easy,
I know it takes some time.
There's a mountain in the pathway,
But it's a mountain we can climb!
We'll all be better off in the end,
And you'll be glad you're in it, friend!

So—let's get organized.
Let's get organized.
Let's get organized.
Get it together, hold that line,
And let's get—organ—ized!

Elise related the most memorable experience of her career in labor, music, and drama:

> In 1988, Bernie Firestone, one of the top leaders of the Amalgamated Clothing Workers' Union in the Midwest, asked if he could join Workers' Lives/Workers' Stories. I was hesitant at first. No one of his stature had ever asked to be part of our group, but he convinced me to give him a chance.
> His first performance was to be his last. In September of 1988 Firestone was shot and killed by a disturbed member of his own union, who later committed suicide. I spoke to Bernie the night before he died, and he said, "I'll see you at rehearsal tomorrow." At the rehearsal that night we held hands, spoke to each other about what Bernie, a true labor leader and hero, meant to us and sang "May the Work That I Have Done":

May the Work That I Have Done
Adapted by Bruce Thomas from a Traditional Song

May the work that I have done speak for me.
May the work that I have done speak for me.

If I fall short of my goal
Someone else will take a hold.
May the work that I have done speak for me.

May the movement I have built speak for me.
May the movement I have built speak for me.
If I fall short of my goal
Someone else will take a hold
May the movement I have built speak for me.

May the songs that I have sung speak for me.
May the songs that I have sung speak for me.
If I fall short of my goal
Someone else will take a hold.
May the songs that I have sung speak for me.

[Repeat first verse.]

In 1998 Bryant left Michigan to become the cultural director at the George Meany Center, a job that would enable her to reach trade unionists from all over the country with her spirit and dynamism.

Tom Juravich

Tom Juravich is a most unusual "new voice of labor." He has a Ph.D. in sociology and is a professor at the University of Massachusetts, where he holds an impressive title: research director at the university's Labor Relations and Research Center. But you can also find him at a coal miners' convention backed by a five-piece rock and roll group or marching and singing on a picket line of striking steelworkers.

Juravich is a burly man of average height with a good head of curly hair and a short beard. He favors well-worn jeans and a dark work shirt. He is not a shouter, even on a picket line, but his warm, sincere baritone cuts through a room clearly, and he has no trouble moving an audience with his message.

At the university, Juravich conducts research on union organizing, collective bargaining, and labor history. He teaches classes in the graduate program and out in the field for trade union leaders and activists. His schedule is flexible enough to permit him to take on singing engagements, usually with unions, up and down the East Coast and occasionally around the country. He has sung at hundreds of union rallies, strikes, and conventions.

Juravich feels right at home with coal miners and steelworkers, his academic credentials notwithstanding. He grew up in a blue-collar family in upstate New

York, and his father, the son of Ukrainian immigrants, was an active officer in his union at the Revere Copper and Brass plant. At age thirteen Juravich had his own band, "The Strikers." He worked one summer at Revere Copper and Brass, long enough to get a good taste of factory life. His interest in singing was ignited during his college days:

> In college in the 1970s I did some folk singing. I listened to records by Woody Guthrie, Pete Seeger, and Malvina Reynolds and began to appreciate the "use value" of their songs. This music has relevance. It could change people's lives. It opened up a whole new world to me. At the University of Massachusetts at Amherst, where I went to graduate school, I began to sing on picket lines as well as in coffee houses. Before long, I was traveling around with guys who were autoworkers, not my classmates, and we were driving not to a concert or a party but to Detroit or to Bridgeport, Connecticut, to a rally. We had a purpose, an idea. It was very exciting.

In 1980 Juravich became intensely involved in a strike of nearly one hundred UAW workers at the Sterling Radiator Company in Westfield, Massachusetts. He sang on their picket lines and at their union meetings, getting to know the strikers and their families intimately and feeling the pride and pain of their long struggle. He also produced a 45-rpm and a ten-inch LP record that included "Trying to Break My Union," written for the strike:

Trying to Break My Union (excerpts)
By Tom Juravich

They're trying to break my union.
They're trying to break my life.
And take all that I've worked for
For my kids and my wife
I was just getting where
Things were starting to go my way.
And now these high-paid lawyers
And these lousy scabs
Try and take my job away.

The strike lasted more than a year and was ultimately lost. It was a heartbreaker for twenty-seven-year-old Juravich, and he still feels the pain of the defeat. The strike taught him two things about labor music. The first was that it had the power to rally workers to their cause, to build their solidarity and spirit, and to strengthen their determination to achieve justice. The second thing was that labor music also had its limits. Pitted against a powerful company determined to break a union and willing to spend whatever it took to do the job, enthusiasm and stirring rallies were not enough.

To conduct the research for his doctoral dissertation, Tom decided to go into a factory instead of a library. "If I was going to write serious studies about workers and their job problems," he reasoned, "I ought to get some serious exposure to workers right on their jobs." In 1980 he spent a year as a trouble-shooting mechanic in a non-union plant in Holyoke, Massachusetts, to gather material.

I asked whether he had difficulty "passing" as a worker in the plant. He was able to get by, he replied, because he had worked with machines when he was young. Some of the workers had trouble figuring him out, however. One wondered why he always carried a pencil and a notebook. (Juravich used the privacy of the men's room to make fieldnotes.) Another suspected that he might not be a legitimate mechanic because he didn't work on his car as the other mechanics did.

At the end of the year he had the raw material for his dissertation, "Chaos on the Shop Floor." And chaos it was. Low wages and haphazard, seat-of-the-pants, know-it-all management led to high turnover, waste, and poor productivity. Supervisors paid no attention to the workers except to push them for more production. The ideas and opinions of those on the line didn't count. Years later Juravich recalled his experience: "I got up every day at 6:15 and went into this little scab shop and repaired machines, came home at 4 o'clock and had a beer and supper. After being at school and out of touch, it really gave me a sense of how many working people spend their lives." The experience burned into his memory and became a part of him. It touched every labor song he wrote and affected every line he sang at labor rallies.

When I asked Tom Juravich about the most memorable experience of the many times he had sung for unions, he answered without hesitation:

> The Pittston coal strike in southwestern Virginia in 1988. I was at the first big rally at the Wise County Fairgrounds. This was probably two or three months into the strike. It was pouring rain. The miners, their wives and kids stood there in the downpour listening to Richard Trumka, the Mine Workers' president, make his speech. I mean it was *pouring*, but eight to ten thousand people stood there as if it wasn't raining at all. Then I got up to sing.
>
> Earlier a miner had told me in disgust about the management at Pittston. "No man would treat us like they have been. These guys are nothing but some roughneck boys." I took that as my theme and wrote "Tell the Boys at Pittston" and sang it to the rain-soaked crowd.

Tell the Boys at Pittston
By Tom Juravich

> Tell the boys at Pittston
> We're gonna stand our ground
> Tell the boys at Pittston
> No one will turn us around.
> Tell the boys at Pittston
> That we're here to stay.
> Tell the boys at Pittston
> We're the UMWA.

We're brothers and we're sisters standing here today
We're here to tell the bosses we'll not run away.
So let me hear your voices ring throughout the land.
Tell the boys at Pittston it's here we'll take our stand.

> Chorus

"When I finished singing," Juravich recalled, "that silent crowd came alive. They stomped their feet; they raised their fists; they whooped and hollered their defiance of the company. You can't buy an experience like that. It's something you don't forget."

Although some of Juravich's most exciting moments have involved singing to coal miners, he realizes that the economy has changed radically:

> The United Mine Workers used to have six hundred thousand workers. Now they're down to a hundred thousand. The old industrial model is a white guy in a blue shirt, a steelworker, or a miner, or a factory worker. But most people don't do that kind of work anymore. I don't think we understand that much yet about these new workers and the conditions they work under. Data entry, food service, telephone sales. When you work all alone behind a cubicle it's harder to see what you have in common with somebody else.

Juravich has captured some of the problems these changes have brought about:

VDT (Video Display Terminal)
By Tom Juravich

You don't know my name but you sure know me.
I work in New York, Boston, and D.C.
I used to be a typist, a secretary,
But now I enter data on my VDT.

> I tell you it's not like I thought it would be
> It's hell to make a living on a VDT.

I'm not here to say that typing was fun,
But at least I could see the work that I'd done.
And the boss couldn't check my productivity
By punching up my number on his VDT.

Chorus

My supervisor says that it's good for me.
She shows me a study done at M.I.T.
You can see what it's done to my eyes.
Heaven only knows what it's doing inside.

Chorus

When you think about union what comes to your mind?
A man driving a truck or working the line.
But if you've ever spent time behind a VDT
You know, no one needs a union more than me.

Chorus

Juravich began as a traditional folksinger, with an acoustic guitar and standard union songs like "Solidarity Forever" and "We Shall Not Be Moved." "But times and jobs change," he observes, "and we've got to change also. Now I am experimenting with different bands. There is room for all forms of music in our work. And we've got to be singing songs that are relevant to the work our people are doing today."

14

New Voices, Part 2

John O'Connor

"When workers hear labor songs for the first time," John O'Connor points out, "there is a special excitement, and I can feel it in my bones." O'Connor has been furnishing that special excitement for more than two decades, singing labor songs for workers and others who need a lift and making up new songs when the occasion calls for it.

I first heard O'Connor sing during the 1980s when he was about thirty. He was average-sized and low-key, with a pleasant voice. He didn't shout or growl on stage, and he didn't jump up and down or wave his arms. Yet he sang some of the hardest-hitting labor songs that audiences were likely to hear. O'Connor stood up in front of the microphone, plucking his acoustic guitar and singing his moving, finely crafted songs to lovely, easy-to-remember melodies. The message was direct, and the poetry was appealing. Every word was clear. The audience loved it.

O'Connor grew up in the Cedar Falls–Waterloo area in northern Iowa. In high school he listened to the Kingston Trio and Woody Guthrie, and their guitar-picking folk styles had a strong influence on him. He attended a community college briefly but found nothing there that interested him. He spent the next eight or nine years working at various unskilled jobs: construction and factory work and washing dishes at a local university. At different times, however, he was active in the International Association of Machinists and the State, County and Municipal Workers' Union. He began singing at union meetings, strikes, and conventions.

One of his jobs was in the pressroom at the Waterloo Register Company, which manufactured heat and ventilation registers. It was a typical monotonous, repetitive, assembly-line job that could drive a sensitive soul up a wall. O'Connor did not last long, but the experience must have stayed with him.

While he drove across Pennsylvania fifteen years later the scene in the press-room at the Register factory flashed into his head. Before traveling many more miles he had worked out a song:

The Pressroom
By John O'Connor

Got me a job in '63
At the Register factory
They put me on a stool on the press room floor
To run this machine forevermore.

    Umchunk, umchunk, all day long
    Umchunk, umchunk, was my song.
    If you think your life is a bore
    You've never been on the press room floor.

Five hundred pieces every hour
The foreman says, "Say, you'll go far.
If you can make it 6–0–2,
There's another machine that's waiting for you."

    Chorus

The days passed slowly by it seems
At night the pressroom filled my dreams
I got a vacation once a year
But even at the beach this sound I'd hear.

    Chorus

I married a machine that cannot feel,
My kids were little pieces of steel.
The foreman must have been their grandpa
'Cause when the bin filled up he said, "Ah."

    Chorus

Now times have changed, machines have too
One day they said, "That's all for you;
Modernization's where it's at,
There'll be a computer where you once sat." [No chorus.]

Umchunk, chunk, no more for me,
I'll sit at home and watch TV.
I'll collect unemployment for a while
And get me a job that has some style. [No chorus.]

So I retrained in '83
No more pressroom, not for me.

I wear a white shirt and my hands are clean.
They put me in front of a TV screen.

Oo peep, oo peep, all day long
Oo peep, oo peep, is my song
If you think your life is a bore
You've never been on the high-tech floor.
Oo peep, oo peep, all day long
Oo peep, oo peep, is my song
And my life is still a bore
And I'm paid much less than ever before.

The area around Waterloo was meat-packing country. Each day thousands of hogs and cattle were driven into one end of the huge Rath, Morrell, and Wilson killing factories, to come out the other end as sides of beef and pork bound for the country's supermarkets, butcher shops, and restaurants.

O'Connor never worked in packing plants, but through conversations with friends and neighbors he became well acquainted with the mean jobs of workers who turned squalling pigs and bellowing cattle into food for the nation's tables. "I remember my girlfriend's father coming home from working in the Rath packing plant after standing in the kill [room] all day," he recalled. "His legs were in terrible shape. If you stuck a finger in the flesh of the leg, the flesh would stay indented. The union had made many improvements in working conditions, but it was still a taxing job. You worked with sharp knives on a fast-moving line. The floor was slippery with blood. The stench was always in your nostrils."

Years later, in 1986, O'Connor was back in the Midwest and singing for striking Morrell workers. "I heard complaints about something called carpal tunnel syndrome," he told me. "It seems that workers who performed repetitive motions—maybe a thousand or two thousand times a day—developed such shooting pains in their hands, wrists, and arms that they could not work. Workers had to wear protective bandages. Physical therapy helped somewhat sometimes. One or more operations on the hand were necessary for some workers. I wrote this song to tell their story."

Carpal Tunnel
By John O'Connor

Early in the morning at the start of the day
I force my fingers 'round the handle of the blade.
I start in to cuttin' just as fast as I can.
By the end of the day I can hardly move my hands.

I got that old carpal tunnel and my hands won't move
But the foreman tells me to stay in the groove
You cut that cattle as fast as I do
You get that carpal tunnel too.

Oh, ten years ago I started in the kill
Now ten years later, well, I got my fill.
But I keep on cuttin' though the line's twice as fast.
Well, I don't know how long these arms will last.

   Chorus

I work with a knife and a blade in my hand
I cut them cows with a big iron band.
But it feels like a knife is cuttin' me all the time
Cause the carpal tunnel lives in the big nerve line.

   Chorus

Now I'll go in for an operation once more
But I'll come right back to the killing floor,
And I'll tell them darling children of mine
"Don't you ever go to work on the packinghouse line."

   Chorus

O'Connor crisscrossed the country, singing old and new songs for workers and other groups in need of inspiration. It was a hard way to make a living, and he had to take part-time jobs to help pay the rent. He also served as president of Local 1000 of the American Federation of Musicians, a special nationwide local of solo traveling musicians. John made such a good impression at this nonpaying job that in May 1996 he was hired as a full-time union organizer of the large and powerful Musicians Local 802 in New York City.

Although he has become more secure financially, O'Connor will always remember his troubadour days and plans to continue singing when he can:

> I remember singing in Olympia, Washington, to a thousand construction workers—all in hard hats and work clothes. They had come to the capitol to protest a proposal to eliminate government-designed "prevailing wage rates" on construction jobs. This would have meant deep wage cuts for many construction workers.
>
> Construction workers are not supposed to be much on singing, and I'm sure that most of them had never heard a labor song, but they bellowed out the choruses of "Solidarity Forever" and other union songs with spirit and gusto. There were some good rabble-rousing speeches by union officials, but everyone agreed the music made the rally. It warmed my heart.

Another memorable event for O'Connor was participating in *Links on a Chain*, a traveling program that included songs and stories about the labor and civil rights movements and the way they are connected:

> I toured with this program, accompanied by David Sawyer, a black folk and gospel singer, through many small industrial towns in Iowa. We were a little nervous about how we would be received since the audiences were almost exclusively white, perhaps even rednecks who would be turned off by any program that emphasized civil rights. But I was pleasantly surprised at the positive impact this program had. I know we got a lot of workers to re-think their traditional prejudices.

My favorite John O'Connor song is "The Triangle Fire," which commemorates one of the most infamous industrial tragedies in U.S. history. He explains, "These are thoughts based on an eyewitness account. One hundred and forty-six were killed, most of them young girls. Victims of business as usual":

The Triangle Fire
By John O'Connor

Come gather around and I'll sing you a song
Of a sight that I saw long ago.
The weather was fair down in Washington Square
It was spring, I was on my way home.
It was 1911 on March twenty-five
I remember as if yesterday.
At the Triangle Shirt Waist Company where the girls
Were all waiting to pick up their pay.

"Fire!" was the cry from the windows up high
I saw, but I could not believe,
Two girls on the ledge as they jumped off the edge
Into the arms of eternity.

On the eighth and the ninth and the tenth floor, this factory
Of workers from the garment trade
Stuffed them into the rooms where so many were doomed
At the end of the Sabbath day.
The doors were all locked and the fire escapes weak,
The building was a trap and a terror
Just to save a few bucks for the rich run-amucks
Who made money from the lives of young girls.

Chorus

What choice for a young girl of sixteen or so
But the sweatshop for the shirtwaists they sell?
And what choice for a soul in a ten-story hole
But the pavement or the fires of hell?
Now the question still looms in the workshops and rooms
The question, I'll pose it to you.
When you stand to defend all the capitalists and their friends
What price for the profits of few?

> And "Murder," I'll cry till the day that I die
> For I saw but I could not believe,
> Two girls on the ledge as they jumped from the edge
> Into the arms of eternity.

After listening to "The Triangle Fire" and other problem-specific songs written and sung by O'Connor, it is easy to understand why he moves labor groups and why, of all the organizations for which he has sung, he most enjoys appearing before them. It's likely that he'll come up with a hatful of new songs for his musicians' union and, whenever possible, for other workers as well.

Julie McCall

As a labor union activist who uses music to motivate, inspire, and rally workers, Julie McCall is unique: She does not accompany herself on the guitar, she does not perform as a solo act, and she does not compose her own music. Her specialty is adapting folk songs or well-known pop tunes. She teaches them in a short time to union members at a strike or a rally, and almost immediately everyone can sing a song that tells the workers' story with humor and fighting spirit.

McCall's trade union career began in 1974 when she was a twenty-eight-year-old clerk at the Washington Hospital Center in Washington, D.C. She helped organize other workers into Local 722 of the Service Employees International Union (SEIU). She also became, in turn, a shop steward, a member of the executive board, and business manager of the local.

She began to use adapted melodies several years later. As she describes it, "We had a rally coming up to put pressure on the hospital to sign an improved union contract. We had trouble generating interest in our meetings, so a group of us wrote a series of song parodies and satirical skits about the hospital. That was in 1980. Prior to that I had done a few picket line songs during a strike by the nurses." One of her first songs, "Your Nursing Heart," was set to the tune of "Your Cheating Heart" by Hank Williams:

Your nursing heart must be your guide
In your profession you must have pride
To care for the injured and tend to the ill
So they will survive to pay their bill.

Julie's background did not indicate that she would become active in unions. She was raised during the 1950s in Middletown, Ohio, a conservative, anti-union town. Her parents were teachers and also anti-union. Other influences prevailed, however. "I was inspired," she says, "by the political and social messages I heard in the folk music of the 1960s while attending Ohio State University. Those messages made a lot of sense to me. Later, I found myself using 'music with a message' in my work with the union."

A good example of her style is a song about the Avondale shipyard in New Orleans. Avondale was heavily subsidized by the U.S. Navy, which continued to do so even though the company brazenly violated the law and refused to bargain with workers, who had voted overwhelmingly for a union.

We're Gonna Get a Union at Avondale
Words: Julie McCall
Music: "Joshua Fit the Battle of Jericho"

Five years ago we organized and voted
"Union yes!"
But shameless union-busting is what
Avondale does best.

>We're gonna get a union at Avondale,
>Avondale, Avondale,
>We're gonna get a union at Avondale,
>It's our right to organize!

"Profits before safety"—that's
Avondale's creed
Your life's not worth a nickel when
You're ruled by corporate greed.

>Chorus

They're bankrolled by the navy and we
Have had our fill
Of seeing our tax dollars go to pay
Lawbreakers' bills.

>Chorus

So brothers, sisters, join us!
Support the workers' cause
It's time the U.S. Navy
Showed respect for labor laws.

Chorus

I found one of her songs particularly useful when I was asked to sing at a rally in the courtyard of the Department of Labor. The event was a protest against using child labor in Pakistan and other Asian countries in the manufacture of soccer balls:

Foul Ball
Words: Julie McCall
Music: "My Bonnie Lies over the Ocean"

In countries far over the ocean
In sweatshops and dark factories
Are children who don't have a notion
Of how it would feel to run free.

Foul ball! Foul ball!
All voices are needed, both large and small
Foul ball! Foul ball!
We're singing for justice for all.

The soccer balls players are choosing
Are stitched by the smallest of hands
The children whose labor they're using
Need us to start taking a stand.

Chorus

We don't know their names or their races
Their language to us may sound strange
But kids deserve rights in *all* places
And we can all help make a change.

Chorus

Over the years Julie McCall has written scores of songs. Just give her the principal issues in a strike or contract dispute, and in an hour or two she will come up with lyrics set to a catchy tune that will be more effective in building workers' solidarity than any rousing speech made by a union leader. I asked her to describe her most satisfying experiences in using music to build union solidarity:

In May of 1994 I did a song-writing workshop at the international convention of the Brotherhood of Maintenance of Way Employees. I taught a group of twenty of those railroad workers who had never written a song before to write a song parody. They performed it in front of the entire convention of four hundred delegates. The place went wild, and we were called back to do the song again to close the convention. The members who wrote the song were very nervous about performing it the first time and were astonished when people sang along, applauded and whistled, and danced in the aisles.

One of the other most moving moments for me was in 1989 when I heard the striking Pittston coal miners in West Virginia sing the Christmas parodies from the colorful songbook I had put together for them with the aid of Mike Konopacki, a top labor cartoonist and artist. The miners had asked for the songs so they could go "caroling" at the homes of coal company executives. I wrote a half-dozen parodies of well-known Christmas tunes. The Labor Heritage Foundation printed them in a colorful booklet, and it was distributed to the miners. The miners sang the songs in the snow and cold at the executives' homes, on the picket line, and in the union hall. The music helped to lift their spirits during a grim Christmas season.

For the union's "carols," McCall wrote "I'm Dreaming of a Fair Contract" to the music of "White Christmas." In a version of "God Rest Ye Merry Gentlemen" ("Arrest Those Union Gentlemen"), she took swipes at the state troopers who went out of their way to harass the Pittston strikers:

Arrest those union gentlemen, arrest the women too
Just lock up everyone in town who disagrees with you
Ignore the rights of many to protect those of a few
Pittston's "finest" as troopers are employed
They are employed
Pittston's "finest" as troopers are employed.

Julie McCall does not think of herself as a musical star performing before huge crowds of cheering workers. She thinks of herself as a teacher. "Most of the union members I work with have better voices than me," she explains, "and they are better acquainted with the local problems than I am. My stuff is simple and direct. All they need are two things to make them good performers—one is technique and the other is confidence. I teach the technique, and once they grasp that they readily develop the confidence to perform effectively before their fellow workers."

One outstanding example of Julie McCall's teaching efforts is the program she developed with the paraprofessional division of the American Federation of Teachers (AFT). Her experience with paraprofessionals ("paras") began in 1987, when AFT organizer Tom Moran asked her to help develop a workshop,

"Say It in a Song or Skit," for their annual conference held in Washington, D.C. The show that workshop participants put on for two hundred delegates on "Solidarity Night" was so popular that it was being continued at workshops ten years later. The event gets bigger and better. Some workers are so fired up from the experience that they return to next year's conference with new songs and skits already prepared.

McCall has led dozens of programs across the country, but she is especially enthusiastic about working with paras. "I have rarely seen the kind of excitement and spirit engendered by the paras," she says. "The crowd is always on its feet, clapping, dancing, and singing along." In a skit during the 1998 show, for example, union members broke into a rousing version of a popular dance tune after defeating an evil boss:

Come on, everybody now, it's time to join the union
When we get together all the workers will be groovin'.
Brothers and the sisters going to get us all a-movin'.
Hey—join the union!

"I've been looking for a way to put some life into our meetings," one excited participant said as he went from row to row after the performance, collecting extra songbooks to take back to his local. "My members won't believe this—I'm going to have them all dancing to union music." That's the kind of enthusiasm Julie McCall generates.

Larry Penn

Larry Penn, a trucker who put in almost forty years behind the wheel of many different trucks before he retired, is another contemporary composer and singer of songs for workers. He's lived through it all: long hauls and short ones, good weather and bad, detours and hazards, dangerous drivers, and the monotony of wheels hitting the road.

Penn's interest in singing was jump-started when he ran across a Leadbelly record. He invested $17 in a guitar, bought an instruction book of guitar chords, and started singing folk songs. Soon he was writing his own.

The editor of the labor newspaper of the Allied Industrial Workers, Ken Germanson, is a neighbor of Penn's in Milwaukee. He liked Larry's style and invited him to sing at a union training school at the University of Wisconsin–Madison. Larry learned some labor songs for the occasion to go with those he had written about truckers and railroads. His songs described working conditions but not unions. Penn was a hit, and his union connection was launched.

When I read about Larry Penn in Germanson's newspaper, I called German-son to track Larry down. Fortunately, I was scheduled to sing at a conference of the Illinois Labor History Society near Chicago, and I arranged for him to be invited.

Larry was fifty when I met him in 1976. He had been driving a truck for more than twenty-five years and still got up at 5:30 A.M. to haul steel for one of Milwaukee's larger steel warehouses. He was a big, burly man with huge hands that made his guitar look small when he held it. He was weather-beaten from years on the road. Although he appeared to be tough, he was actually a gentle man and spoke softly. His singing voice, however, was gruff and gravelly and easily filled a big room. And what songs! He could turn day-to-day experiences into poetry.

Larry and I talked after his performance. He had written songs about working conditions, job safety, unemployment, and all kinds of injustice, but he wrote his first true union song after he sang at the School for Workers in Madison. He was shocked to find that only three of the group of fifty-three union members had heard of Joe Hill. "I had to do a song about that," he said:

Union Man (excerpts)
By Larry Penn

Union man, union man,
Tell me who Joe Hill is.
Do you know how many others
Paid a price like his?
And do you know the reason?
Why it is that you don't know?
You ought to wonder why, union man.

I asked Larry Penn what he thought about the truck-driving songs played on country music stations, and he smiled: "A lot of songs about trucking come out of Nashville, but I get the feeling that those writers haven't spent much time in the cab of a truck. Maybe you'd like to hear a song written by a real truck driver." And then he sang:

Truck Driver Man
By Larry Penn

Where have you been today, truck driver man?
Where have you traveled across the wide land?
I've been to the East, I've been to the West,
The North and the South and the roadside to rest.

I've been to the centers of commerce and trade
And every big city that industry made.

> Been rolling so long, but I'm still in the hole
> The fever is gone and the coffee is cold.
> And each mile of highway has calloused my soul
> Rolling it all home to you.

What did you haul today, truck driver man?
What did you carry across the wide land?
Peanuts and lumber and parts for machines,
Castings and cookies and rose-colored dreams.
There were boxes and bags and barrels of oil,
Cement by the yard and steel by the coil.

> Chorus

What took you so long today, truck driver man?
What was the delay as you traveled the land?
It rained in the morning, it snowed in the night.
I made a left turn, I should have gone right.
I watched for the crazies, I watched for the bears.
I waited for scales, I was down for repairs.

> Chorus

What did you think about, truck driver man?
What were your dreams as you traveled the land?
I dreamed about playing all day in the sun
While somebody younger is making the run.
I dreamed about finding two perfect fried eggs,
Resting my eyes, and the waitresses' legs.
Never, no more, nights all alone
Not being more than an hour from home.

> Chorus

Where have you been today, truck driver man,
Where have you traveled across the wide land?
I've been to the East, I've been to the West,
The North and the South and the roadside to rest.

As a member of Teamsters Local 200, Larry has been able to make a decent living for his family over four decades of trucking. Yet he has seen enough poor management to have suffered the booms and busts of the economy. "There must be a better way to pace the workload," he insists. "Overtime" reflects that sentiment:

Overtime (excerpts)
By Larry Penn

Last month it was overtime
Home late every day.
This month it's just a long line
For my unemployment pay.

I'm supposed to earn my bread
By the sweat of my brow like the good book said.
How come they wrote a line for me
They never wrote none for the company?

Larry Penn writes many songs about truckers and railroads, trains being one of his chief interests. I learned of his fascination in Ashland, Wisconsin. We had been campaigning for Ed Garvey, who was running for the U.S. Senate (and lost despite the good music we provided). Between the meetings Larry said, "Let's go down to the railroad and see if we can find some spikes." He enjoyed scouting abandoned railroad rights of way for six-inch steel spikes once used to attach rails to wooden ties. "I polish the spikes and mount them on a nice piece of wood," he explained. We walked along the tracks and did indeed find a half-dozen spikes nearly hidden in the grass and gravel.

About a month later I received a package from Larry. In it was a burnished railroad spike mounted on a beautifully polished piece of cherry wood, upon which was fastened the red logo of the Milwaukee Road. Etched into the wood were the words "Handcrafted by Larry Penn." Accompanying the spike was a poem:

A Spike (excerpts)
By Larry Penn

It's a spike
It's a railroad spike
And it was laying there on the cold ground
It was left there to rust itself back into dust
And the tracks were no longer around
But when it was new it was gun metal blue
And a steel driver hammered it home
And the whole thing sang while the cold steel rang
To the sound of a spike driver's moan

It's a spike
It's a railroad spike
And it's worn from the work that it done

And it doesn't seem fair to just leave it there
Without any place in the sun
It ought to be picked up and polished and mounted
And hung by the mantel and shown
And then each time it glistens, if anyone listens
They could still hear that spike driver's moan.

Larry has written a wonderful song called "My Grandmother's Quilt," which is about brotherhood and multi-ethnicity and quite popular. The one that moves audiences the most, however, is "I'm a Little Cookie." As he explains, "My wife Pat, who works with damaged kids—Down's Syndrome, emotionally disturbed, slow learners, etc.—said one night, 'They sure don't write many songs for this kind of kid.' It got me thinking—we had a cookie factory here in Milwaukee that used to hang up a sign every week or so. It read, 'Broken Cookies!' You could buy five pounds of broken cookies for $1.25. When you ate them you realized they tasted as good as the cookies you bought in the store in a package of maybe eight for 89 cents."

I'm a Little Cookie
By Larry Penn

I'm a little cookie, yes I am
I was made by the cookie man.
On my way from the cookie pan
A li'l piece broke off me.

> A li'l piece broke off-a me, um hmm
> A li'l piece broke off-a me, um hmm
> But I can taste just as good, um hmm
> As a regular cookie can.

I'm a little chocolate bar, yes I am
I was made by the chocolate man.
On my way from the chocolate stand
I got a li'l bend in me.

> Got a li'l bend in me, um hmm
> Got a li'l bend in me, um hmm
> But I can taste just as good, um hmm
> As a regular chocolate bar can.

I'm a little tootsie roll, yes I am
I was made by the tootsie roll man.
On my way from tootsie roll land
I got a li'l twist in me.

Got a li'l twist in me, um hmm.
Got a li'l twist in me, um hmm.
But I can taste just as good, um hmm.
As a regular tootsie roll can.

I'm a little gum drop, yes I am
I was made by the gum drop man.
On my way from the sugar can
I got a li'l dent in me.

Got a li'l dent in me, um hmm.
Got a li'l dent in me, um hmm.
But I can taste just as good, um hmm
As a regular gumdrop can.

I'm a li'l cookie, yes I am
I was made by the cookie man.
On my way from the cookie pan
A li'l piece broke off-a me.

Now I'm not as round as I might be
But I'll taste good just wait and see
And I can love back just twice as hard
As a regular cookie can.

Most of Penn's songs, however, are about workers and working conditions. He has retired from trucking runs. When he is not singing on picket lines and at union meetings he is performing in coffeehouses, clubs, festivals, and church basements. He advises that trucking is still hard work despite the fact that trucks have become wonderful pieces of machinery: "The younger truckers who still have miles to go, they'll run you around the country like some kind of gypsy and then wonder why you get tired from sitting down so much. In the meantime, stay between the ditches and don't be afraid to stick to the union. It'll get you there."

Harry Stamper

Harry Stamper is a longshoreman in Coos Bay, Oregon, and writes and sings songs with a modern, folk-rock style. Not for him the songs of the 1940s. "I found," he explains, "that 'Hold the Fort' was not moving a twenty-one-year-old longshoreman with the Sex Pistols blasting into the headphones of his Walkman. So I began to write my own. My intent was to make them interesting, current, and universal all at the same time. Nobody could say I wasn't doing the song right if they had never heard the song before."

In 1981 Stamper telephoned me to ask, "Is this the Joe Glazer that does the labor songs?"

Glazer: That's right.

Stamper: Well, my name is Harry Stamper. I'm a longshoreman in Oregon, and I write labor songs.

Glazer: Do you sing them too?

Stamper: Sure. I write and sing them and I play the guitar. Would you like to hear them?

Glazer: Why don't you put some of your best songs on a cassette and send them to me?

The woods are full of wannabe, would-be, and hope-to-be songwriters who write songs that will never be sung because they are no good. I wasn't holding my breath while I waited for Harry Stamper's cassette. When it arrived and I got around to listening to it, however, I was blown over. Stamper was good, very good. He was a fine picker and had a driving, folk-rock style. His songs had a strong union and working-class message. More important, he had a nice poetic touch. And I could understand every word he sang. I liked that.

Stand by Your Union (excerpts)
By Harry Stamper

You think you got it made, boy,
You got yourself three rentals on the hill.
You got a new pickup in your driveway,
You got money in your pocket for your bills.
You got to keep in mind, boy,
A train runs both ways on the track;
And the man who let you have all those things
Anytime he can, he's gonna take them back.

Better stand by your union,
The one that got you your house and home
You know, a working man never had a chance
Out on the street with his money, alone.

They treat you okay at work.
Who do you think got that for you?
Now you're sitting there thinking
There's nothing left for you to do.

If you sit on your hands, son,
You're gonna find that it's true
That if you don't do the doing
You get the doing done to you.

Chorus

The Western Workers Heritage Festival would take place in Oakland, California, in a few months, and I quickly made arrangements for Stamper to attend. The annual West Coast festival was co-sponsored by the Labor Heritage Foundation, and because I was scheduled to lead a workshop and also perform I would have a good chance to see Stamper in action.

In Coos Bay, where Stamper works on the docks, they ship out more logs than any other port in the country. I was expecting a great hulk of a man, rough around the edges—my image of a longshoreman. Instead, Stamper turned out to be of average size and quite handsome. He had youthful features and was well-spoken and neatly dressed. In his late thirties, he could have passed for a yuppie lawyer in a downtown law office. But when he introduced "We Just Come to Work Here, We Don't Come to Die," you knew a true longshoreman was talking. Stamper explained how he had come to write the song:

We load a lot of logs in Coos Bay. One day all of the logs didn't quite fit in the way they were supposed to, and we ended up with a pile of them about half as high as this hall—all piled up in the wrong place. There was no way to roll them down into the wings of the ship where they belonged.

The boss turned to me, "Stamper, what we'll do is we'll pass a thick cable around something up here, and you crawl down there and fasten it on to something down there so that when we pull tight all those logs will roll down into the hold." (Hopefully after I'd had a chance to climb back up.) "Why don't you do that?"

I answered with a good longshoreman expletive that I can't repeat to you. So he fired me.

I told him, "You can't fire me on a health and safety beef. You call up the arbitrator, and I'll just go out in the lunchroom and wait." So we went and got some beer, and I got my guitar out of the car. By the time the arbitrator got through I had made up this song, and I had taught it to all the guys in the lunchroom. By the way, the arbitrator put me back to work.

We Just Come to Work Here, We Don't Come to Die
By Harry Stamper

I've been working here for fifteen years
And I've seen some changes come.
I've seen some Oakies called Californians

I've seen some poets called bums.
I've seen some people working for safety
There must be a reason why.
It's maybe we just come to work here
We don't come to die.

I'd like to end up with all of my fingers
I don't want my brains to get numb
I'd like to have my ears when retirement nears
I'd like to hear that applause come.
I'd like to see my grandchildren
Be able to pick them up if they cry.
That's why I just come to work here
I don't come to die.

> 'Cause if it's always level
> On the floor where you're working
> And your telephone is OSHA approved,
> When you tell me how much you're spending on safety
> Pardon me if I'm not moved.
> Ever since 1970 the law has been on my side.
> That's why we just come to work here
> We don't come to die.

You and I know that the things that aren't code
Could be fixed with relative ease.
But we never did get anything
By asking on our knees.
So now we're looking you straight in the eye
Shoulder to shoulder and side by side.
We're saying we just come to work here
We don't come to die.

> Chorus

Stamper sang his song at the big public show that closed the three-day festival. An audience of four hundred trade unionists jammed the union hall in
Oakland, and he had them stomping and yelling out the chorus with him: "We
just come to work here, we don't come to die." I've been to a few thousand
union meetings in my day, but I've rarely seen the kind of emotional high that
Stamper achieved with that song. Every worker could identify with his defiant
challenge.

Before returning to the docks in Coos Bay, he told me how he had begun to
write labor songs. He graduated from high school in 1962 and tried college as

a music major but soon lost interest. There was, he said, too much emphasis on piano. He first went to work on the docks in Ashland, Oregon, became a member of the International Longshoreman and Warehouseman's Union (ILWU) in 1967, and has been working as a longshoreman ever since. Stamper recalled receiving his first guitar:

> My father presented me with a Martin guitar on my thirteenth Christmas. It was quite a financial gamble for a little kid, but he was right. I took it running and never really looked back. I passed it on to my daughter on her thirteenth birthday, and she plays it today.
>
> My first ILWU strike was in 1970. The power I felt as a union member was a revelation. I began to sing traditional union songs at this time. After this strike I transferred to Local 12 in Coos Bay, where I became active in the union. I was first a member and then chairman of the Safety Committee, then served on the Labor Relations Committee.

It was at this time that Stamper changed his singing and playing style. He claims to have drawn freely from the styles of Pete Seeger and Woody Guthrie, but his new with-it style has a modern, rock flavor.

Stamper not only sings for groups within his own union but also is in demand by other union groups. He makes up many songs about conditions on the job and also touches on problems of working people off the job. He has worked on the docks for more than thirty years and has moved into "labor prose"—short stories about life on the job. The ones I've read still sound like good labor music to me.

Anne Feeney

Anne Feeney is one of the new voices of labor who seeks out strikers on the battlefields of labor's struggles, belting out her songs in the manner of Ethel Merman or Bessie Smith. I met her in 1988 at the AFL-CIO George Meany Center, where she was attending the Great Labor Arts Exchange sponsored by the Labor Heritage Foundation.

A trim, attractive woman in her late thirties, she was sitting quietly in a crowd of a hundred trade union activists who had come from all over the country to learn and exchange labor songs. Although she made no initial impression, when she picked up her big guitar and started singing she became a growling, roaring, snarling tiger on the hunt for scabs and union-busting bosses. She belted out her songs in a voice that bounced off the walls of the room and set hands clapping and feet stomping:

NEW VOICES, PART 2

Scabs (excerpts)
By Anne Feeney

There's an alien life form been creeping round my job site
They look almost human but something about 'em ain't right.
They just cross right over a picket line
Pay no attention to a picket sign.

They're called scabs . . . scabs
The lowest life form found in nature's labs.
They got no brains, they got no heart
Scabs are tearing our communities apart . . .

Now before we had our union let me tell you conditions were bad—
Understaffed, overworked, underpaid—till we finally got mad.
But then when we walked out to protect our rights
They just gave our jobs away to these parasites

To those scabs . . . scabs
The lowest form of life found in nature's labs . . .

Anne had spent twelve years practicing law in Pittsburgh. On the side, she played guitar and sang her songs at union rallies and anti-Vietnam protests. Music was much more satisfying than the law, and in 1990 she became a full-time musical agitator. She calls herself a "hell-raiser," which is just what she is.

Anne Feeney is not one for singing union songs in someone's living room. She is always in the trenches, marching on picket lines and rousing the troops with her music and driving energy. In 1992 she went to Las Vegas to sing at the first anniversary of the strike at the Frontier Hotel and Casino. The Frontier Hotel was the only major hotel in Las Vegas that refused to sign a standard contract with the Hotel and Restaurant Employees Union. Two years later Anne was back again to sing at the third anniversary of the strike. "The strike was still solid," she said enthusiastically. "During those three years not a single one of the four hundred strikers had crossed the picket line. The hotel is owned by the Elardi family. For those brave men and women I wrote this song to the tune of 'That's Amore'":

With three years on the line
Who's the boss that's a swine?
That's Elardi.
Tell me who's gonna whine
'Bout their big OSHA fine?
That's Elardi.

Feeney continued:

> At the hotel where I was staying, the waiter who brought me coffee the morning I was leaving noticed all the rally posters and buttons in my room and asked me if I had come for the rally. I sang "That's Elardi" to him, and he remarked that it was a shame that no one had Spanish translations of the songs since most of the workers at Frontier were Latinas. I mentioned that I had written one song in Spanish, "Me Casé Con un Heroe" (I married a hero).
>
> I sang it for him. Twenty minutes later there was a knock at my door. He brought the whole kitchen staff up to hear me sing the two songs. They cried, they hugged me, and they gave me a huge basket of fruit, caviar, nuts, champagne, and champagne glasses. It was overwhelming.
>
> There is one fascinating bit about this Frontier strike. At the beginning of the strike, white union men were running the show. Later the Latina women who were the kitchen help, hotel maids, and laundry workers came into their own, taking charge. It changed them forever.
>
> I look forward to the day when the strike is won. I plan to be there, marching triumphantly with hundreds of strikers into the hotel singing "Solidarity Forever" loud enough so that even the zonked-out, glassy-eyed slot machine players will stop dead and ask, "What's going on?"

The strike was finally won, but it took five long years. Not one single Frontier worker ever crossed the line. Sure enough, Anne Feeney was at the big victory rally in the hotel's parking lot, singing her songs of solidarity to Frontier workers as they cheered and yelled and cried tears of happiness at the triumphant outcome of their historic struggle.

Anne Feeney and her guitar cannot stay away from a hard-fought strike. She is outraged by powerful and profitable corporations that force workers out on strike and hire "replacement workers" with the intent to smash the union. That is why she made eight or ten visits to Decatur, Illinois, during the mid-1990s when several thousand workers were engaged in three major strikes to save their unions and preserve the working conditions they had built over many years.

The workers called the city of Decatur the "war zone" because they were fighting for their jobs, their standard of living, their homes, and their families. Anne Feeney marched and sang with them, but the lack of "direct action" in the campaign frustrated her. At the close of one large rally on October 16, 1994, she laid on a main street, intending to block traffic. She was arrested. She believes as Mother Jones did that "it is an honor to go to jail when your cause is just."

When Staley workers were locked out in June 1993 (they lost their struggle after three years on the picket line), Anne wrote a song:

War on the Workers (excerpts)
By Anne Feeney

Listen up. We've got a war zone here today,
Right in our heartland, but our union's here to stay.
These multinational bastards don't use tanks and guns it's true,
But they've declared a war on us—
Fight back, it's up to you.

    It's a war on the workers.
    [All] War on the workers.
    It's a war on the workers.
    [All] War on the workers.
    It's a war on the workers.
    And it's time we started callin' the shots . . .

They can lock us out or lock us up
We will not give in.
No more lies, no compromise
We'll battle till we win.

    It's a war on the workers
    [All] War on the workers.
    It's a war on the workers.
    [All] War on the workers.
    When they boost your co-pay—
    [All] It's a war on the workers.
    Don't you know what to say?
    [All] It's a war on the workers.
    When they want privatization—
    [All] It's a war on the workers.
    And cooperation—
    [All] It's a war on the workers.
    How about flexibility?
    [All] It's a war on the workers.
    Any working stiff can see—
    [All] It's a war on the workers.
    It's a war on the workers.
    It's a war on the workers.
    And it's time we started calling the shots.

Most of Anne Feeney's songs are about contemporary issues and struggles,
but sometimes she delves into labor history to tell the story of a labor martyr.
Fannie Sellins, an organizer for the United Mine Workers, was brutally mur-
dered by the Pennsylvania State Police during the Great Steel Strike of 1919.

Fannie Sellins
By Anne Feeney

In labor's joyous history was many a union maid
Who stood up to the bosses so staunch and unafraid
Molly Jackson, Mother Jones fought for a better way
But let's sing of Fannie Sellins and remember her today.
All over Pennsylvania, Fannie spread the union word
In the coalfields and the company towns her voice was always heard.
United we will bargain but divided we must beg
Fannie Sellins spread the dreams of the UMWA.

> A widow with four children toiling eighty hours a week
> She found time to fight injustice and bring power to the meek.
> She fought with tireless energy no duty would she shirk.
> Though murderers cut short her life we carry on her work.

In the company slums of Ducktown in the summer of nineteen
An unarmed striking miner was gunned down by deputies.
When Fannie cried out "Spare his life!" they shot her down as well.
And hundreds watched in horror as this fearless woman fell.
Now the ones who gave the orders faced no charges of any sort
And the men who pulled the triggers were acquitted by the court.
When companies own the courthouse, justice fails for you and me,
So let's work like Fannie Sellins now for true equality.

> Chorus

In 1997 Anne Feeney was elected full-time president of Musicians' Local 60-471 in Pittsburgh. The job involved organizing, settling grievances, and negotiating contracts. She worked fifty, sixty, and even seventy hours a week, which left little time for musical agitation at strikes around the country. But like a fire horse ready to go at the sound of the firehouse bell, she was off again on June 20, 1977, to support a twenty-month strike against the two major Detroit newspapers. She marched and sang "Scabs" to the cheers of 120,000 workers at a rally culminating in a march through the streets. Afterward, she drove home to Pittsburgh, recharged and ready more than ever to carry on.

In 1999 Feeney was defeated when she ran for a second term as president of her local. But that didn't upset her too much. It just gave her more time to do the thing she loves: uplifting the spirit of workers with her music.

Eddie Starr

"I am a steelworker, just like a million other steelworkers, getting mill grease on my elbows and slag dust in my hair, hacking out a living, a good living, by the sweat of my brow, thanks to the good old United Steel Workers of America." Eddie Starr is a singer-songwriter of union songs and brings the drive, excitement, and enthusiasm of rock and roll to his music. He is a full-time steelworker, proud of being a worker and a staunch union member.

I first met Eddie Starr in 1990 at the annual Great Labor Arts Exchange in Silver Spring, Maryland. He was from Granite City, Illinois, and his reputation as a rock and roll union singer had preceded him. I was eager to meet him. A vibrant man of thirty-four who could easily pass as ten years younger, Starr had a relaxed manner, a ready smile, and a head of red, unruly hair. He took his big electric guitar and amplifying equipment wherever he went.

He was a third-generation steelworker. His grandfather had worked in the Granite City mill, and his father worked as a maintenance man on the blast furnace. Almost everyone he knew inevitably wound up working in the dirty, hard world of industrial mills and plants after graduating from high school. He had no intention of doing the same.

Starr was born in East St. Louis, on the industrial side of the Mississippi River where there are steel mills, copper mills, zinc mills, rubber plants, chemical plants, and petroleum plants, all union-organized. He likes to point out that his birth in the 1950s coincided with the birth of rock and roll. After seeing the Beatles on the *Ed Sullivan Show* in the 1960s he was determined that one day he would be a rock and roll star. He learned to play guitar at age nine, joined the musicians' union at sixteen, had his own band at nineteen, and made enough money playing in nightclubs to buy a new car and finance a house at twenty-two.

During the disco craze of the 1970s, live musicians lost work to disc jockeys. Starr's agent told him that the only way to keep the band booked was to put them on the road. But Starr had a family and needed a job with a pension plan and health insurance, so he hired on at the Cerro Copper Mill. It was a traumatic change for someone accustomed to singing in nightclubs, where he was patted on the back after a performance and told how good he was.

He spent ten years in the copper mill, writing songs and singing them to workers in break shacks and locker rooms with no thought of receiving any sort of recognition for his music. Yet he needed to sing to protest the oppressive manner in which the workers were being treated, and the workers were receptive. "In the Cerro Copper Mill," Starr explained, "new workers had a probationary period of forty-five days. During that period you could be fired for any, or no, reason. Once you had put in your forty-five days, you were a full union member protected by all the provisions of the union contract. But some foremen would fire a worker when he got close to the end of his probationary period. It was a cruel thing to do. I wrote a song about this injustice called 'The Probationary Blues'":

Probationary Blues (excerpts)
By Eddie Starr

I done landed me a job in these trying times
But they say I've got forty-five days in which I'm
Supposed to work real hard and not make no plans
If I wanna keep my job and be a union man.
So I sweated and I slaved until I dropped to my knees
But you won't believe what that company done to me.

Well, I met a girl, who said she wants to hold me tight
I said, "I'd be glad to meet you after work tonight."
Well, the boss came up at ten o'clock, he looked real pleased,
He said, "You do the kind of work I like to see.
You wanna make the union, boy, then stick with me.
There's gonna be some overtime on furnace three."

> And I said . . . I got the blues
> And I just can't wait to start paying those union dues.

The other verses describe missing other dates with his girlfriend because of compulsory overtime. Yet he is still laid off on his forty-fourth day, one day short of becoming a permanent employee with union protection. Starr put the song on a record and sold it to the workers for one dollar to help cover the cost of the recording.

In 1989 Eddie left the copper mill and went to work at Granite City Steel, where his father worked. Local 67, which represented the workers at the mill, was more militant and better organized than the workers at the copper mill, and Eddie liked that. More important, Larry Ross, one of the union's chief stewards, knew about the Great Labor Arts Exchange. Eddie described his experience:

> When I attended my first Labor Arts Exchange I found out I was a labor singer. Up until that point I had no idea what a labor singer was or that there were ever such things as labor singers. At the Exchange I met a whole national cadre of labor singers, poets, and artists who were just like me. Exchanging experiences with these fellow artists and poets left me not only spiritually charged but intellectually fulfilled. The things I learned there have made me not only an effective picket-line singer but also a confident speaker and motivator at both labor rallies and political demonstrations.
>
> Since that time, I have led marches and demonstrations with my guitar. I have sung on picket lines and rallies, spoken in schools and on radio and television talk shows. I have appeared at various labor jams, union banquets, and conventions around the country along with my fellow steelworkers and helped to start our own annual labor jam in the Granite City area.

Starr is proud of some of the highlights of his union singing career:

I remember singing on a picket line with Joe Glazer in the industrial Mississippi River town of Sauget, Illinois, where we strummed our guitars in front of a burning barrel of wood surrounded by a weary-looking bunch of scruffs who had just been locked out and replaced by scabs at the Midwest Rubber Reclamation Plant.

I have sung on the same stage as Pete Seeger himself at the Solidarity Day concert in Washington, D.C. in which three hundred thousand union workers of all races, religions, and creeds marched in unity to the Capitol for the cause of labor legislation, job security, and national health care.

I have sung "I Am Union and I'm Proud" in the far north country of Hibbing, Minnesota, to a crowd of over a thousand who packed the local hockey arena to hear International union president George Becker of my own Steelworkers' Union shout his anger to the emotional cheers of the 750 locked-out iron ore miners, their families, and community supporters.

I Am Union and I'm Proud
By Eddie Starr

> I am union and I'm proud
> And my membership talks loud.
> Where I'm concerned
> And I won't get burned.
> Cause the union is my shield
> My protection when I feel
> They've done me wrong.
> It makes me strong.

> I'm trying to make a living
> So I'll give 'em all I got
> And I'll work real hard, but I'm never gonna give in.
> But when it comes to corporate greed
> I'm on my guard
> I've got my card.

> 'Cause I'm union and I stand
> And no company's demand
> Will make me fall.
> And I will not crawl
> 'Cause the union is the key
> To make working people free
> And I won't back down and lose my ground.

> Chorus

Starr continued:

> I've strummed my guitar in the drizzling rain, as the grief-stricken wife and children of fallen worker, Ronald Schmitt, stood silently in tearful meditation. The participants of the Workers' Memorial Day ceremony stood arm in arm, heads bowed in silent tribute to all those who senselessly and often violently died on their jobs. With only the sound of raindrops on umbrellas and my voice and guitar, singing Pete Seeger's beautiful song from Ecclesiastes, "Turn, Turn, Turn" ("to everything there is a season"), did the family and friends find solace in their sorrows. I, too, allowed the raindrops to mask my own tears, which inevitably found their way down my cheeks and onto the top of my resonating guitar.
>
> And last of all, but certainly not least, I still play my harmonica in the mill, in the locker rooms and break shacks, and down at the union hall, singing my songs about the workers and the bosses.

Starr has put the story of his life into a song:

We Are the Working Class
By Eddie Starr

When I graduated high school I had a plan
To seek fame and fortune with a rock and roll band.
It was a pointless dream
But I was too young to see.
Now after fifteen years I'm on a cold-roll stand in a steel mill and I've been
Reflecting on something my father said,
And here's what he said to me,

> "There is no disgrace in standing side by side with working people
> Sweating for an honest wage I'll never be ashamed of.
> So take it in stride, we've still got our pride.
> 'Cause we are the working class and that's the place to be."

Now I'm strumming the guitar in the picket lines
And at the union hall, and in the middle of the Labor Day street parade
And I think I've got it made.
And at the end of my story, when it all comes down
I'll be remembered as the guy with his feet on the ground
Whose very life was led
By the words that his father said:

Chorus

"We Are the Working Class" expresses Starr's pleasure at composing and singing songs for union members—something he plans to keep doing for many years.

Kenny Winfree

The title of one of Kenny Winfree's cassettes, *Blue Collar Bluegrass,* accurately describes the kind of labor music he writes. He is a proud member of two unions ("that makes me feel twice as good") in Nashville, Tennessee: Musicians' Local 257 and Machinists' Local 735.

Winfree started out as a textile worker in his hometown of Lebanon, Tennessee, about thirty miles east of Nashville. The Amalgamated Clothing and Textile Workers' Union (ACTWU) tried to organize the plant in 1980 but lost by seventeen votes. "The defeat didn't discourage me one bit," he says. "It fired me up and made me a stronger union man. Involvement in that campaign changed my life forever." As it turned out, the mill was finally organized in 1984.

Winfree played guitar and wrote country tunes but soon found himself writing labor songs. During the organizing campaign, "Cotton Mill Dreams" was one of his first:

Cotton Mill Dreams
By Kenny Winfree

The cotton mill it sits just outside of town
From where I live you can hear the weaving sound,
Where the looms they weave all day and sewing machines seam
While I lie here dying in my cotton mill dreams.

I used to work there several years ago
Until my lungs they got to hurting me so
They're never any better; they're only worse it seems
But I just keep on dreaming my cotton mill dreams.

The pain, it's immense, there's thunder in my head
You know, the doctor says that soon I'll be dead.
Then angels, they can carry me away on moonlit beams
We can glide away into my cotton mill dreams.

I'm going to where there's never ever been a cloudy day
To a place where I can rest and still draw my union pay.
Where the mills are made of marble and there's crystal flowing streams
I can live forever in my cotton mill dreams.

Winfree grew up and has lived all his life in the Nashville area. Country music was in his bones. All his songs are country-flavored but have a labor theme. They are easy to sing and easy to remember. Winfree could have been a successful Nashville songwriter had he wanted to, but that was not his interest. What he enjoys is putting his talent to work for the labor movement.

I thought Winfree's work deserved wider dissemination and had him record a dozen songs on my Collector Records label. Here is one:

Down at the Union Hall
By Kenny Winfree

I can remember when I was a kid
Some of the things that my daddy did.
Worked hard for a living and helped raise us all
He taught us to cherish the old union hall.

We'd go to the meetings in that smoky old place
I could see union spirit in my daddy's face.
Fiery speeches and solidarity
Will live forever in my memory.

    Down at the union hall
    Down at the union hall
    Calling all workers to come one and all
    Down at the union hall.

I remember the year that the union got in
I remember the slogan that helped us to win.
We said, "United we stand, divided we fall."
We took that pledge at the old union hall.

    Chorus

My working days are over, now I'm old and gray
Let's not let solidarity slip away.
It's not too late, there are battles to win
So let's all get together and revive it again.

    Chorus

In the cover notes for *Blue Collar Bluegrass,* I wrote, "Kenny Winfree is this generation's Woody Guthrie." That embarrassed him, but I felt that he had Woody's knack for writing catchy, moving songs with a message—they are easy to sing and easy to remember. One example is "I'm a Union Card":

I'm a Union Card
By Kenny Winfree

I was thumbing through my wallet just the other day
I came to a certain spot, and I could have sworn I heard someone say,
"Howdy, I'm your union card; now don't you forget about me.
Listen to this story and see if you don't agree.

You may not know it but I do a lot for you;
I protect your benefits and all your wages too.
I might even keep you from getting fired
Praise the Lord that I'm a union card.

   Praise the Lord that I'm a union card
   Could have been a Visa, could have been a Master Charge.
   Don't worry about your money as long as I'm on guard.
   Praise the Lord that I'm a union card.

Could have been the joker, could have been the old maid,
Could have been the rooker, could have been the ace of spades.
Living in your wallet here, it sure is hard,
Praise the Lord that I'm a union card.

   Chorus

I'm a postal worker who delivers mail to you;
I'm a textile worker and I work on airplanes too,
I'm carried by millions over near and far,
Praise the Lord that I'm a union card."

   Chorus

Winfree left the textile mill in 1981 to work at the Textron Aero Structures, a large aircraft factory in Nashville. It had been organized by the International Association of Machinists' Local 735, and he immediately became an active union member, rising to the rank of vice president after a few years. When the Machinists' Union celebrated its hundredth anniversary, Winfree wrote a song for the occasion:

Long Live the IAM
By Kenny Winfree

Well, it all started back in 1888
Down in Atlanta, Gee-Ay:
Nineteen machinists, that's how it got started
And look where we are today.

   Long live the IAM.
   Long live the IAM.
   Let's all get together
   And sing this little hymn,
   Long live the IAM.

Now there's even a legend of the "Fighting Machinists"
And how they worked to right the wrong.

We've picked the battle, we're "Fighting Machinists"
And we're fighting as we sing this little song.

Chorus

The industrial union department of the AFL-CIO asked him in 1988 to take a leave of absence from his job at the aircraft plant and become a full-time organizer for three years. He carried his trusty guitar with him to organizing meetings and found it was a useful means of winning the confidence of intimidated and sometimes skeptical workers. "It was not easy organizing in the South," said Winfree. "A lot of the bosses would call organizers like me snake-oil salesmen. I wrote a song about it":

Snake Oil (excerpts)
By Kenny Winfree

Well, the boss came by here yesterday
He said, "Boy, I've been good to you,
And I heard that the union is coming to town
And I hope they pass on through.
Cause the danged old union it makes me so mad
Sometimes it makes my blood boil.
But don't you be listening to them, son,
Cause the union is selling snake oil."

Oh, please give me a bath in snake oil
'Cause you know that's just what I need.
Grease me up, please don't wipe me off
'Cause I've got a family to feed.
Wash my back, then my neck
You can scrub till I'm black and blue
I'm taking a bath in snake oil.
Come on now, you take one too.

"I've had a lot of exciting times playing my music for the labor movement," says Winfree. "But without a doubt my most moving moment was one day when I was to perform at a big labor dinner in Paterson, New Jersey. A young man came up to me and said he had recently purchased a copy of my cassette *Blue Collar Bluegrass*. He told me, 'I carry it with me wherever I go. Whenever I get depressed or down I listen to your tape. It is my inspiration. It brings me back to reality. Thank you, Kenny.' Red Skelton used to close his show by saying, 'If I have reached one person, it was all worth it.' I guess he was right!"

Other Voices

There are many more labor singers who should be included in this group of new voices. For example, Joe Uehlein is a labor activist and guitar-picker who helped me organize the Labor Heritage Foundation. In the 1990s he put together the Bones of Contention, a four-piece labor rock and roll band in Washington, D.C. The group peps up large rallies and union conventions. Their first CD and cassette contains seventeen high-energy versions of traditional union songs as well as contemporary freedom and protest songs.

Mike Stout, a steelworker from Homestead, Pennsylvania, is another singer-guitar player who makes union music with a rock and roll band, the Human Union. His CDs and cassettes are a rocking collection of workers' songs and ballads, written mostly by Stout. The band played at the 1997 convention of the AFL-CIO in Pittsburgh.

The New York City Labor Chorus is the largest of its kind in the country, with 120 members from twenty-five different local unions. It has performed on picket lines, at union rallies, at Madison Square Garden, at Carnegie Hall, and at the 1992 Democratic Party convention. It was organized by Bobbie Rabinowitz, vice president of Social Service Employees' Union, Local 371. Geoffrey Fairweather is the dynamic and talented director of the chorus.

Susan Lewis and Janet Stecher of Washington state are the Rebel Voices and sing in beautiful harmony about women at work and other topics of social significance.

Baldemar Velasquez is the president of the Farm Labor Organizing Committee, which has headquarters in Toledo, Ohio. He is also an excellent musician and songwriter who leads a band, Aguila Negra, that plays and sings union songs in Spanish to help organize Hispanic farm laborers in Ohio, Michigan, and other states.

John McCutcheon is one of the nation's finest singers-songwriters-musicians. Many recordings of his songs have social significance, including a number that have a labor angle. He has composed labor anthems for several unions and with Si Kahn has produced an album to help children understand the significance of trade unions.

The many labor singers and songwriters I have discussed should dispel the notion that there is no more singing in the American labor movement. As long as there are struggles for justice on the job, there will be a poet, a singer, or a guitar player who will put labor's side of the story to music.

15

Wrapping Up

I was twenty-six on May 1, 1944, when I went to work for the Textile Workers Union of America. Now, more than fifty years later, I have allowed myself a long look back as well as a look to the future. I have spent those fifty-odd years working in and around the labor movement and with the U.S. Information Agency, interpreting the labor movement for overseas audiences. During much of that time the guitar was my assistant, my friend, and my entrée to people and places I would not otherwise have been able to approach.

I spent many of those years singing on picket lines in the cold, snow, and rain; speaking and singing in shabby union halls to twenty-five or thirty workers or to three hundred thousand at a rally in the shadow of the nation's Capitol; and singing at noisy union picnics to beer-drinking workers gorging on hot dogs or at elegant union dinners in fancy hotels where white-gloved waiters poured wine and served prime roast beef, French style.

I have taught thousands of new union members the basics of trade unionism and seen them develop over the years into skilled, effective leaders who helped give other members a real voice on the job.

I have been angry and ashamed when I saw labor leaders misuse their power, abuse their trust, and besmirch the good name of the labor movement. I have mourned lost strikes and cheered union victories.

It has been a good ride, with many heartwarming experiences and few regrets. I have been blessed with a loving and supportive wife, Mildred, through all those many years; with three healthy children; fine in-laws; and four feisty grandchildren. I have lived beyond the biblical marker of three score and ten and except for thinning, white hair, bifocals, and the usual aches and pains that come with the territory for senior citizens, I am in reasonably good shape. Most of all, my voice seems to be as strong as ever. For example, in August 1997 I belted out chorus after chorus of "Solidarity Forever" at a huge outdoor rally for United Parcel Service (UPS) strikers in the Washington area. When I finished, an old friend who had heard me sing for forty years rushed over and said, "Joe, you sound better than ever!" I don't know about that, but that day I felt I could out-sing anyone fifty years my junior.

I feel good about making some important and permanent contributions to the music of the American labor movement. In 1960 I published *Songs of Work and Freedom* (later retitled *Songs of Work and Protest*) with the distinguished Canadian folklorist Edith Fowke—a book of one hundred songs, including music and a detailed historical analysis of each song. Many experts consider this a classic in its field. Years later it remains in print, still useful for those who want to learn labor songs and the history of the American labor movement as told through its music.

In 1970 I established Collector Records, which specializes in recordings of labor, protest, and political songs, with special emphasis on labor and union songs. I began the company because I was frustrated with the various small companies that had put out records of my songs early in my career. They would go out of business, and the recordings would go with them. Or, if the pressings sold out and the companies decided they couldn't make money on reissues, the record would be dropped. I was more interested in keeping the music alive than in making money.

My first catalog was a one-page sheet promoting four of my own records. In a few years I began recording other labor singers, especially those who had never been recorded. Then there was a growing list of labor and union singers who were making LPs and cassettes on their own. I added them to my catalog. By the 1990s Collector Records' catalog listed more than one hundred cassettes and CDs (we dropped LPs from the catalog in 1996). It became one of the largest depositories of recorded labor and union songs in the nation.

Another source of great satisfaction has been my involvement with the founding of the Labor Heritage Foundation in 1978 and serving as its chair throughout the years. The foundation has nurtured labor artists and promoted the use of labor music and the arts to help build solidarity. It has taken over many of the functions of Collector Records, especially distributing recordings of labor music.

As I review my life in the labor movement, certain scenes flash by. In one, I am singing on a stage on the south lawn of the White House before a thousand trade union leaders on Labor Day in 1980. Jimmy Carter is in an open-collar sport shirt and sitting on the grass not more than twenty feet from me.

What should I sing for a president from Plains, Georgia, who has surely never heard a labor song before? This is how I handled it:

> Mr. President, I am certain you are acquainted with the old hymn "Jesus Is My Captain, I Shall Not Be Moved"? Well, fifty years ago in the West Virginia coalfields, when the miners and their families were driven out of their company-owned houses during a strike, they made a union song out of that hymn. I want to sing that for you now.

We Shall Not Be Moved

The union is behind us,
We shall not be moved.
The union is behind us,
We shall not be moved.
Just like a tree that's planted by the water
We shall not be moved.

All the union folks joined in on the chorus, and I could see President Carter's lips moving tentatively as he tried out new words to a song he must have sung many times in church. He smiled and applauded with the others when the song was over. I'll bet he would have signed a union card right then and there had someone asked him.

The scene now shifts across the country to Portland, Oregon. The year is 1960. I am singing to a convention of the International Woodworkers of America (IWA), the union that organizes lumber workers and loggers.

Ralph Chaplin, who had been an editor, poet, and songwriter for the Industrial Workers of the World (Wobblies) and had written the American labor anthem "Solidarity Forever," lived nearby in the state of Washington. I had arranged to have him speak to the convention. In the early days of the century, the Wobblies had organized the lumber camps and sawmills in the Northwest, and I thought that Chaplin could give modern-day woodworkers an important message. What a message it was: "It isn't a question of saying to young people, 'Oh, we were great guys in our days. We were the real men.' That isn't it. We were no bigger, no smarter, than you are. If you had been there in those times, under those conditions, you would have fought just as hard as we did to build the union."

Chaplin's speech lasted ten minutes, and the delegates were enthralled. He received a standing ovation. He was then in his seventies and still a powerhouse on the platform—what a stemwinder he must have been in his youth! To close the session I led the delegates in "Solidarity Forever" in his honor. Chaplin later told me, "When I wrote that song on my living-room floor in Chicago back

in 1915 I never imagined they'd still be singing it forty-five years later." Did I
see tears in his eyes, or were they just glistening from the warmth and joy of
the occasion?

In a flash I am back on the East Coast. I am walking on a picket line in New
York City in a strike of hospital workers—people who make beds, mop floors,
empty bed pans, wash towels, cook food, and work in the laboratories. A strike
at a hospital is never a popular activity, but these workers had been underpaid,
overworked, mistreated, and ignored for many years. Many were not covered
by health insurance. They had become desperate enough to walk out. The leader of the New York City Labor Council, Harry Van Arsdale, had asked me to
sing on their picket lines to lift the spirits of the strikers.

Workers at five large private hospitals were striking, but a city ordinance
prevented making noise near a hospital. As I walked the picket line, I carried
my guitar. Later there would be a rally, and I would sing in a nearby park. A
law officer walked over to me, pointed his nightstick at my guitar case, and
belted out, "Whatduyuh got in there?" When I told him, "A guitar," he said
gruffly, "Open it up." He seemed surprised that it really was a guitar in the case.
I explained that the instrument was valuable and I couldn't let it out of my
sight. He was puzzled. He didn't want me walking around with a guitar case
but was unsure what to do about it. Finally, he said, "Look here, buddy. Give
me that guitar case, and I'll watch it while you're on the line."

My guitar was well guarded. When the picket line dispersed I retrieved it and
used it for rallies that afternoon and evening. The strike was won, and it helped
launch what would become the most powerful hospital workers' union in the
country.

Another memory concerns the George Meany Center for Labor Studies. The
year is 1985. Pete Seeger is talking about his new book of labor songs to a hundred labor activists attending the Great Labor Arts Exchange sponsored by the
Labor Heritage Foundation. "We want to do the right thing and pay royalties
to the composers of all these labor songs," he says. "Unfortunately, some of
the old-time composers, like John Handcox who wrote 'Roll the Union On'
are dead." I raised my hand. "Pete, your information on Handcox is wrong. I
sang 'Roll the Union On' with him last week in Memphis, and he is very much
alive." Handcox, the legendary black poet of the Southern Tenant Farmers
Union had been out of circulation for forty years. We reintroduced him to the
labor movement, where he inspired a new generation of union members with
his songs, poems, and stories.

Next my mind takes me to Toledo, Ohio, and a plant organized by the Textile Workers' Union. It is 1948. I will be teaching a class of shop stewards in the

evening, but in the afternoon I am sitting in on a labor-management grievance session. The union is represented by its regional director, Charlie Bubb,
and the workers' committee. On the company side are the labor relations director, a lawyer, and several plant supervisors. Bubb is one of the smartest,
toughest negotiators I have ever seen. He knows every line in the hundred-page
union contract. He demolishes every point raised by the company, which ultimately concedes on every one of the four grievances presented that day. The
union committee walks out happy. Bubb is humming to himself as we ride back
to the hotel. He breaks out in a big grin and says, "Hell, I wouldn't trade this
job for a million dollars."

When Frances Perkins, the secretary of labor in Franklin D. Roosevelt's cabinet, was asked which of the government jobs she had held during her long
career she prized the most, she answered without hesitation, "Years ago I was
a member of the New York State Appeals Board which heard workman's compensation cases. That was my favorite job because I was able to render justice
every day."

I have known hundreds of Charlie Bubbs—organizers, business agents, and
negotiators—dedicated men and women who have devoted their lives to the
labor movement. Because of their jobs, they are able "to render justice every
day." These are people who rarely get their names in the newspapers; they are
unheralded, almost anonymous, except to the workers they serve. They work
evenings and weekends, running from meeting to meeting, local to local, and
town to town, doing their best to render justice every day. Add to this group
of full-time union employees several hundred thousand volunteer shop stewards, local committees, and local union officers, and you have a picture of what
I call the true glory of the labor movement.

In my own way, I have tried to render justice—or at least to help others do
so—through my work in the labor movement, in politics, and around the
world. I have gotten to know outstanding leaders of the labor movement:
George Meany, Walter Reuther, Phil Murray, Lane Kirkland, John Sweeney,
Cesar Chavez, and a host of others. In my political work, I shared platforms
with Harry Truman, Eleanor Roosevelt, John F. Kennedy, Robert Kennedy,
Lyndon Johnson, Ladybird Johnson, Jimmy Carter, and Bill Clinton in addi-
ton to Hubert Humphrey, George McGovern, Herbert Lehman, Wayne Morse,
and Paul Douglas, to mention only some members of Congress, a number of
whom I worked with and got to know well. Overseas, I met with ambassadors,
prime ministers, secretaries of labor, foreign trade union officials, and many
rank-and-file workers.

I know that mills will not be made of marble here on earth. I know that machines will not be made of gold. Workers will become tired and grow old. But I hope that through the years I have helped, through my songs, to make life a bit better for others. I have been called a "musical agitator for all good causes," and I hope to continue in that role.

Discography

Eight New Songs for Labor. 1950. CIO Department of Education and Research. (Unnumbered.) Two twelve-inch, 78-rpm records in stiff album jacket. Sung by Joe Glazer and the Elm City Four, with guitar accompaniment by Fred Hellerman: "We Will Overcome," "The Mill Was Made of Marble," "Great Day," "That's All," "Shine on Me," "Humblin' Back," "Too Old to Work," and "I Ain't No Stranger Now."

Les Ouvriers Chantent (Workers sing). 1951. Recorded in France. (Unnumbered.) Four ten-inch, 78-rpm records in soft album jacket. Sung by Joe Glazer with guitar and backed by a French workers' quartet: "Solidarity Forever," "The Mill Was Made of Marble," "Great Day," "Tarriers Song," "Union Maid," "That's All," and "Roll the Union On."

Ballads for Sectarians. 1952. Labor Arts. (Unnumbered.) Three ten-inch, 78-rpm records in an album accompanied by eight-page pamphlet with lyrics and historical notes. Satirical songs about the twists and turns of the Communist Party line sung by Joe Glazer and Bill Friedland with their own guitar accompaniment: "Old Bolshevik's Song," "Land of the *Daily Worker*," "Unite for Unity," "The Last International," "In Old Moscow," "The Cloakmakers Union," "Bill Bailey," and "Our Line's Been Changed Again."

Ballads for Sectarians. 1953. Labor Arts. (Unnumbered.) Reissued as a ten-inch LP record. Same as above but with one additional song: "Little Joe the Rustler" (the story of Joseph Stalin).

Songs for Political Action: Folk Music, Topical Songs and the American Left—1926–1953. 1996. Bear Family, Germany BCD 15720 JL. 10 CDS. The entire album of *Ballads for Sectarians* (1952 edition) is included. Accompanied by a two-hundred-page book that includes the lyrics and historical notes for *Ballads for Sectarians* and a biography of Joe Glazer.

Two Songs by Joe Glazer. 1953. Labor Arts. (Unnumbered.) 78-rpm record in paper jacket. Sung by Joe Glazer, with guitar: "Joe McCarthy's Band" and "The Giveaway Boys in Washington." These two songs are also included in the Bear Family collection, *Songs for Political Action.*

The Songs of Joe Hill. 1954. Folkways Records FA 2039. Ten-inch LP album. Sung by Joe Glazer with guitar accompaniment. Booklet with lyrics includes: "Casey Jones," "Scissor Bill," "The Rebel Girl," "There Is Power in a Union," "Preacher and the Slave," "Joe Hill's Last Will," "Mr. Block," "The Tramp," "Joe Hill," and "The Commonwealth of Toil."

Songs of the Wobblies. 1954. Labor Arts. (Unnumbered.) Ten-inch LP album. Sung by Joe Glazer and Bill Friedland with their own guitar accompaniment. Booklet with lyrics and historic notes includes: "Hallelujah I'm a Bum," "The Rebel Girl," "The Tramp," "Boom Went the Boom," "The Popular Wobbly," "The Commonwealth of Toil," "Dump the Bosses Off Your Back," "Scissor Bill," "Workingmen Unite," "The Preacher and the Slave," "Down to the Soup Line," and "There Is Power in a Union."

Joe Glazer and the PAC Bucks. 1955. CIO Education and Research Department. (Unnumbered.) Two 78-rpm records in paper sleeves. Sung by Joe Glazer with guitar and accompanied by the PAC Bucks vocal trio: "You Gotta Go Down and Join the Union," "A Promise Ain't a Promise Anymore," "The Giveaway Boys in Washington," and "Solidarity Forever."

Image of History: Twenty Years of the CIO. 1956. UAW Education Department. (Unnumbered.) Twelve-inch LP album. Historical narration with accompanying songs presented at the final convention of the CIO in December 1955. Music by Joe Glazer and the Workmen's Circle Chorus. Narration by Melvyn Douglas; script by Hyman Bookbinder: "I'm Gonna Call the Roll of the CIO" written by Joe Glazer, plus excerpts of traditional labor songs.

A Douglas for Me and Other Songs of the New Democratic Party of Canada. 1956. Woodworth Book Club of Canada. (Unnumbered.) Seven-inch LP album. Sung by Joe Glazer with guitar: "A Douglas for Me," "That Brand New Democratic Party Train," "This Land Is Your Land" (Canadian version), "It Could Be a Wonderful World," "Solidarity Forever," "The Farmer Is the Man," and "We Shall Not Be Moved."

Ballads for Ballots. 1956. Sound Studios. (Unnumbered.) Ten-inch LP album. Songs for 1956 presidential campaign. Sung by Joe Glazer with guitar. First three songs written by Joe Glazer: "Love That Team," "The Ballad of Richard Nixon," "The Giveaway Boys in Washington," and "The Dixon-Yates Song."

Two Songs by Joe Glazer. 1958. Sound Studios. (Unnumbered.) Seven-inch, 45-rpm album in paper sleeve. Two songs written and sung by Joe Glazer accompanied by Charlie Byrd on guitar: "Chins Up" and "Unemployment Compensation Blues."

Union Songs. 1958. UAW Educational Department. (Unnumbered.) Ten-inch, 78-rpm record in paper sleeve. Sung by Joe Glazer with guitar: "The Song of the Guaranteed Wage."

Songs of Work and Freedom. 1960. Washington Records. WR-4601. Twelve-inch LP album. Sung by Joe Glazer accompanied by Charlie Byrd on guitar and Mike Seeger on banjo and guitar: "Solidarity Forever," "Talking Union," "Dark as a Dungeon,"

"West Virginia Hills," "Union Man," "My Sweetheart's the Mule in the Mines," "The Mill Was Made of Marble," "The Farmer Is the Man," "Planting Rice," "Automation," "The Man That Waters the Workers' Beer," "Kevin Barry," and "It Could Be a Wonderful World."

Newspaper Guild Strike Song. 1960. (Unnumbered.) Portland, Oregon Newspaper Guild. Seven-inch, 33⅓-rpm record in a paper sleeve. Joe Glazer sings song written for the Portland Guild strike against the *Oregon Journal* and the *Oregonian:* "On the Portland Picket Line."

Ballads for Ballots. 1960. Labor's Committee for Kennedy and Johnson. (Unnumbered.) Twelve-inch LP album. Songs for the 1960 presidential campaign sung by Joe Glazer, assisted by the Dynamic Democratic Dixielanders: "The Democratic Party March," "I Like Ike" (originally "Love That Team")," "A Home for Checkers," "Balance the Budget," "Democratic Victory Train," "Sweet Music in Washington," "Ballad of Richard Nixon," "Dig Down Deep," and "I'm an Old Republican." The record has the same title as one issued in 1956 but is a completely different recording.

Democratic Music. 1960. Democratic Committee for John F. Kennedy for President. (Unnumbered.) Twelve-inch LP album in paper sleeve. Sung by Joe Glazer: "Democratic Party March," "Democratic Victory Train," and "Sweet Music in Washington."

Songs of Coal. 1964. Sound Studios. (Unnumbered.) Twelve-inch LP album. Sung by Joe Glazer with guitar at 1964 UMWA convention: "A Miner's Life," "Dark as a Dungeon," "Ludlow Massacre," "Company Store," "Sixteen Tons," "We Shall Not Be Moved," "Solidarity Forever," "Which Side Are You On?" "Union Maid," "No Irish Need Apply," "Drill Man Blues," "Talking Union," "Joe Hill," and "Coal Miner's Heaven."

Your Vacation in Mexico. 1965. (Unnumbered.) Ten-inch LP album. Two original songs about Mexico plus four Mexican folk songs sung by Joe Glazer with guitar and accompanied by others. The Mexican songs are sung in Spanish, with English singing translations: "Talking Mexico," "Acapulco, Xochimilco," "Adios Mi Chaparrita," "La Sandunga," "Gavilan Pollero," and "El Abandonado."

The Golden Presses—That Heavenly Newspaper Plant. 1966. The American Newspaper Guild. (Unnumbered.) Twelve-inch LP in a paper sleeve. On side one, Joe Glazer sings six songs at the 1966 Newspaper Guild convention: "His Name Is Heywood Broun," "A Newspaper Man Meets Such Interesting People," "A Newspaper Man for Me," "The Pickers' Song," "On the Portland Picket Line," and "That Heavenly Newspaper Plant." Side two contains a speech made at the convention by George Meany, president, AFL-CIO.

My Darling Party Line. 1968. Sound Studios. (Unnumbered.) Twelve-inch LP album. Irreverent songs about the twists and turns of the American Communist Party line, sung by Joe Glazer and Abe Brumberg. An updated version of the ten-inch LP album, *Ballads for Sectarians*, recorded in 1953 by Joe Glazer and Bill Friedland. The earlier record contained nine of the fifteen songs included here: "Old Bolshevik's Song," "The Cloakmakers Union," "Our Line's Been Changed Again," "The Land of the *Daily Worker*," "In Old Moscow," "Unite for Unity," "Bill Bailey," "The Last International," and "Little Joe the Rustler." New songs are: "The Lady with the Popular Front," "The Ballad of Harry Pollitt," "Nikita's Lament," "Something Has Gone Awry," "The Lady from Siberia," and "Sovietology." Includes booklet with lyrics and historical notes.

My Darling Party Line. 1988. Collector Records 1990C. Cassette. Same songs as above.

AFSCME Sings with Joe Glazer. 1968. (Unnumbered.) Twelve-inch LP album. Sung by Joe Glazer with guitar and recorded live with members of the American Federation of State, County and Municipal Employees (AFSCME): "The AFSCME Song," "We Shall Not Be Moved," "Miners' Strawberries," "Hard Times in the Mill," "We Are Building a Strong Union," "The Mill Was Made of Marble," "Union Maid," "Roll the Union On," "That's All," "Solidarity Forever," "It Could Be a Wonderful World," "Union Train," "Joe Hill," "John Henry," "Automation," "Too Old to Work," "We've Got a Lot of Work to Do," and "On Our Way with AFSCME."

Singing about Our Union—an Evening with Joe Glazer and AFSCME Members. 1969. (Unnumbered.) Twelve-inch LP album. Sung by Joe Glazer with guitar and recorded live with a group of AFSCME members: "Talking Union," "On Our Way with AFSCME," "Four-Day Week," "Which Side Are You On?" "John Brown's Body," "Battle Hymn of the Republic," "Solidarity Forever," "Desde Delano Voy," "Garbage," and "The AFSCME Song."

Joe Glazer Sings Labor Songs. 1971. Collector Records 1918. Twelve-inch LP album. A remastered and edited version of *AFSCME Sings with Joe Glazer* (1968). Includes all the same songs except for two: "On Our Way with AFSCME" and "The AFSCME Song."

Joe Glazer Sings Garbage—and Other Songs of Our Times. 1971. Collector Records 1919. Twelve-inch LP album. Joe Glazer sings songs of social commentary, nine of them written by him, accompanied by the Charlie Byrd Trio: "Ping Pong Diplomacy," "I Belong to a Private Club," "Automation," "Looking for the 'R' in Hahvad," "Ballad of Robert Briscoe," "Garbage," "Four-Day Week," "Fashion," "Ecology," "Fight That Line," and "Twenty-Two Minutes from Town."

Joe Glazer Sings Garbage—and Other Songs of Our Times. 1980. Collector Records 1919. A reissue of the 1971 record of the same name and number, with two new songs: "The Ballad of Richard Nixon" and "Don't Tear It Down." Omitted were "Ping Pong Diplomacy" and "Fashion."

Joe Glazer Sings Garbage—and Other Songs of Our Times. 1993. Collector Records 1919C. Cassette. New songs added to the records of the same name were: "Kugelsburg Bank,"

"Touch Tone Telephone Blues," "Teacher's Lament," "Friend of the Fetus," and "I Dreamed of Martin Luther King."

The Ballad of Bobby Fischer. 1972. Collector Records 1920. Seven-inch, 33⅓-rpm album. Joe Glazer with guitar: "The Ballad of Bobby Fischer," "Ping Pong Diplomacy," and "Four-Day Week."

Joe Glazer Live at Vail. 1973. Twelve-inch LP album issued by the Central Pension Fund of the Operating Engineers International Union (OEIU). (Unnumbered.) Joe Glazer sings at an OEIU meeting in Vail, Colorado: "I'm an Operating Engineer," "When a Fellow Is Out of a Job," "Solidarity Forever," "Union Maid," "Automation," "Too Old to Work," "The Mill Was Made of Marble," "Pie in the Sky," "We Shall Not Be Moved," "That's All," and "It Could Be a Wonderful World."

Songs of Steel and Struggle—the Story of the Steelworkers of America. 1975. Collector Records. (Unnumbered.) Twelve-inch LP album. Sung by Joe Glazer accompanied by the Charlie Byrd Quartet. One song, "The Spirit of Phil Murray," is sung by the Sterling Jubilee Singers. Includes a twelve-page illustrated booklet with essay by Archie Green, lyrics of the songs, and historical notes: "Pittsburgh," "Red Iron Ore," "The Ballad of John Catchins," "United Steelworkers Are We," "Amalgamate as One," "The Homestead Strike," "Memorial Day Massacre," "The Spirit of Phil Murray," "Too Old to Work," "Corrido Del Minero," "Steel Mill Blues," "1913 Massacre," "I Lie in the American Land," "When a Fellow Is Out of a Job," and "Solidarity Forever."

Down in a Coal Mine. 1974. Collector Records 1923. Twelve-inch LP album dedicated to George Korson. Sung by Joe Glazer accompanied by Charlie Byrd on guitar. Side one contains seven songs collected by George Korson: "Down in a Coal Mine," "My Sweetheart's the Mule in the Mines," "The Young Lady Who Married a Mule Driver," "When the Breaker Starts Up Full Time," "Jolly Wee Miner Men," "Death of Mother Jones," and "Old Miner's Refrain." Side two is a shortened version of the recording of Joe Glazer singing at the United Mine Workers' convention in 1964 (see *Songs of Coal*): "A Miner's Life," "Ludlow Massacre," "We Live in the Company Houses," "Sixteen Tons," "Which Side Are You On?" "Union Man," "Drill Man Blues," and "Coal Miner's Heaven."

Down in a Coal Mine. 1997. Collector Records 1923C. Cassette. Same songs as above.

Songs about Operating Engineers. 1974. Collector Records. (Unnumbered.) Seven-inch, 33⅓-rpm album. Sung by Joe Glazer: "I'm an Operating Engineer."

Textile Voices—Songs and Stories of the Mills. 1975. Collector Records 1922. Twelve-inch LP album. Sung by Joe Glazer with guitar and recorded live with a group of textile workers: "Let Them Wear Their Dresses Fine," "Factory Girl," "Babies in the Mill," "Weave Room Blues," "On the Picket Line," "We Live in the Company Houses," "We Are Climbing Jacob's Ladder," "We Are Building a Strong Union," "Hard Times in the Mill," "Cotton Mill Colic," "Shine on Me," "I Ain't No Stranger Now," "Humblin' Back," "Give Me That Textile Workers' Union," "The Mill Was Made of Marble," and "Solidarity Forever."

Textile Voices—Songs and Stories of the Mills. 1985. Collector Records 1922C. Cassette. Same as above.

Singing BRAC with Joe Glazer. 1975. Collector Records 1924. Twelve-inch LP album of railroad songs produced for the seventy-fifth anniversary convention of the Brotherhood of Railway and Airline Clerks (BRAC). Sung by Joe Glazer accompanied by members of the Seldom Scene Bluegrass Band: "Talking BRAC," "Daddy, What's a Train?" "Casey Jones" (Joe Hill version), "Many a Man Killed on the Railroad," "Union Train," "Solidarity Forever," "This Train's a Clean Train," "Danville Girl," "Pat Works on the Railroad," "Ballad of Eugene Victor Debs," "That's BRAC," and "We Shall Not Be Moved."

Union Train. 1975. Collector Records 1925. Twelve-inch LP album. Sung by Joe Glazer accompanied by members of the Seldom Scene Bluegrass Band. The first eight songs listed were originally recorded for the album *Singing BRAC* (Collector 1924): "Daddy, What's a Train?" "Casey Jones" (Joe Hill version), "Many a Man Killed on the Railroad," "Union Train," "Solidarity Forever," "This Train's a Clean Train," "Danville Girl," "Pat Works on the Railroad," "Ballad of Eugene Victor Debs," "Bye, Bye Black Smoke Choo Choo," "Casey Jones" (traditional version), "Wreck of the *Royal Palm*," and "Hobo's Meditation."

Goodbye Uganda, Israel Shalom. 1976. Collector Records 1926. Seven-inch, 33⅓-rpm record in paper album cover. Two songs sung by Joe Glazer accompanied by members of the Seldom Scene Bluegrass Band: "Goodbye Uganda, Israel Shalom" (written by Joe Glazer to celebrate the rescue of Israeli hostages at Entebbe Airport) and "Mene, Mene Tekel."

Songs for Woodworkers. 1977. Collector Records 1929. Twelve-inch LP album. Produced for the International Woodworkers of America (IWA) for their fortieth anniversary. Sung by Joe Glazer accompanied by a varied group of musicians and vocal groups: "Fifty Thousand Lumberjacks," "The Frozen Logger," "The Shantyman's Life," "The Raftsmen," "The Lumberjack's Prayer," "The Lumber Camp Song," "Talking IWA," "IWA Marching Song," "Grand Hotel," "The Jam on Gerry's Rocks," "The Jones Boys," "The Lumberman's Alphabet," "Ralph Chaplin Speaks," and "Solidarity Forever."

Songs of the Wobblies. 1978. Collector Records 1927. Twelve-inch LP album. Sung by Joe Glazer accompanied by a varied group of musicians and vocal groups. A completely new edition of the ten-inch LP with the same title produced in 1954 by Labor Arts: "The Commonwealth of Toil," "Mr. Block," "Fifty-Thousand Lumberjacks," "Pie in the Sky," "Workingmen Unite," "Dump the Bosses Off Your Back," "Joe Hill,"

"Hallelujah I'm a Bum," "Rebel Girl," "There Is Power in a Union," "Boom Went the Boom," "Solidarity Forever," and "Ralph Chaplin Speaks."

Songs of the Wobblies. 1988. Collector Records 1927C. Cassette. Same as above.

Service Employees International Sings with Joe Glazer. 1980. Collector Records. (Unnumbered.) Twelve-inch LP album made for the Service Employees International Union (SEIU). Sung by Joe Glazer accompanied by various musicians: "Union Maid," "Which Side Are You On?" "We Shall Not Be Moved," "We Shall Overcome," "MCA Song," "Solidarity Forever," "Hold the Fort," "Casey Jones," "This Land Is Your Land," "Bread and Roses," "That's All," and "Talking SEIU."

Joe Glazer Sings Labor Songs. 1982. Collector Records 1918. Twelve-inch LP album. A completely new edition of an album with the same title and number (1971). Most of the song titles are the same as in the earlier album, but the versions are different. Backup is by various musical and vocal groups: "We Shall Not Be Moved," "Roll the Union On," "Hold the Fort," "That's All," "Joe Hill," "Union Maid," "Casey Jones," "Which Side Are You On?" "The Mill Was Made of Marble," "Solidarity Forever," "Automation," "Hard Times in the Mill," "Look for the Union Label," "John Henry," "Too Old to Work," and "Union Buster."

Joe Glazer Sings Labor Songs. 1988. Collector Records 1918C. Cassette. Same as above.

Joe Glazer Sings Labor Songs. 1994. Collector Records 1918CD. CD. Same as above but with two additional songs: "Downsized" and "Union, Union."

Jellybean Blues. 1982. Collector Records 1935. Twelve-inch LP album. Sung by Joe Glazer accompanied by members of the Seldom Scene Bluegrass Band: "Jellybean Blues," "Around the Corner—Prosperity," "Ronald Reagan Had a Ranch," "Social Security Song," "Gentleman Jimmy Watt," "Don't Blame Me," "Hood Robin's My Name," "The Fox and the Chickens," "The Moral Majority," "A Handful of Jellybeans," "Don't Wake the President Up," "The Fox Is Not Your Friend," "A Sweet Fellow Like Me," and "Jobs, Jobs, Jobs."

Jellybean Blues. 1982. Collector Records 1935C. Cassette. Same as above.

Jellybean Blues, Volume II. 1984. Collector Records 1935. Twelve-inch LP album. Sung by Joe Glazer for the 1984 presidential campaign. A revised and updated version of *Jellybean Blues* (1982 and also numbered Collector Records 1935). Eight new songs replace eight out-dated songs: "Jellybean Blues," "Hood Robin's My Name," "The Giveaway Boys in Washington," "Teflon Man," "Balance the Budget," "Casey and Ronnie," "Don't Blame Me," "The Fox and the Chickens," "Democratic Party March," "Sweet Music in Washington," "Social Security Song," and "Don't Wake the President Up."

Jellybean Blues, Volume II. 1984. Collector Records 1935C. Cassette. Same as above.

A Century of Labor Songs. 1981. Collector Records 1934. Twelve-inch LP album. Produced for the American Federation of Teachers in celebration of the hundredth anniversary of the American Federation of Labor. Sung by Joe Glazer accompanied by various musicians and vocal groups: "Hard Times in the Mill," "No Irish Need Apply," "John Henry," "Which Side Are You On?" "Joe Hill," "Union Maid," "Solidarity Forever," "We Shall Not Be Moved," "Roll the Union On," "Babies in the Mill," "Look for the Union Label," "When a Fellow Is Out of a Job," "Farm Workers Song," "Too Old to Work," and "We've Only Just Begun."

Songs for USIA. 1985. Collector Records. (Unnumbered.) Cassette. Deals with the work of the United States Information Agency around the world. Joe Glazer sings, plays guitar, and provides background commentary. All songs except "We Shall Overcome" written by Joe Glazer: "A USIA Job in Heaven," "The VOA Mines," "The Silent Majority," "USIA Retirees' Song," "We're Spreading Culture All over the World," "Ping Pong Diplomacy," "Twenty-two Minutes from Town," "Looking for the 'R' in Hahvad," "I Belong to a Private Club," "Congressman's Blues," and "We Shall Overcome."

Fifty Years of the UAW. 1985. Collector Records 1934C. Cassette. Joe Glazer sings with guitar and provides historical commentary: "We Shall Not Be Moved," "Roll the Union On," "Soup Song," "Sit Down, Sit Down," "We Are the CIO," "UAW-CIO," "Automation," "Fight That Line," "Too Old to Work," "Song of the Guaranteed Wage," "Ain't Gonna Sing No Company Song," and "Solidarity Forever."

Bricklayin' Union Man—Songs and Stories by Joe Glazer. 1987. Collector Records 1991C. Sung by Joe Glazer with guitar in a live performance before a group of union bricklayers: "A Bricklaying Job in Heaven," "Down at the Union Hall," "I'm Union and Damn Proud of It," "Casey Jones," "Bricklayin' Union Man," "Joe Hill," "Why Paddy's Not at Work Today," "Too Old to Work," "Union Maid," "That's All," and "Solidarity Forever."

Old Folks Ain't All the Same. 1987. Collector Records 1942. Twelve-inch LP album. Produced for the Labor Heritage Foundation. Deals with various aspects of aging— ageism, stereotypes, loneliness, Social Security, wisdom, dignity, health, and struggle. Sung by Joe Glazer accompanied by various musicians and vocal groups: "Old Folks Ain't All the Same," "Hello in There," "Ida Mae (Social Security Song)," "Old Age Pension Check," "Too Old to Work," "Senior Citizen's Battle Hymn," "What the Old Folks Know," and "My Get Up and Go."

Old Folks Ain't All the Same. 1987. Collector Records 1942C. Cassette. Same as above.

Joe Glazer Sings Labor Songs, II. 1989. Collector Records 1944C. Cassette. Sung by Joe Glazer accompanied by a varied group of musicians and vocal groups: "Operating Engineer," "Fight That Line," "The Dancing Boilerman," "I Never Did It," "I'm Union and Damn Proud of It," "Taxi Song," "Down at the Union Hall," "To Labor,"

"Truck Driver Man," "Press Room," "Babies in the Mill," "Hospital Workers," "Buffalo Creek Flood," "Talking Import Blues," and "VDT."

The Jewish Immigrant Experience in America—Songs and Stories by Joe Glazer. 1989. Collector Records 1945C. Cassette. A live performance by Joe Glazer with guitar: "America, America," "Bulbes," "Lidl Fun Goldenem Land," "Rock-a-Bye Baby," "Mayn Yingele," "Di Grineh Kusineh," "Mayn Rue Plats," "Hail the Waistmakers of 1909," "Poem of the Triangle Fire," "Anthem of the ILGWU," "Glory, Glory Amalgamated," "Motl Der Opraytor," "The Cloakmakers Union," "Brivele Der Mamen," "Ballad of Robert Briscoe," "Goodbye Uganda, Israel Shalom," and "Mene, Mene Tekel."

Folk Song America. 1990. Smithsonian Collection of Recordings RD046; A4 21489. Four CDs and cassettes. Joe Glazer accompanied by the Elm City Four sings "We Will Overcome."

Don't Mourn—Organize! 1990. Smithsonian/Folkways SF-40026. Songs of the labor songwriter Joe Hill. Joe Glazer recites "Joe Hill Listens to the Praying," a poem by Kenneth Patchen.

Build and Sing—Songs for Architects, Builders and Planners. 1991. Collector Records 1950C. Cassette. Live recording with commentary. Sung by Joe Glazer with guitar: "Working on a Building," "Boll Weevil Song," "Starving to Death on My Government Claim," "Why Paddy's Not at Work Today," "I'm an Operating Engineer," "I Wouldn't Live in New York City," "Rocky Top," "The Streets of Baltimore," "Little Boxes," "Hey Rocky," "Student Architect Blues," "Don't Tear It Down," "Running the Bums Out of Town," "The Past Is a Bucket of Ashes," "Moving Father's Grave," and "God Bless the Grass."

Welcome to America—Songs of the American Immigrants. 1990. Collector Records 1952C. Cassette. Joe Glazer accompanied by various musicians and vocal groups sings: "America, America," "No Irish Need Apply," "Pat Works on the Railway," "Kilkelly," "When I First Came to This Land," "Oleanna," "Swede from North Dakota," "Song of the Golden Land," "Mayn Yingele," "The Raftsmen," "I Lie in the American Land," "Farm Workers' Song," "Deportee," "Welcome to America," and "We Shall Overcome."

We Just Come to Work Here—We Don't Come to Die. 1993. Collector Records 1953C. Cassette. Joe Glazer sings Drill Ye Tarriers Drill; Taxi Song; We've Got a Right to Know; Corrido Del Minero.

Folk Songs of the American Dream. 1995. Collector Records 1954C and 1954CD. CD and cassette. Joe Glazer accompanied by various musicians and vocal groups sings: "America, America," "No Irish Need Apply," "When I First Came to This Land," "Oleanna," "Starving to Death on My Government Claim," "Swing Low, Sweet Chariot," "Hard Times in the Mill," "Babies in the Mill," "Anti-Suffragette Song,"

"Brother, Can You Spare a Dime?" "Ida Mae (Social Security Song)," "It Could Be a Wonderful World," "I'll Be Home for Christmas," "Twenty-two Minutes from Town," "Truck Driver Man," "Garbage," "Touch Tone Telephone Blues," "I Dreamed of Martin Luther King," "The World of Tomorrow," "I Wanna Be President," and "The Mill Was Made of Marble."

The Music of American Politics. 1996. Collector Records 1955CD and 1955C. CD and cassette. Joe Glazer accompanied by Magpie (Greg Artzner and Terry Leonino) and bassist Ralph Gordon sings political campaign songs in a live performance: "Happy Days Are Here Again," "Row, Row, Row with Roosevelt," "Tippecanoe and Tyler Too," "Henry Clay and Frelinghuysen," "John Brown Medley," "Benjamin Harrison Song," "Suffragette Song," "Silent Cal," "If He's Good Enough for Lindy," "Brother, Can You Spare a Dime?" "Ida Mae (Social Security Song)," "Leaning on a Shovel," "REA Song," "We've Got FDR Back Again," "Dewey/Bricker Song," "Wild about Harry," "I Like Ike" (1952), "I Like Ike" (1956), "Joe McCarthy's Band," "Ballad of Richard Nixon," "John F. Kennedy Song," "We Shall Overcome," "Goldwater for President," "Don't Wake the President Up," and "Politics."

Index

Joe Glazer, long known as "Labor's Troubadour," is the chairman and a founder of the Labor Heritage Foundation, which promotes labor music and arts inside and outside the labor movement. For fifty years his voice and guitar have been heard in a hundred union halls, on dozens of picket lines, and at scores of labor, political, and protest rallies. He has recorded more than thirty albums, cassettes, and CDs of labor, political, and social commentary songs and has performed in almost every U.S. state as well as in sixty countries around the world.

Music in American Life

Typeset in 10.5/13 Minion
with Serifa Bold display
Designed by Dennis Roberts
Composed by Jim Proefrock
at the University of Illinois Press
Manufactured by Thomson-Shore, Inc.

University of Illinois Press
1325 South Oak Street
Champaign, IL 61820-6903
www.press.uillinois.edu